BONATTI

ON HORARY

Treatise 6 of Guido Bonatti's
Book of Astronomy

Translated by Benjamin N. Dykes, Ph.D.

From the 1491 and 1550 Latin Editions

The Cazimi Press
Minneapolis, Minnesota
2010

Published and printed in the United States of America
by the Cazimi Press
621 5th Avenue SE #25, Minneapolis, MN 55414

ISBN-13: 978-1-934586-08-2

PUBLISHER'S NOTE:

This reprint of Treatise 6 of Guido Bonatti's *Book of Astronomy* has been excerpted from the out-of-print 1st edition, published in 2007. The text reflects the original pagination, and has not been revised or updated to reflect new translation conventions or citations in more recent translations. The Table of Arabic Terms has been removed. A more recent version can be found at: www.bendykes.com/reviews/study.php

Students should also consult *Works of Sahl & Māshā'allāh* (2008), which contains much horary material, now translated into English.

Dr. Benjamin N. Dykes
The Cazimi Press
April, 2010

PUBLISHER'S NOTE.

TABLE OF CONTENTS

Book Abbreviations:

Abu 'Ali al-Khayyat:	*The Judgments of Nativities*	*JN*
Abū Ma'shar:	*Liber Introductorii Maioris ad Scientiam Iudiciorum Astrorum (Great Introduction to the Knowledge of the Judgments of the Stars)*	*Gr. Intr.*
	On Historical Astrology: the Book of Religions and Dynasties (On the Great Conjunctions)	*OGC*
	The Abbreviation of the Introduction to Astrology	*Abbr.*
	The Flowers of Abū Ma'shar	*Flowers*
Al-Biruni:	*The Book of Instruction in the Elements of the Art of Astrology*	*Instr.*
Māshā'allāh:	*On Reception*	*OR*
	On the Revolutions of the Years of the World	*De Rev. Ann.*
Pseudo-Ptolemy:	*Centiloquium (Centiloquy)*	*Cent.*
Ptolemy	*Tetrabiblos*	*Tet.*
Sahl ibn Bishr:	*On Elections*	*On Elect.*
	On Questions	*On Quest.*
	Introduction	*Introduct.*
'Umar al-Tabarī:	*Three Books of Nativities*	*TBN*
Vettius Valens:	*The Anthology*	*Anth.*

Table of Figures

TREATISE 6:
QUESTIONS

On the parts of judgments, or
a brief introduction to the judgments of the stars

[PART 1]

Chapter 1

If you intended to attain to the judgments of astrology, let it be your first concern to consider whether he who has come to you in order to pose a question, asks with a purpose, just as is said elsewhere.[1] Likewise it is said there *how* you can know whether he asks from an intention or not, in a more extensive way than can be touched upon here; [but] here are certain things which are not dealt with there: for if the Lord of the Ascendant and the Lord of the hour were of the same triplicity, or of the same complexion, or if the Lord of the Ascendant and the hour were the same [planet], the question will be from an intention and is rooted. But if it is otherwise, it does not appear that it comes to be from an intention or to be rooted, unless perhaps in an unexpected case, you will assign the Ascendant to the querent.[2] And if it were necessary, yield to the person, and see the sign that signifies the quaesited matter,[3] and the planet ruling that sign, and the aspect of the significators; also attend to the conjunction of the benefics and malefics to the significators, both by body and by aspect.

And may you know that the corporal conjunction of the Sun, which is called combustion, is harmful beyond all other impediments. Likewise you will consider whether the significator of the querent or of the quaesited matter is in its own domicile or in any domicile from it, and whether it is free from impediments or not, and that it is not in the *via combusta*; likewise, whether the significators (among which the Moon is always to be counted) are in strong

---

[1] See e.g., Tr. 5, Considerations 1, 2, 7, 143.
[2] In other words, if it is an emergency, go ahead and take the chart regardless of whether or not the Lord of the Ascendant and the Lord of the hour fulfill the requirements listed.
[3] In accordance with modern usage, I will use the term "quaesited matter" in place of Bonatti's "the matter inquired about."

places or weak ones, or mediocre ones, and whether they are in the beginnings of the houses, the middle, or their ends. In the same way you will look for helpers or hinderers of any one of them, according to their nature [or condition].[4] All these things having been diligently considered, you will be able to weigh your judgment of the question proposed to you: because the benefics signify good, but the malefics on the contrary will herald evil. If however you were to find an equal balance of benefics and malefics, they portend a judgment in the middle. But if [you were to find only] benefics, they will have power over fortunate things; and if the malefics, you will judge the opposite.

You will even judge the people asking the questions, how and in what way it matters to them that they are asking whatever they are–whether the querent asks for himself, or through another and [or] for another, and by what houses the people asking are signified;[5] and likewise with the quaesited, and what is signified by whatever house, the significations of which you have from the chapter above on the things signified by the twelve houses.

Chapter 2: How one ought to reach a judgment

Since judging about future things is most difficult (and that this is true, is clear by the Considerations assigned to you above);[6] nor did Hippocrates pronounce on a vain and difficult judgment (because nothing is more difficult in the world than predicting the truth about future things).[7] Before [making] judgments is arrived at, I will tell you certain things which pertain to the business of judgments, without which it would be impossible for me to believe

---

[4] *Esse,* "to be." In what follows I will translate this word as "condition" or "nature." By "condition," I mean when Bonatti refers to it as being in a dignity or weakness, afflicted, helped by the benefics, combust, in a weak or strong house, etc. By "nature," I mean when Bonatti refers to a planet as being primarily benefic or malefic in itself, regardless of its extrinsic condition.

[5] Bonatti is hinting that the houses are allocated differently, depending on who the client is and why he is there. He clarifies this in below in Part 2, 5th House, Ch. 4, when he says that if a man is asking for a woman (in this case, presumably his wife) who has given her consent and is aware he is consulting an astrologer, then she is the true querent and is given the 1st house; but if the man is there of his own accord, and she is unaware, then he is the querent and is given the 1st house (she is given the 7th). The issue, then, is whether the person actually facing or writing to the astrologer is the one with the question, or is a messenger on the true querent's behalf. See also Part 2, 6th House, Ch. 1.

[6] I.e., in Tr. 5.

[7] Bonatti frequently begins his chapters with incomplete sentences that declare what the chapter is about or why it is important; I will try to make these as natural-sounding as possible, but in this case I must leave it as it is.

you are able to know how to judge according to the march of truth[8] (even though I made some mention of these very things above).

Wherefore it is important to know first, before you presume to judge, what are the causes perfecting matters,[9] and which of them disclose the truth, and which are those that prohibit them so they are not perfected, and from what causes the effecting of matters will come; and from what will come their detriment; and what is signified by whatever perfecting [cause] or even by whatever destroying or prohibiting cause; and what would signify the time when they ought to be perfected, or when they ought to be destroyed or prohibited. And [this] is a function that the highest creator of everything gave to the planets and signs, and even to the fixed stars. And Māshā'allāh[10] and others said that the effecting and detriment of matters in this world must come to be by three[11] principal ways.

Namely, the first way is when the Lord of the Ascendant and the Lord of the quaesited matter are joined, and the Moon at the same time.[12]

Second, when the aforesaid are not joined together, so that there is some planet who transfers the light between them, namely so that it is separated from one and is joined to the other.[13]

The third,[14] when there comes to be a collection of light from some other planet which is heavier then they, and they themselves are both joined to

---

[8] *Veritatis incessum.*

[9] Note that while Bonatti is primarily concerned with horary questions here, these principles have a broader application, i.e., that translation of light and so on are how matters *of all sorts* are perfected. Thus horary rules are special cases of the universal linkages between the planets and human events.

[10] Bonatti is probably drawing on material throughout OR.

[11] Later Bonatti will implicitly add two other ways: by location (of which there are a couple of kinds), and what I am calling "benefic reception." Receiving disposition is also accounted for in Māshā'allāh's OR.

[12] Let us call this the mode "by joining." Note that in his use of "join," Bonatti includes both corporal conjunction and aspects. Bonatti does not require that the Moon also be involved, but it would definitely be a surer sign of perfection (as we will see, Bonatti often slips in "and the Moon" at the last moment to remind us that she is a significatrix in every question).

[13] This is commonly called "translation of light." I will use "transfer" instead of "translate," since it is more accurate both linguistically and in terms of the mechanics described.

[14] This is "collection of light."

it, and any one of them commits its own disposition to it; because [the heavier planet] itself is the one who perfects the matter.[15]

And sometimes a matter is perfected wholly as the interrogator wills it; and sometimes it is perfected in part, and sometimes neither wholly nor in part; and I will set out all of this for you, so that you may understand it better and may comprehend how you can judge about matters that are presented to you.

On the exposition of the first way[16]

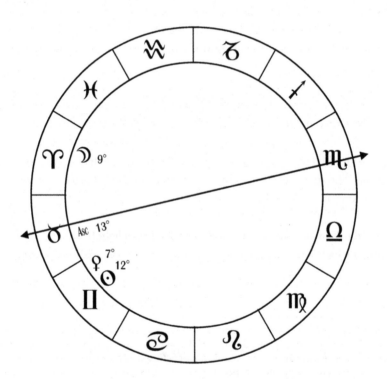

Figure 1: Perfection by Joining

---

[15] This seems to mean that they must *both* be joined to it, but that *only one* of them must commit disposition to it (under a technical meaning of committing disposition). The rationale (if this is correct) must be that each of the significators by itself has enough authority that, if they were joined directly, the matter would be perfected; but a third planet collecting their separate rays of light would not by itself be able to perfect the matter unless it had the disposition committed to it by at least one of them.

[16] This is the mode "by joining."

The exposition of the first way by which matters are perfected, is when the Lord of the Ascendant and the Moon are joined with the Lord of the quaesited matter: for then the matter is perfected.

For example, a certain question was posed, whether a certain man was going to obtain a certain manor estate which he wanted to buy. And the Ascendant was Taurus, 13°; and Venus was in Gemini, 7°; and the Sun was in Gemini, 12°; and the Moon in Aries, 9°. And the Lord of the Ascendant (namely Venus, who was going to a corporal conjunction of the Sun) and the Moon (who was going to its aspectual conjunction) signified that the matter ought to be perfected;[17] And it would be perfected if the one who had posed the question wanted to pursue it so that it would be perfected;[18] and especially since the Sun, who was the significator of the quaesited, received the Moon from Aries by a sextile aspect. And if not by sextile, the matter would perfect even by square or opposition, provided that reception intervened, even if it were with difficulty and anxiety and the greatest labor, and likewise obstacles and unfitness.

---

[17] In this example, the querent is represented by Venus, who rules the Ascendant; the quaesited (the estate) is represented by the Sun, who rules the 4th. The Moon is a co-significator. All three are joined by applying corporal conjunction or aspect, fulfilling the criteria of perfection "by joining."

[18] The important point here is that something may be fated, but only if the agents who can make it happen, do act. In this sense, horary is something of a cross between elections and straightforward prediction (as with natal or mundane techniques), because it assumes a degree of fate, but in many cases it must also assume that the agents take advantage of good timing.

On the exposition of the second way[19]

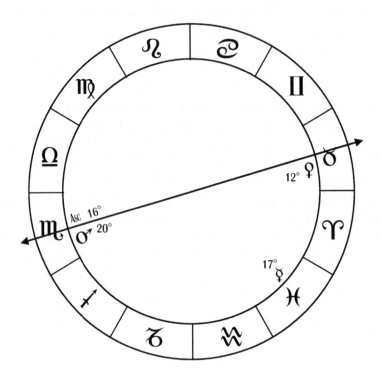

Figure 2: Perfection by Transfer of Light

The exposition of the second way is when one planet is separated from another, and is joined to [yet] another, and commits the disposition he had accepted from the first, to the one with which he himself is joined. For example, a question was put to me: a certain man asked whether he was about to have the goods of a certain uncle of his (who had no sons), the Ascendant of which was Scorpio, 16°; and Mars in it, 20°; and Venus in Taurus, 12°, going toward the opposition of Mars; and Mercury in Pisces, 17°. And Mercury was separated from Venus by a sextile aspect, by which he had been joined to her; [and] she received him from Pisces, which is her exaltation, and she committed her disposition to him. And Mercury carried it to Mars, and committed it to [Mars] by a trine aspect. And this signified that the man was going to possess his uncle's goods, on account of Venus, who was the significatrix of the goods of the querent's uncle, [and] who committed her disposition to Mercury, and

---

[19] Transfer of light.

Mercury carried it to Mars, who is the significator of the querent. For the 6th house is the significator of the uncle, namely the father's brother, just as was said above in the chapter on the houses. Because the 6th is the 3rd from the 4th (which is the house of the father); and the 7th (which signifies the uncle's substance) is the 2nd from the 6th. And the transfer of light signified that the matter would come to be through the agency of legates,[20] who intervene in it; and it seemed that it ought to come to be through the agency of an ally of one of the querent's partners;[21] which if he did not have a partner, it would come to be through the agency of a certain ally of his enemy or his wife. If his wife did not live in the house with him, and if [such an] ally were not to be found, it will come to be through the agency of a certain servant of the querent's brother;[22] which if the brother did not have a servant, it would come to be through the agency of some stepson of the querent;[23] which if he did not have a stepson, it would come to be through the agency of a certain friend of his;[24] which if he did not have a friend, it would come to be through the agency of a certain soldier or ally of the king;[25] which if such people were not found, it would come to be through the agency of a certain person in whom his secret enemies trust.[26] And if such a person is not found, then it will come to be through the agency of one who is signified by the house in which the Moon is.

---

[20] Mercury is in the 5th, signifying legates.

[21] The word for "ally" here is *familiaris*, which can indicate a member of the household or a slave–basically, someone who personally attached to and beholden to the querent. In war charts the 2nd is the ally of the querent waging war, just as the 11th represents the ministers and advisors to the king (2nd from 10th). In this case, Mercury rules Gemini on the 8th house, which is the 2nd (ally) from the 7th (partners).

[22] The 8th (ruled by Mercury) is the 6th (servants) from the 3rd (siblings).

[23] Mercury rules the 11th, the other children (5th) of the spouse (7th).

[24] Mercury also rules Virgo on the 11th (friends).

[25] The 11th is the 2nd (allies) from the 10th (king).

[26] I.e., people in the household of the enemy (the 8th is the 2nd from the 7th).

On the exposition of the third way[27]

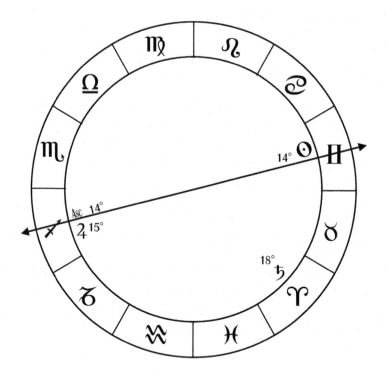

Figure 3: Perfection by Collection of Light

The exposition of the third way is when one planet who is the significator of the quaesited matter is not joined to the Lord of the Ascendant of the question, but they are both joined to another who is heavier than they, and they both commit their own virtue to it, and the heavier one perfects the quaesited matter. Just as for example, [when] a certain man asked whether he was about to obtain a certain church [position] for which he strove: the Ascendant was Sagittarius, 14°; and Jupiter in it, 15°; and the Sun (who was the significator of the church position) in Gemini, 14°; and Saturn in Aries, 18°. And each one was joined to Saturn, and [Saturn] himself collected the light of each;[28] indeed this collection

---

[27] Collection of light.

[28] This example is unusual, because since the Sun is in an earlier degree than Jupiter, he should be able to perfect the matter at least somewhat by opposition–i.e., by the first way of "joining." But their opposition lacks perfect reception: so perhaps Bonatti is suggesting that it is easier for Saturn to perfect the matter by collection, than it would be for the Sun and Jupiter to do so by opposition without reception. Or perhaps the reason it is pertinent is

of the light of Jupiter and the Sun that Saturn was making, signified that the matter would be perfected, and that he would obtain the church position inquired about. Because the Sun, who was the Lord of the 9th house (which signified [the church position]), committed his own disposition to Saturn, because [the Sun] received [Saturn] from [the Sun's] exaltation; and Saturn entrusted and committed to Jupiter the quaesited matter which was being committed to him by the Sun,[29] and the matter would have been perfected all the more preferably if the querent had sought the quaesited matter for another than if he sought it for himself. Because even though [Jupiter] was joined to [Saturn] from a trine aspect, Saturn however did not receive him by perfect reception, because he did not receive him except by triplicity.[30] And it seemed that a brother of the querent would be the one by whose agency the matter was perfected;[31] which if he did not have a brother, it would have been the brother of someone who pretends to love him when he [really] does not.[32] And if there were no such person, it would have been a son of a friend of his;[33] and if such a person is not found, it would have been the slave of a magnate;[34] and if such a person were not found, it would have been a certain enemy of the church; and if such an enemy of the church were not found, it would have been an enemy of the querent's son; and if he did not have a son, or the son had no friend, it would have been a certain hidden enemy of the querent's father; which if the client did not have a father, or the father did not have such an enemy, it would

---

because both the Sun and Jupiter are joined to Saturn already by orbs, so that Saturn's participation needs to be taken into account in any case–here, by a collection of light. But Bonatti also mentions below at the end of Ch. 4, that an opposition (even with perfect reception) will not show a durable perfection. See the other variants on these aspects and reception that follow below.

[29] Bonatti did not say that the collecting planet would have to commit the disposition he receives from one significator to the other in turn. This could be an elaboration of the definition, or else Bonatti is just pointing out that this in fact is what Saturn happens to be doing here.

[30] Bonatti seems to be saying that since there is no perfect reception, the disposition from the Sun (which was committed to Saturn) will not be able to be fully committed to Jupiter, because the reception is not perfect. Therefore, the matter will not be perfected in the best way for the *querent* (Jupiter) but since the dignity of triplicity is compared to having allies and helpers and friends (Tr. 2, Part 1, Ch. 19), it could perfect for a friend the querent is helping.

[31] Saturn rules the 3rd (siblings).

[32] Saturn rules the 2nd, which is the 3rd (siblings) from the 12th (secret enemies).

[33] The 3rd house is the 5th (children) from the 11th (friends).

[34] The 3rd is the 6th (servants, slaves) from the 10th (magnates, important people).

have happened then through simony;[35] and this way of perfecting the matter is lasting.[36]

On another way of perfecting matters

And there is another way of perfecting matters which can be said to be subordinate to the preceding one, which is neither lasting nor perfect, namely if two planets were joined to another one heavier than they, and they committed disposition and virtue to him (just as was said about Jupiter and the Sun, as to how they committed virtue to Saturn); and this heavier one who received the disposition were impeded (namely cadent or retrograde or combust or joined to malefics who impede him), or he were besieged by the malefics.[37] I say that he can perfect the matter, and sometimes perfects it, but after the matter is arranged and perfected, it is destroyed and does not remain in its perfection. Whence you can make the judgment to the one who asks you, that it seems the matter will be perfected, but it will be destroyed after it is perfected.

On certain other accidents of matters which are perfected

Sometimes something happens in matters which are perfected, namely that certain ones of them come to be with difficulty and duress, and labor, and the greatest complications; others come to be with ease, others come to be with striving and inconvenience, certain ones come to be with striving and great inconvenience, certain ones come to be without striving and any difficulty–on the contrary, they come without any thought at all.

On those matters which come easily

Those which come easily and without striving or any difficulty, as unhindered things, are when the Lord of the Ascendant or the significator of the querent and the significator of the quaesited matter are joined by a trine or sextile aspect, and with reception.

---

[35] Simony is the purchasing of ecclesiastical offices.
[36] This almost seems like a joke on Bonatti's part. He undoubtedly means that collection of light is lasting; but he could also be cynically noting that simony is a surefire way to get a lasting position.
[37] This is an example of collection of light, but where the collecting planet is afflicted.

On those matters which come to be shortly

Indeed those matters which come to be shortly and without striving (even if hope is not had, concerning them, that they will come to be) are when the Lord of the Ascendant is joined with the Lord of the quaesited by a trine aspect without reception, or by a sextile with reception.

On those matters which come to be with striving[38]

Indeed, those which come to be with the querent's striving and effort, are when the Lord of the Ascendant is joined with the significator of the quaesited matter, by a square aspect with reception, or a sextile aspect without reception.

On those matters which come to be with striving, effort, and labor

However, those which come to be with striving and effort and obstacles and labor, and great trouble, are when the significator of the querent is joined with the significator of the quaesited matter by opposition, or by a square aspect without reception.

On those matters which come to be with labor, yet are hardly perfected

Those things which come to be with the greatest labor, and obstacles, and striving and effort and distress, likewise sadness, and as though after the desperation of friends and blood relations, and yet hardly or never perfect (and if they were perfected their effect will be slow for a long time, and even then with expenses)–are those in which the Lord of the Ascendant (or the Moon) and the Lord of the quaesited matter, are joined by opposition without reception.

When a matter someone wishes for, comes to be without reception

And there is another way that a matter (which someone intends to have) may be perfected, and it is easier than all other aforesaid ways: namely, when the significator of the quaesited matter is joined to the significator of the one

---

[38] *Petitione.* Hand translates *petitio* as "suit," i.e., a lawsuit. But the term has a broader meaning for any kind of striving for a goal, whether a lawsuit, candidacy, petition, request or application (*peto*, "to strive for, demand, entreat"). Bonatti clearly reserves the word for "lawsuit" (*lis*) in the section on the 7th house.

desiring it, from a sextile aspect with reception, or from a trine without reception; or if the significator of the matter were in the Ascendant or in the house signifying the one for whom the matter is pursued.[39] May you understand the same concerning corporal conjunction as with aspects, for then the matter will come to be most easily.

When the matter which is sought is a magistracy or dignity

If perhaps the matter which is sought were a magistracy or lay dignity, which is hoped for by someone, and the querent hoped to get it from the king or from some lord of his, and the significator of the aforesaid matter were in the Ascendant, or were joined to the Lord of the Ascendant, or with the Moon from a trine or sextile aspect, or corporally and with reception, it signifies that the quaesited matter will perfect without his own striving, or by another on his behalf.

When some matter is hoped for from some magnate—how the matter will come to be

And if someone hopes for something from one who is lower [in status] than the king, or from some friend of his, or from a commoner of some land, or the like, the matter will come to be and will come by means of a fortuitous occurrence.[40]

When a conjunction or aspect does not intervene[41]

If however there were no conjunctional aspect between them, but there were a transfer of light, the matter will come to be through the agency of legates, who introduce themselves into the situation so that it may be perfected. Indeed, in order to know who these legates are, you would look to the house whose Lord is the significator of whichever of [the planets it is], or to the house in which you were to find them, as has been sufficiently explained to you. For it would be tedious to explain it everywhere. And then look likewise at the Moon: because if she were then separated from the significator of the one desiring the matter (or even from the querent of [the matter]), and she were joined to the significator of

---

[39] Let us call this the "fourth way" of perfection, that "by location."
[40] I believe the only point of this paragraph is to note that 11th house matters, when they perfect, will do so in an 11th house way—with fortunate circumstances and fulfilled hopes.
[41] I.e., when the mode "by joining" does not apply—then we look for translation or collection of light.

the matter, it signifies that those who are running to and fro among them come from the side[42] of the one desiring the matter; and with his knowledge and will. If however she were separated from a planet signifying the matter, and she were joined to the significator of the one desiring the matter, it signifies that they originate from the side of the thing or from those who can perfect it. And if the matter were perfected by legates, the legates themselves will be of the sort of persons signified by the houses of which they are Lords: look, then, to see what persons are signified by those houses, and judge according to them, whether it is an ally, or brother or neighbor, or father, or child, or slave, or partner, or [the partner's] ally, or a religious figure, or a king or master, or friend or hidden enemy.

And you must know that even though I told you that matters are perfected by trine or sextile aspects, you must however understand well: because if [1] the place from which the Lord of the Ascendant (or the Moon) is aspected by the Lord of the quaesited matter (namely by which the matter itself is signified), or [2] the place from which the Lord or significator of the matter is aspected by the Lord of the Ascendant (or the Moon) is [3] the detriment of the one aspecting, the matter is not perfected, even if the aspect is a sextile or trine. Just as, for example, the Ascendant was Leo, and the question was about a marriage–whether it would take place or not–and the Sun is joined with Saturn or the Moon (which signifies women) from Aries, which is the detriment [fall] of Saturn. Even if the aspect (however great in itself) is with reception, Saturn however will not perfect the matter, but rather impedes it so that it does not perfect–he not only impedes, but tries to destroy it if he can. And if [the Sun] were joined to [Saturn] from Cancer or Leo, he would do the same, because both of them are his fall. Likewise if the significator of whatever matter (or the Moon) were joined to the Sun from Libra (which is his descension), or from Aquarius (which is his fall),[43] because then the Sun would not receive any of them, and thus he would destroy the matter and not permit it to be perfected. Or if he were joined to Venus from Scorpio or Aries or Virgo, or to Jupiter from Capricorn or Gemini or Virgo. And may you know the detriment of whatever planet [you are dealing with]: nor does any aspect suffice (unless reception intervenes), that will break its malice.

And may you understand the same if the significator or the Moon were joined to a planet which is in the detriment of that significator itself (or of the

---

[42] *Ex parte.* In other words, they are people known to him, working for him, etc.
[43] Note Bonatti's loose use of "descension" and "fall." See Tr. 2.

Moon): like if Mercury were the significator, and were joined to a planet which is in Sagittarius or Pisces, or the Moon were joined to a planet which is in Scorpio or Capricorn, or a planet were joined to any planet located in its own descension; or [if] the one who is in the descension of the other, is joined to him whose descension it is,[44] it always tries to destroy the matter and annul it.

There is even something else which introduces fear into matters, as when a planet which is the significator of the quaesited matter is a malefic, and it shows that the matter ought to be perfected by an aspect[45] or by opposition, then the querent fears lest some trouble will come to him from it, whence he hopes more strongly that it will not perfect, than he does that it will perfect. But if the aspect were a trine or sextile with reception, it will be secured; if however without reception, it will not be evil in the way that he fears, even if it is not very secure in the way the querent wants.

Moreover, if the significator of the querent and the significator of the quaesited matter were the same planet, just as often happens, nor were he received in the place in which he is, it signifies that the matter ought not to be perfected; indeed if he were received, it signifies that the matter ought to be perfected with a good perfection, unless he who is receiving him were impeded by fall[46] or combustion or retrogradation; because even if it comes to be, it is not be perfected by a good perfection (as [it would be] when it is not impeded).[47]

And there is another thing: when the planetary significators are aided to perfect the thing, namely when signs agree in nature with the planets, and help them, and some exhibit their testimonies by means of them.[48]

And Sahl said[49] it behooves [us] that, if the Ascendant is a fixed or common sign, understand that the Ascendant is made diverse according to the diversity

---

[44] These last two clauses sound complicated, but are simple: if one is joined to the other, or the other to it.

[45] Presumably by square, since Bonatti almost always pairs it with the opposition.

[46] I take this to mean the essential weakness of "fall" (casus) and not being cadent (which also has connotations of falling); presumably it also includes detriment. But it could certainly also mean cadence.

[47] This paragraph suggests that a planet can still receive if in fall, retrograde, or combust–but it will not be an effective reception.

[48] He has already discussed how dignities and debilities affect planets, so I believe here he is simply saying that the signs the significators are in, can sometimes signify types of people and events.

[49] This seems to be based on a section in Sahl's On Quest. §8, "The testimonies of the signs in the effecting of a matter." Sahl says: "And know wherefore the testimonies of the signs in the effecting of matters are like if the Ascendant is a fixed sign or a common one, and the angles stable: that is, like when the Midheaven is the tenth sign, and the angle of earth the fourth

of the persons, by beginning from the 1st house all the way to the 12th; and the angles should not be wide, but of the proper size, that is, so that the 10th house is the tenth sign from the Ascendant, and the angle of the earth is the fourth sign from the Ascendant (indeed so that the 10th house is not the ninth sign from the Ascendant, nor the 4th house the third sign from the Ascendant).[50]

By what significations it is known whether matters ought to be perfected

Likewise, you ought to know the significations by means of which it is known whether matters ought to be perfected or not, of which the first is the Lord of the Ascendant. The second is the Moon, because, as is said elsewhere, she herself participates in every matter. The third is the planet signifying the quaesited matter. Which, when they are all joined together, they signify the effecting of the whole matter in the houses signifying the matters.

And may you always be mindful to diversify the Ascendants just as I told you now: indeed if two of them (namely the Lord of the Ascendant and the Lord of the [quaesited] matter, or the Moon and the Lord of the quaesited) were joined together, it signifies that the matter will come to be by two thirds. But if only one of them were attested to, it signifies that the quaesited matter will be perfected for the querent by one-third. Understand this in matters which are susceptible to division, because if there were a matter which could not be divided, either it will come to be wholly, or it will not come to be wholly. If however in matters which are not divided, you were to have two of the aforesaid testimonies, declare the effect of the quaesited to be entire. If perhaps you were to have only one of them, it can hardly or never be perfected, but if it were perfected it would come to be with hardship and delays, and with the greatest labor besides, and complications, like a marriage which either comes to be

---

sign—and the Midheaven is not the ninth sign, nor were the angle of the earth fall in the third sign. This exposition of the angles is of the stable ones."

[50] Here we see a clear distinction between quadrant houses and signs. The point seems to be that for matters to be effective, it is preferable that (a) the rising sign be fixed or common, and (b) there be only one sign per quadrant house cusp. The first point seems to be related to the notion (seen especially in elections) that movable signs show things changing quickly, which is to be avoided if the matter to be perfected should last a long time (fixed signs show lastingness, common ones repetition). The second point seems to be related to the doctrine of "removal" (mentioned in my Introduction), that the timing of events and the promise of their perfection changes when there are intercepted signs or two quadrant house cusps land on the same sign. It would seem that Sahl is listing ideal conditions for certain judgment and lasting perfection. Perhaps the connection between "diversification" here is simply that it is more difficult to be certain about assigning significators when we have intercepted signs and signs that have two cusps.

entirely or does not come to be entirely, and the like: if a marriage, I say there would be a single one. For if there were multiple marriages at once, as sometimes happens when it is sought by multiple women and multiple men—as when someone were looking for himself, and for his father or brother or son or someone else—then certain ones of them could be perfected, and certain ones not, according to how you were to see the significations and testimonies occurring in the question.

And these three testimonies or significations should be considered in any matter; which if all were strong, then without a doubt whatever the matter is, it will be wholly perfected for the querent. For the significators (namely the Lord of the Ascendant, and the Moon, and the Lord of the quaesited matter) are strong when they are free from combustion, fall, retrogradation, the square aspect and opposition of the malefics (and from their besiegement), and from the corporal conjunction of the same—which rarely happens. And if in addition to their being strong, they were received by the malefics from any aspect, the matter will be perfected, and for the good. Indeed, if they were received by the benefics, again the good will be increased, as though the querent did not know how to strive better, nor believed that the matter he sought would come to be perfectly.

And may you not dismiss these words, because they have proven accurate in each matter, and work for every question and every thing which someone intends to do. However, much is discovered by considering the helpful and harmful fixed stars which help or do harm (as they are accordingly discussed in the chapter on them).

PART 2: On the Particular Judgments of the Stars

Chapter 1: That which signifies the querent's person, and what happens to him in any question[51] and any matter which he intends to undertake or begin, inasmuch as questioning or beginning pertains to him, and likewise on those things which naturally appear to pertain to this

In this first chapter we must deal with those things which pertain to the 1st house (which is the rising sign, and signifies the querent), in accordance as the question pertains to [the 1st house]. And I will tell you certain things which you ought to know about these. For diverse questions can be made, and of diverse types, in accordance as their qualities diversify them. For questions can be made diverse according to their own nature, as when one is about one matter and another is different from it. They can even be diverse according to other diverse significations, for at one time someone asks when he asks for himself, at another time when he asks on another's behalf. And I will tell you in what way you ought to look in each case, and likewise at what house when someone asks. For it is not always necessary that you should look at the 1st house for the Ascendant of the thing signified[52] in every question.

But you might say, "Why didn't any of the sages write down what you're saying?" The reason for this is this: they themselves let it remain for the industry of the wise; because they did not then speak to those who had to be introduced, but for those who had been introduced, and for the overflowing and the wise, and the instructed.

For if someone were to ask about himself, you ought to look at the 1st. But if he were to ask about his own substance or other things signified by the 2nd house, you ought to look at the 2nd. If he were to ask about siblings or about other things signified by the 3rd house, you ought to look at the 3rd. If he were to ask about his father or about other things signified by the 4th house, you ought to look at the 4th. If he were to ask about children or about other things signified by the 5th house, you ought to look at the 5th. If he were to ask about slaves or about other things signified by the 6th house, you ought to look at the 6th. If he were to ask about a wife or about other things signified by the 7th

---

[51] Bonatti alternates between using *quaestio* and *interrogatio* (and their paronyms) to indicate questions and querents. I will simply use the same words, "question" and "querent."
[52] This may be a key to the business about diversifying topics and Ascendants (see above)—because he equivocally uses the term "Ascendant" here to refer to any cusp.

house, you ought to look at the 7th. If he were to ask about death or about other things signified by the 8th house, you ought to look at the 8th. If he were to ask about religion or about other things signified by the 9th house, you ought to look at the 9th. And if he were to ask about a kingdom or about other things signified by the 10th house, you ought to look at the 10th. If he were to ask about friends or about other things signified by the 11th house, you ought to look at the 11th. If he were to ask about hidden enemies or about other things signified by the 12th house, you ought to look at the 12th. And may you always remember these things.

Chapter 2: How you ought to look at the shadow when questions are posed to you

And when you are asked about some matter, concerning which the questioner wishes to pose a question to you, take the altitude of the Sun, if it is a diurnal question. If however it were a nocturnal one, take the altitude of whichever fixed star is inscribed on the astrolabe, or with another instrument suitable to this [purpose], as soon as you can, accurately, immediately, without any delay or any length of interval, once the words leave the mouth of the one asking about the matter.

And take care that you do not deviate in anything, lest some error take place in the matter about which the question was posed to you. And observe the method which I told you, in looking at the house which signifies the quaesited matter. And likewise beware lest you mix diverse topics together with questions at diverse times. For if some question had been made to you, let us say about marriage, and you examine it; and a little while afterwards the same man (or perhaps another) poses another question to you, on whatever topic, do not mix it with the other, already-examined one.[53] For the Ascendant has already changed, and thus it is necessary that the judgment be changed; whence you could thereby be guilty of being deceived in your judgment. But you can take it up with the required altitude, and it will be another judgment than the first one. Nevertheless, however, you can accept more than one question under multiple headings under one Ascendant, if the querent thinks of them; and should he have it in his mind for one day, or a day and a night, so that the whole heaven has revolved at least once, provided that the questions are different, indeed so

---

[53] In other words, do not use the same chart as before. One must cast a new chart for every consultation, whether by the same person or another.

that one is not on the same topic as another. And likewise beware lest he who asks should come to you with the purpose of testing or deceiving you, as certain people tend to do, or that he does not have the question in his heart for a day and a night, just as was said elsewhere (if you remember it well).[54] For matters spring up according to the amount of worry, and hope, and money of the querent. For when someone asks about a matter, the house and places of the planets, and their disposition, signifies what will be so about the matter which he himself seeks, for the whole of the time of his life. Likewise in nativities, even though nativities sometimes are altered by the revolution of years, sometimes according to increase and sometimes according to decrease.

And in universal questions about fortune (namely whether someone's question [covers the whole course of life] or a determinate [amount of time]), as for one or more years or months, or a week or a day, and the like: because whatever an agent intends the end of his acts to be, he acts according to his estimate of his intended ends, and according to the result which he foresees. And let this be known to you, because everyone who asks, does not ask except about this, and according to that which the planets and signs (and their disposition concerning any good or evil) prevail over, in the root of his nativity.

Chapter 3: What is the trunk and what are the branches of this tree

For questions are the trunks of this tree, and the Considerations[55] which you must have about questions, are its branches. And thus by considering, you will see how the Lord of the Ascendant of any question, and any nativity, and any beginning [election], and any matter, is made fortunate; and how the Moon is made fortunate, and how the Lord of the house signifying the topic (on which a question were) is made fortunate. For nobody asks about this except as I have told you now, and according to that (unless perhaps he were to ask knowingly—for you ought not to look for him, just as is said elsewhere).[56] For no one is born or asks in a good hour, and under a good and fortunate Ascendant, unless he is fortunate and one whom goods and fortunes are supposed to surround. And no one is born or asks under an evil and unfortunate Ascendant, unless he is an unfortunate man whom evils and misfortunes are supposed to surround.

---

[54] Tr. 5 (2nd Consideration).
[55] I.e., the 146 considerations from Tr. 5.
[56] Bonatti refers to people who try to deceive the astrologer, already knowing the answer to the question.

Thence it is that we see that certain people are fortunate, certain ones unfortunate.

Chapter 4: That the astrologer ought not to cast a chart for himself

It seemed to the ancient sages, and especially to Māshā'allāh,[57] that the astrologer ought not to cast a chart for himself,[58] lest perchance he be deceived in his own matter; because it rarely happens but that he himself has some regret over the Ascendant; whence it is necessary that he ask someone else according to the aforesaid procedure. Indeed, after the other person were to understand his question, he would be able to look for himself and answer his own question, or he may give his own question to another (whether in writing or not)– naturally to such a person who is concerned about his matter. And he may offer it on his own behalf after he has posed it, when he wishes. Or [else] he would put [it] in his mind, saying, "when such a sign will have occurred to me, let it be for the Ascendant of the question, which I intend to undertake on my own behalf, and it will be just as effective."

Whence if it were a question on a matter which ought to last or be stable, or which ought to be improved or made worse, or be concluded quickly, or changed, one must look then at the Lord of the Ascendant, and see whether he himself is joined to the Lord of the quaesited matter (or the Lord of the quaesited matter is joined to him), and by what aspect. Because if they are joined by a trine or sextile, and in the angles or from the angles, or from succeedents, it signifies the effecting of the quaesited matter. It even signifies durability, and stability, and its improvement; and even better than this is if the aspect were with reception. Because then it signifies the whole goodness of the thing, without any decrease.

But if the aspect were a square, it reduces much of the querent's intention and the goodness and durability of that same matter, even if it were with reception. It even diminishes if it were a trine or sextile without reception, even if less so [than if it were a square]. If it were a square or opposition without reception, it signifies the destruction of the matter itself and that no good nor durability will be in it. But if the Lord of the Ascendant and the Lord of the quaesited matter are joined to some planet which is heavier than they, and he receives their disposition, and he aspects the Ascendant or were to aspect some

---

[57] OR, Ch. 2.

[58] Lit., "ought not to look for himself" (*non debet aspicere sibi ipsi*).

planet aspecting the Ascendant (and having some dignity in it [the Ascendant]), nor is he impeded, it signifies goodness and the effecting and durability and stability of the matter. Indeed if the receiver of the disposition did not aspect the Ascendant, nor were he joined to a planet which aspected it from its own place, it will be evil, for it signifies annulling and malice and the destruction of the matter itself.

If however the Lord of the Ascendant were heavier than the Lord of the quaesited matter, and the Lord of the quaesited matter were joined to him from a good aspect–or from any besides the opposition–with perfect reception, it signifies the goodness and the durability of the matter. Likewise, if the Lord of the quaesited matter were heavier than the Lord of the Ascendant, and the Lord of the Ascendant were joined to him with perfect reception, it signifies the goodness and durability of the matter itself. May you understand the same thing about a conjunction with the Lord of the quaesited matter, if the Lord of the quaesited matter is not joined with the Lord of the Ascendant. And may you always understand this: that the significators (as much the Lord of the Ascendant as the Lord of the quaesited matter, and the receiver of disposition, and the Moon) would be free from the malefics and their impediments.

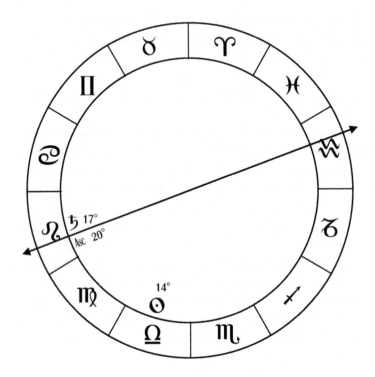

Figure 4: A Question About Marriage

For example, a certain question was posed about a marriage–whether it would be perfected or not–and the Ascendant of this question was Leo, 20°; Saturn in it, 17°; the Sun in Libra, 14°. It signified this, that the matter would come to be and be perfected freely, without contradiction, because each of the significators received the other; and that its perfection would be good and durable, and likewise peaceful and happy. May you say the same concerning other questions. If however the Sun were put in Libra at 20°, and Saturn in Aries at 25°, even though each of the significators receives the other, it signifies the impediment of the matter, whatever the topic of the question was; and the diminution of the good which was signified on account of the reception; and that it would hardly or never be perfected. And if it had been completely perfected, [it would be] with obstacles and the greatest labor and anxiety. Nor however will the perfection be good or durable, but rather it appears that it would be destroyed after its perfection; and if it were not destroyed by evil and unpeaceful means, it will endure; because their aspect is from the opposition, and each of the significators is impeded.

Another example which Sahl put in his book of judgments[59]

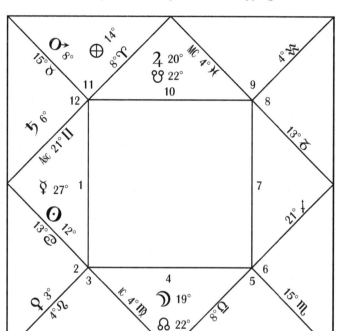

Figure 5: A Question from Sahl

A certain soldier asked whether he would get a position of authority in that year. And his question was absolute, because he did not specify which position. Still, he hoped to have a particular one. The Ascendant of which question was Gemini, 21°; Cancer was the 2nd house, 13°; Leo the 3rd house, 4°; Virgo the 4th house, 4°; Libra the 5th house, 8°; Scorpio the 6th house, 15°; the remaining six houses opposite the aforesaid ones. The locations of the planets were thus: Saturn was in Gemini, 6°; Jupiter stationary in Pisces, 20°; Mars in Taurus, 8°; the Sun in Cancer, 12°; Venus in Leo, 3°; Mercury in Gemini, 27°; the Moon in

---

[59] From the introductory sections of *On Quest*. §9, "Testimonies of the planets in the effecting of matters." This chart suggests a latitude at approximately 30°N (for example, near Basra, Iraq). But Sahl himself gives 20° Gemini for the Ascendant and 0° Pisces for the Midheaven (suggesting a latitude of approximately 34°N, close to Baghdad's latitude), and omits *all* other cusp locations. The fact that Bonatti has filled in the other cusps as well as having gotten a different Midheaven value, suggests that he has recalculated the chart. I would also point out that this passage is a paraphrase, with some elements out of order, and with Sahl's clear references to whole sign houses (in the Latin translation) omitted.

Virgo, 19°; the Head of the Dragon in Virgo, 22°; the Tail opposite to it. The Part of Fortune was in Aries, 14°.

[Sahl] said, therefore I looked at this question, naturally at the Ascendant and its Lord and at the Moon (which are the significators of the querent); and at the Midheaven and its Lord (which are the significators of the quaesited matter). But Mercury, who is a significator of the querent, is in the 1st house, clearly in the Ascendant near the end of the sign, and he was separated from Jupiter (who is a significator of the quaesited matter). And this signifies that he will not have a position of authority in that year. Then I began to operate through the Moon, which was in opposition to Jupiter (signifying the quaesited). Whence insofar as it is from this that she[60] was joined to him, it signified that he would have a position of authority in that year (even though the conjunction was by opposition), but with labor and inconvenience, and likewise obstacles and distress and the greatest anxiety, which would not have been the case if his conjunction had been by trine or sextile aspect; but rather he would have attained it easily, and without labor, and moreover with the greatest ease. Then I looked at Jupiter, the significator of the quaesited, and he was in a house signifying the matter the question was about; [and] he would have signified the effecting of the matter if he himself had been of good condition, and well disposed. But he was in his first station, wanting to go retrograde. Whence, even if he received the disposition of the Moon, still, because of his weakness he was not able to uphold the matter, and this showed that the man who is laboring at this so that the matter would perfect, could not bring it to conclusion; and thus the poor disposition of Jupiter signified the destruction of the quaesited matter, and its annulment; and it seemed that he who then had the position of authority was the reason why [the querent] would not attain it. Because Jupiter, who was destroying the matter, was the Lord of the 10th house, which signified the position of authority. And if the Lord of the 11th house were the one who was impeded, it would have seemed that the detriment and destruction of the matter would have to come from the side of a certain friend of the querent. And if he were the Lord of the 12th, it would be because of a certain person who pretended to be his friend, when he was [really] his hidden enemy. And if the Lord of the Ascendant was the receiver of the disposition who impeded, and who was impeded, it would have signified that the querent himself is the reason for the destruction of the quaesited matter: because he would have committed the act [explaining] why the matter would not come to be nor be perfected for him. And because the Lord

---

[60] Reading *ipsa* for *ipse*.

of the Ascendant was changed from own domicile to another, it signified that the querent changed his own purpose quickly [from one] to another, and because he was changed to the 2nd house, it seemed that the change would be the reason that he would acquire for himself substance which he did not have.[61] And it seemed that the change would come to pass into a certain place in which he himself had already been at another time on the occasion of acquiring money for himself.[62]

Moreover it seemed that Mars, who was the Lord of the 6th house, was harmful to him so that the matter would not come to be for him. Because it seemed that the querent was going to take ill in the place to which he intended to go; and this was signified through Mars, who received the Lord of the Ascendant, but on the other hand made [the Lord of the Ascendant] unfortunate. Which if he was not taken ill, such things would happen (and come before his hands)[63] that he himself did, which would be the reason why he was not going to have the quaesited position of authority. And his slaves (or others under his power) would have risen up against him, resisting him so that he would not get it. Or perhaps it would be the general populace and other vulgar people who do not have any other employment except for shouting and spreading rumors, not knowing what they are shouting about.

Likewise, it was signified by Jupiter (the significator of the quaesited) that some detriment would happen to the querent, or some sadness, on account of which he did not obtain the dignity. And even if he had not expressed that he had the intention of possessing it, still, Mercury (who was his significator) seemed to show that he already hoped for it, because [Mercury] himself was separated from Jupiter (the significator of the matter). Whence it seemed that [the question] was already posed as though out of desperation, but he did not lose all hope, since Mercury, even though he was separated from Jupiter (the Lord of the 10th house), still aspected him. Whence you would be able to say to him, that even if he himself pretended to be ignorant of what he asks about, he knows about it very well, [that] he already had hoped for it, and feared he would not be able to perfect it. And just as I have told you about the position of authority, may you understand in any matter which can be signified by any of the twelve houses.

---

[61] *Illa mutatio esset causa ut acquireret substantiam.* This seems to relate to the notion that he changed his mind, from seeking a position of authority to seeking money.
[62] But why?
[63] *Prae manibus,* i.e., matters he is directly involved in.

Chapter 5: How to inspect planets that impede matters so they do not come to pass

Even though it might have seemed more suitable to put this chapter some-where else, still it seems to me that it should be put here, because if it is deferred until the Treatise on nativities, you could [still] need it in more than one place; for it has a place not only in nativities, but indeed even in all interrogations, in all journeys, and in all beginnings[64] of whatever things which we want or plan to undertake. And [the point of] this is that you look for the planet which impedes matters so that they do not come to pass, or are not perfected. And this planet can be called the strong "killing" or "prohibiting" or "destroying" one, or abscisor, because it is he himself who cuts off the life of a native, and destroys it, and does not permit the native to achieve a long life, namely to old age; and who corrupts a matter and destroys it after it has been thought to be arranged and seems that it must be perfected. And it is this which our ancients called the abscisor or "the one cutting," and which you ought to look at in nativities and in questions; and this, so that you know whether matters ought to be perfected or not and come to the required effect. And we take it from the planet with which the Lord of the Ascendant or significator of the quaesited (or the Moon, if she herself participates with the Lord of the Ascendant, or is the significator of the quaesited) is joined.

For you ought to consider the planet to which the significator of the querent, or the significator of the quaesited, or the Moon, is joined; and see how that planet is disposed, and the one to whom *this* planet is conjoined. Because if the Lord of the Ascendant, or the Moon, or the significator of the quaesited is joined to a planet that is malefic and badly disposed, without reception–or if it is not badly disposed but joined to another malefic who is badly disposed, who does not receive him–it signifies the destruction of the quaesited matter.

I understand a "badly disposed" malefic planet, to be peregrine, and retro-grade, and combust, and cadent from the Ascendant or from the house of the quaesited matter (so that it does not aspect it, or at least [the house's] Lord–although an aspect to the house is stronger than an aspect to [the house's] Lord in this)–or which is in its own fall or descension. Indeed he is the one who is called the abscisor or destroyer.

---

[64] That is, elections.

Moreover, if the significator of the querent (or the quaesited matter, or the Moon, or a planet to which the Moon is joined, or if she herself were significatrix or participator with the Lord of the Ascendant), were joined to some unfortunated planet, that is to say retrograde or combust or cadent, you will see then if reception intervenes. Because even if by burdens and fatigue, the perfection of the quaesited matter is signified [in that case]. If however reception did not intervene, it signifies the corruption of the matter and the destruction of the same, and that the matter will not be perfected after it is thought to be arranged. If however (a) he who receives the Lord of the Ascendant or the Moon or the Lord of the quaesited matter; or (b) a planet to whom one of them is joined, were free, and neither the received[65] nor the receiving [planet] were made unfortunate, it signifies the perfection of the matter with ease.

And if the planet to which the Lord of the Ascendant, or the Moon or the Lord of the quaesited matter is joined, were free from the malefics, but were joined to some benefic planet who was joined to some malefic who is impeded, nor receives him[66]–and may you understand, by a planet among the seven planets[67]–the matter will not be perfected, nor come to a good end.

May you always understand this: if those conjunctions come to be without reception (because with reception it will be perfected, even if with weariness), this having been first considered and discerned, that if some planet cuts off the light of one of the aforesaid planets when it wishes to be conjoined to a malefic, that it takes away the harm, and it is not prohibited without the matter being perfected. But if the cutting-off of light intervenes,[68] the matter is prohibited and does not perfect; and if it is perfected, it is destroyed. But you will consider this: if reception were to intervene–except do not let it be by the opposition or a square aspect; for if the planet were then badly disposed, a reception which is by square aspect[69] or by opposition will not profit, and especially if the receiver is impeded. But if the reception were by trine or sextile, it is strong and it is believed that the matter ought to perfect. Indeed if a planet who receives were then well disposed, by whatever aspect the reception were, it perfects the

---

[65] Reading *receptus* for *receptor*.

[66] *Nec recipiat eum.* Based on the scenarios Bonatti considers below, he is speaking about the malefic receiving the other planet.

[67] I do not understand why Bonatti feels it necessary to emphasize the seven planets here–what else might we be talking about?

[68] Omitting *non*: otherwise Bonatti would be saying that the cutting of light *allows* things to be perfected, directly contradicting the whole point of this passage.

[69] Reading *aspectu* for *respectu*.

matter, and neither the square nor opposition will stand in the way. If however it were by trine or sextile, it perfects the matter because of the one who is well disposed, to which the significator is joined (whether with reception or without reception). However, [this is only so provided] that the aspect or conjunction is not yet complete [nor] that it begins to be separated in any way.

And if the significator is joined with an unimpeded benefic, the matter is perfected. And if one of the planets transferred light or virtue between the significator and some other planet, and he to whom he transfers the light is a malefic, and who is (as was said) impeded, the matter is corrupted unless the impeding or receiving malefic were received in turn. If indeed the significator of the querent (or the Moon) and the significator of the quaesited matter were joined to some planet who collected the light of both, and he were a malefic or made unfortunate, he destroys the matter and does not permit it to be perfected unless he himself receives both significators; [and] even if he receives [only] one of them, nevertheless the matter is destroyed.

You will even consider whether the significator of the querent is found in the house of the quaesited matter, or going toward a conjunction with its Lord, because this signifies that the querent goes to the quaesited matter. If however the significator of the quaesited matter is found in the Ascendant, or going toward a conjunction with the significator of the querent, it signifies that the quaesited matter will go to the querent, however with the receptions and aspects and the Moon remaining in their own [current] state.[70]

---

[70] Esse.

ON THE SECOND HOUSE

Chapter 1: On substance which the querent hopes to possess for himself

If someone were to inquire of you whether or not he will possess substance which he hopes to have, you will learn from him of what sort of substance it is which he intends to have or acquire.

And then look to the Ascendant, and its Lord, and the Moon (who are the universal significators of the querent). Nor let this deceive you: whatever person it was who asked you about substance, who hopes to acquire it for himself, the 1st is given to him–whether he is a king, or someone else, whether cleric, or layman, or Pope, or any prelate, or noble or any other person. For no one has prerogative in this case, nor is [any] condition, or order, or sex, preferred. All are equal in this case, provided that whoever it is asks for himself. And you will give the second sign and its Lord to the substance, unless the querent specifies otherwise.

If the Lord of the Ascendant or the Moon is joined to the Lord of the house of substance, or the Lord of the house of substance to the Lord of the Ascendant; or the Lord of the house of substance were in the Ascendant; or the Lord of the Ascendant or the Moon were in the house of substance; or the Moon or one of the other planets were transferring the light between the Lord of the Ascendant and the Lord of the house of substance (namely from one of them to the other), it signifies that the querent will get the substance he asks about. And if this was not the case for the Lord of the Ascendant, or the Moon, or the Lord of the house of substance, then look to see if Jupiter (who is the natural significator of substance) or Venus (who is naturally a benefic), or the Head of the Dragon were in the house of substance without an aspect to any malefic: [then] the querent will acquire the substance, and he will obtain it.

May you understand the same if the question about substance were absolute, namely when the querent does not specify otherwise in his question, but says only: "Will I acquire substance or not?" You must look just as you looked above. Which if you did not find something [indicating] substance, tell him that he will not find substance, but will remain in his condition, unless the malefics (which are Mars and Saturn and the Tail of the Dragon) are in the house of substance, without aspect to any benefic: [for] they destroy substance, unless perhaps they were received by the Lord of the house of substance or were themselves the Lord of the said house, and otherwise of good condition (not retrograde, not combust, nor impeded in another way); because then their malice is decreased.

And if even the Tail were with them in the house of substance, their malice will be increased, and they will be made worse. While if the Tail were in the house of substance with the benefics, he greatly decreases their goodness, and even takes away a fourth part of the substance after it is acquired, and somewhat more. And if you were to find one of the malefics in the house of substance, of bad condition, [and] you were to find the Moon void in course or joining herself to malefics impeding her, this will signify that he will not acquire substance for the entire time of his life: on the contrary will see that what he has is reduced, and that he will always be needy and a beggar.

Chapter 2: Whence he will acquire substance, and whence he will lose it, and from what cause

If indeed you were to see that the querent is going to acquire wealth, and you wished to know from whence he will acquire it, and from what cause—or if he is going to lose it, then in what circumstances he will lose it—look to the planets I told you about above, which participate in the affairs of substance. And you will consider the one to which the other is joined;[71] because he who is heavier than the one joined to him, will signify by what means, and whence he will acquire substance.

Likewise, see of which house the heavier one (to whom the other is joined) is the Lord, and see in which house is this heavy planet who receives the disposition (namely to whom the other is joined).

For if he were in the Ascendant, or were the Lord of the Ascendant, the querent will acquire substance by the labor of his own hands and through his own person.

If however it were in the second, or were the Lord of the second, he will acquire it with his own substance, as through commerce and the like, like those who work with their own possessions[72] to acquire other things which they do not have.

---

[71] Or simply, see what planets are in conjunction or aspect.
[72] *Rebus.*

If it were in the third, or were the Lord of the third, he will acquire it from his brothers; which if he did not have brothers, he will acquire it from neighbors, or from fellow citizens, or from certain notable people who pretend to be his friends but are not perfect friends, or by circumstances of the aforesaid.

And if it were in the fourth, or were Lord of the fourth, he will acquire it from his father or uncle or father-in-law, or another of his more senior ancestors; which if he did not have such parents, he will acquire it from lands and estates [or farms], or immovable things.

And if it were in the fifth, or were Lord of the fifth, he will acquire it from children; which if he did not have children, he will acquire it from certain people in whom he has confidence [or from whom he has a pledge], so that they make him to win profit, even if they are not true friends.

And if it were in the sixth, or were Lord of the sixth, and the sixth sign were a human one, he will acquire it from slaves and clients.[73] Which if he did not have slaves or clients, he will acquire it from small domesticated animals, like sheep, goats, pigs, and the like (if the sixth sign were quadrupedal). And if he did not have animals, he will acquire it from sick people, or at least from low-class persons.

And if it were in the seventh, or were itself the Lord of the seventh, he will acquire it from women (if the seventh sign were a feminine sign); or he will acquire it from enemies, or perhaps in estates [or farms]; or he will acquire it from partners or from a contention he will have with some people.

And if it were in the eighth, or were itself the Lord of the eighth, he will acquire it from the goods of wives, and from inheritances of the dead, or he will acquire it in foreign lands to which he goes freely (not by force).

---

[73] "Clients" here is meant in the ancient sense: people below you in status who depend on you for your money and influence. It does not refer to people who hire you for your services.

And if it were in the 9th house, or were the Lord of the ninth, he will acquire it from religious people; and if not from religious people, reckon [it to be] all consecrated clerics, or by reason of religion, or in circumstances of the teaching of divinity; or he will acquire it on the occasion of a long journey which he will make to parts far from his own land, just as do the Venetians, Pisans, Genoans, Florentines, and all similar people profiting by long journeys.

And if it were in the tenth, or were the Lord of the tenth, he will acquire it from kings; and if he did not acquire it from kings, he will acquire it from other great men [or magnates], or he will acquire it from offices or positions of authority, if he is such a person that it is proper for him to have an office. If indeed he were not such a person who is fit for this, he will acquire it from his own mastery,[74] with his own honor.

And if it were in the eleventh, or were the Lord of the eleventh, he will acquire it from friends or from those persons in which he has great hope; or he will acquire it from merchants with whom he does business, as much in his own land as in a foreign one (however it is stronger in his own land), and from things which come to him unexpectedly through his own good luck.

And if it were in the twelfth, or were the Lord of the twelfth, he will acquire it from hidden enemies or from those placed in confinement (if the twelfth sign is a human sign). Indeed, if the twelfth sign were quadrupedal, [it would be] from large animals; if it were Taurus, from cows. If it were the last half of Sagittarius, from horses or beasts of burden.

However, may you not forget this, because in whatever house you were to find the Tail with a significator, it always reduces what is signified. And if you find the Head there, it increases what is signified. I retain what was said about their significations in the 2nd house.

---

[74] *De suis magisteriis. Magisterium* in this context can also mean "profession," and refers to special skills that are exercised.

Chapter 3: On the reason why he will not acquire substance

If perhaps it will not seem that he ought to acquire substance, and you wished to know the reason why he will not gain it, what is the reason prohibiting it so that he will not gain substance: look at the receiver of disposition, according to the way I told you above in that same chapter.

And if he who prohibits the acquisition of wealth were the Lord of the Ascendant, the same man who asks the question is himself the reason that he does not gain substance.

And if it were the Lord of the 2nd, his substance will be the reason that he does not gain substance.

If it were the Lord of the 3rd, brothers are the reason he does not gain substance.

And understand this about the significators of all houses: that any one at all, by its place and time will be the reason that substance is not gained by the querent, according to what was said, that the reason for getting it is through the same method, all the way up to the end of the twelve houses.

Those are the things signified by the twelve houses. Whence wherever you were to find the significator of substance, you ought to judge the obtaining of substance through that house; and wherever you will find the prohibitor of substance, you ought to judge the prohibition of substance (so that it is not acquired by the querent) through that house. And look through all the houses for the things signified by all matters which pertain to you.

Moreover, he whom God willed to be a Master,[75] said: because if the question were absolute (or not), it may be said whence he ought to have substance, that we ought to determine the Ascendant, and the house of substance, which is the 2nd from the Ascendant, just as was said elsewhere.[76]

And we ought to look at the Lord of the house of life (which is the Lord of the Ascendant); and if we were to find him aspecting the Ascendant, or

---

[75] This is Māshā'allāh as described by Sahl (*Introduct.*, §5.3).
[76] OR, Ch. 5. What follows is Māshā'allāh's own method for determining which planet (between the Lord of the Ascendant or the Moon) will be best suited to signify the querent.

if he were joined to a planet which renders his light to the Ascendant, we ought then to work with him.

Which if he did not aspect the Ascendant, nor aspected some planet which aspected and rendered his light to the Ascendant, then we ought to look to the Moon; which if she aspected the Ascendant, or aspected some planet which aspects the Ascendant, and renders his light to the Ascendant, work through her.

If indeed the Lord of the Ascendant and the Moon did not aspect the Ascendant, nor were they joined to a planet which aspects the Ascendant, we ought to look then to which of them (namely the Lord of the Ascendant and the Moon) is in more degrees in the sign in which it is; which will leave the sign it is in the fastest, and enter into another; and we ought to work with that one. And it appears [that] if it itself, after it exits the sign in which it is, were joined to the Lord of the house of substance immediately before another were joined to him, or he to the other, the said philosopher said that the querent will gain substance–whether or not the Lord of the Ascendant or the Moon, after its change from the sign in which it was, to another, were received by the Lord of the house of substance.[77]

Nor does [Māshā'allāh] relate whether the Lord of the house of substance should be a benefic or malefic, because[78] the conjunction of the Lord of the Ascendant or the Moon with the Lord of the house of substance causes the obtaining of the matter, namely the substance that was sought.

Still, you ought to look to see that the Lord of the house of substance is not joined to some planet, or some planet joined to him, before the Lord of the Ascendant (or the Moon) joins to the one to which the Lord of the house of substance commits his disposition. And therefore I said "immediately," so that some planet may not cut off the light nor prohibit the conjunction of the Lord of the Ascendant, or of the Moon, with the Lord of the house of substance.

If indeed the question were about a determinate substance, see by what house this substance (which the question concerns) would be signified; and see if the Lord of the Ascendant and the Moon, or either of them, is joined with the

---

[77] Here ends the quote/paraphrase of Māshā'allāh.
[78] The rest of this sentence is a paraphrase of a paragraph in Māshā'allāh.

Lord of the house signifying the matter: because the obtaining of the quaesited matter will come to be through the conjunction of the Lord of the Ascendant (or the Moon) with the Lord of the house signifying that matter about which the question was. If however there were no conjunction of the Lord of the Ascendant or the Moon with the Lord of the house signifying the quaesited matter, then look in all places, just as I told you about the conjunction of the Lord of the house of substance in its mutation from a sign to a sign, and in the conjunction with the Lord of that matter about which the question was. If indeed the Lord of the house of substance or of the quaesited matter were to commit his own disposition to another planet before he himself were joined with the Lord of the Ascendant (or the Lord of the Ascendant or the Moon were joined to him), see which is that planet to whom the Lord of the house of substance or of the quaesited matter is joined, and say that *that* planet is the significator of the impeding reason why the matter will not be perfected. And see which house it is Lord of, because the person who is signified by that house is striving to make it so that the matter will not perfect; and especially if the planet to whom the Lord of the house of substance committed his disposition, is impeded–that is, if it were retrograde or combust, or in its fall, or in its descension, or cadent from the angles. Because if the receiver of the disposition to which the Lord of the house of substance (or of the quaesited matter) is joined, were not impeded by any of the aforesaid impediments, and were a benefic, it will not impede, but the quaesited matter will be perfected, whether or not it were to receive the Lord of the Ascendant.

If indeed it were a malefic, and were not impeded by one of the aforesaid impediments, and it were to receive the Lord of the Ascendant or the Moon, the matter will be perfected likewise by means of the aspect by which it were received. If indeed the malefic did not receive the Lord of the Ascendant, and there were a conjunction by a trine or sextile aspect, the matter will be perfected, even if with labor and delays. And if it were a conjunction by square aspect or by opposition, the quaesited matter will hardly be perfected at any time; and if it were perfected, it would be with so much anxiety and so much of the querent's labor, that he may frequently say "If only I hadn't gotten myself involved in that!"

But if reception were to intervene, the matter will be perfected. If a benefic were the one to receive, the matter will come to be easily and in a short time; if a malefic were the one to receive, the matter will come to be with burdens and delays. And if reception intervenes, it can in no way be but that the thing will be perfected; and there is nothing which can prohibit it so that it does not come to be, unless the querent wanted to give up on his proposal, so that the matter would not be perfected. But if the receiver of the disposition were in an angle, the effecting of the matter will hasten; if in a succeedent house, it will be delayed, and hasten less; if in the cadent houses, it will be prolonged even more again, even if there is reception there. Still, reception is of such strength, that it does not permit the matter to be annulled; for even if it is delayed, ultimately it will achieve the quaesited effect, whether the question concerns substance or whatever matter at all.

Moreover, if the Lord of the Ascendant and the Moon (or one of them) were joined to the Lord of the house of substance or of the quaesited matter, or they were joined to some benefic which is in the house of substance or of the quaesited matter, the querent will obtain the thing or substance. And if one of them (namely the Lord of the Ascendant or the Moon) were not joined to a benefic in the house of substance, but were joined to some malefic which was in the house of substance or of the quaesited matter, and that malefic were to receive the Lord of the Ascendant or the Moon, the matter will come to be, and the Lord of the Ascendant or the querent will acquire it. And if the malefic did not receive the Lord of the Ascendant, nor the Moon, then if he himself had dignity in the house of substance or of the quaesited matter, the querent will yet acquire the substance or quaesited matter, even if it will be put off for a space of time.

And if the Lord of the house of substance or of the quaesited matter were lighter than the Lord of the Ascendant, and it were joined to him (or some other planet which was in the house of substance or of the quaesited matter were likewise lighter than the Lord of the Ascendant, and were joined to him) by a trine or sextile aspect, the substance will be acquired, or the quaesited matter will come to be with ease. If indeed the conjunction were by a square aspect, the matter will come to be if reception intervenes, likewise without great hardship.

But if the Lord of the Ascendant were lighter and were joined to the Lord of the second house or of the quaesited matter, the matter will not come to be easily nor without the querent's effort. If the Lord of the quaesited matter were joined to the Lord of the Ascendant (or of the querent), and he were to receive him by a trine or sextile aspect, substance or the quaesited matter will come to him even more so than he had hoped, and more easily. If however the Lord of the Ascendant or the Moon were not joined to the Lord of the house of substance, or of the quaesited matter, nor to any planet which is in it, you must then see to which of the planets the Lord of the Ascendant or the Moon were joined. Because if one of them is joined to a benefic, well disposed, who is not impeded, or is in an angle, nor is the benefic joined to another planet, nor is another planet joined to her whom she receives or to whom she commits her own disposition, the querent will acquire the substance and the quaesited matter will be perfected. But if that planet (to whom the Lord of the Ascendant is joined) were to receive another and not the Lord of the Ascendant, or the Moon is joined to him [the other planet] by a similar conjunction, nor does he receive her,[79] it is otherwise: because the conjunction of him who receives, annuls the conjunction of him who does not receive. Indeed, if the Lord of the Ascendant (or the Moon) were joined to a malefic who did not receive him, it signifies the destruction and annulling of the substance, or of the quaesited matter, so that the querent does not acquire it, nor will the quaesited matter be perfected for him: because the malefic planets, insofar as they do not receive, do not strive except for the destruction of things, just as the benefics strive to perfect and furnish [them], whether they receive or not. Indeed the malefics strive to the contrary unless they receive (because then they restrain their malice and perfect things just like the benefics do).

Chapter 4: Whether he will acquire the substance he seeks, or has lent, or put in someone's trust[80]

If indeed there were a question from someone who asked whether one from whom he seeks money would give it to him, look at the Lord of the Ascendant and the Moon (who are the significators of the querent); and the 2nd will be the house of his own substance. The 7th and its Lord will be the significators of him from whom it is sought, and the 8th and its Lord will be the significator of the substance of him from whom the substance is sought.

Then see if the Lord of the Ascendant or the Moon were joined to the Lord of the 8th house (which is the significatrix of the substance of him from whom he seeks substance), or one of them were joined to a planet located in the 8th house: if it [the latter] were a benefic, he will acquire the substance about which

---

[79] Reading *eam* for *eum*.
[80] *Deposuit.*

he asks.[81] If he asks for something else (namely of him from whom he seeks), he will give it to him. If he seeks substance that he has lent or put in someone's trust, he will get it, too, whether [the Lord of the Ascendant or the Moon] were to receive that benefic or not. If indeed it were a malefic and it received the Lord of the Ascendant or the Moon, likewise he will acquire the substance about which he asks. If indeed [the malefic] did not receive [the Lord of the Ascendant or the Moon], he will hardly or never recover it; and if he will have gotten it, he will hardly or never have the whole amount, and he will have it with burdens and duress and obstacles, which he will have because of it.

Likewise if the Lord of the 8th were in the 1st, or were in the 2nd, and the Lord of the 2nd were to receive him, it signifies the attainment of the matter which is sought. But if the Lord of the 7th or the Lord of the 8th were in the 1st or 2nd, and the Lord of the Ascendant or the Moon or the Lord of the 2nd did not receive him, it signifies that the querent will lose yet more of his substance, and his original injury will be increased. If however the Lord of the Ascendant or the Moon were joined to a benefic which had dignity in the Ascendant, the matter will come to be; or if one of them were joined to a malefic which had dignity in the Ascendant and received the Lord of the Ascendant or the Moon, the matter about which the querent asks will come to pass. And if the benefic to which is joined the Lord of the Ascendant or the Moon, were in a strong place, the matter will come to pass even without reception.[82]

But understand all of the above statements [to be] about matters which are considered or which exist among lesser or even common people, like the dwellers of cities, military camps, villas, and similar people, which do not exist among people where one exceeds many others.[83] By "people who exceed," understand kings, and magnates who are fit to be kings, like the greatest dukes and greatest marquises, for whom kingdoms are suitable—or unless [the matters] exist between religious men or between laymen and religious men, in matters which do not belong to them themselves. And I will make mention to you

---

[81] I take this to be the fourth method of perfection in Bonatti: let us call it perfection "by location." I take this to happen in two ways: either by the significator being in a key house, or else by a planet in that house being joined with—or collecting the light of—the other significators. See, e.g., the 9th House, Ch. 1.

[82] I take this to be the fifth mode of perfection: let us call it perfection by "benefic reception." My understanding of this is that it happens by a benefic (or perhaps a malefic, but only with reception) which is well-disposed, and/or angular, being joined with reception to a significator, without another joining to the significator who would get the disposition. But I should note that this might only be a special example of perfection by "joining."

[83] In other words, one cannot ask for (or expect) money from the king as one does from a friend.

about these matters which are considered in their own place and time, if it should please Jesus Christ our Lord and True Man.

Chapter 5: If he will obtain the substance of the king

Likewise, sometimes other questions on substance come into the hands of astrologers, as when someone asks whether he is going to get the money of some king, like the soldiers of kings and of other magnates sometimes do, [as when] someone asks about the aforesaid, whether he is going to get his soldier's pay from the king. And it is the same if he asked [for it] from the deputy of the king, or if it is someone who asks about substance which he believes he will have.

Look then at the Ascendant and its Lord, and the Moon (which are the significators of the querent); and the second from the Ascendant (which is the house of the querent's substance), and its Lord; and look at the tenth and its Lord, which are the significators of the king or his deputy, and of magnates who receive service; and look at the eleventh and its Lord, which are the significators of the substance of the king or magnate. If the Lord of the Ascendant or the Moon were joined to the Lord of the 11th[84]or if one of them were joined to a planet located in the 11th (which is a benefic and is neither impeded nor badly disposed), the querent will acquire that which he seeks from the substance of the king or magnate, whether he who asks is a soldier or anyone else, [and] whether or not that benefic were to receive the Lord of the Ascendant or the Moon. Indeed if it were a malefic and received them, he will likewise get what he seeks. If however that malefic did not receive the Lord of the Ascendant or the Moon, he will hardly or never attain the quaesited matter.

Chapter 6: On the time of the aforesaid things

If he who asked you even still wanted to know when the matter he seeks will come to be, then look at the planet to which the Lord of the Ascendant or the Moon are joined, and who had signified the effecting of the matter; because if he were to aspect himself[85] with the Lord of the Ascendant or with the Moon

---

[84] *Undecimae*; now we switch back to the feminine, suggesting quadrant houses–then again it could mean "domiciles," indicating whole-sign houses.

[85] *Aspexerit se.* Bonatti rarely uses this wording; it seems to mean that the two planets are aspecting each other.

by a trine or sextile aspect (whether or not he who received the Lord of the Ascendant or the Moon were a benefic), consider if he projects his light or rays upon the rays[86] of the Lord of the Ascendant or the Moon. And see how many degrees are between them by degree, namely in which one projects his rays upon the rays of the other, up to the perfection of the aspect, degree by degree. And say that there will be so many days until the time of the effecting of the matter, if they were both in cadent houses; if they are in succeedent houses it will be weeks, if they were in angles it will be months. And if the matter seems like it could be greatly prolonged, you could say that there are years–and especially if both significators, namely the Lord of the Ascendant (or the Moon), and the planet to which it is joined, are in angles.

Indeed, if one were in an angle and the other in a succeedent, then they signify months. If one were in a succeedent and the other in a cadent house, they signify weeks. If indeed one were in an angle, the other in a cadent house, they signify months. And if it were the Sun (or Venus or Mercury or the Moon), the degrees which were between them likewise signify days; or perhaps the Sun and Venus could signify weeks or more.

Likewise, Māshā'allāh said[87] that if it were not so, then it will be when the said planet is joined corporally with the Lord of the Ascendant, or with the Moon, degree by degree. If indeed at the hour of the question the planet which signifies the effecting of the matter were in the same sign as the Lord of the Ascendant, the matter will come to be when they are corporally conjoined in the same degree and minute–*if* the Lord of the Ascendant were heavier[88] (whether or not he who is joined receives him). But if the Lord of the Ascendant were lighter, indeed so that he went to the conjunction of the planet signifying the effecting of the matter, and he received the Lord of the Ascendant, then the matter will come to pass. If indeed he did not receive the Lord of the Ascendant, then the matter will not be perfected then, unless that significator were in the angles when the conjunction happens, or in the sign that[89] is said to be its joy. Which if it were not so, it will not be perfected then; but it will be perfected when that planet to whom the Lord of the Ascendant or the Moon is joined (or who is joined to the Lord of the Ascendant), goes toward the Sun, or the Sun goes to him. And were he combust and going out from combustion, then [it will

[86] *Super radios.*

[87] The following statements seem to be largely paraphrases of statements by Māshā'allāh in OR, Chs. 2 and 5.

[88] Emphasis mine.

[89] Adding *quod.*

be perfected] when he has begun to appear from under the rays of the Sun, whether he were before or after the Sun when he escapes combustion, indeed so that he is seen outside the rays of the Sun; and if he were under the rays of the Sun at the hour of the question, the matter will be when that planet begins to appear from under the rays.

ON THE THIRD HOUSE

Chapter 1: On brothers and their condition

If someone asked you about his brother, see in what way he is asking, namely whether he asks about a brother who is present, or about an absent brother, or a healthy brother, or a sick brother, or in what sort of condition[90] is the brother of the one who asks.

You will give the 1st to the querent, because the Ascendant signifies him, and then you will give the 3rd to the brother. If he asks about an absent brother, then look to the Lord of the 3rd house, which signifies the brother, and see where the Lord of the brother's house were found. Because his condition and own disposition will have to be according to what the Lord of the house in which he is, signifies. And see how the planets aspect him, whether he is in the aspect of benefics or malefics, and by what aspects they aspect him, and he to them, or if they were conjoined together corporally.

Because if the significator of brothers were in his own house (namely the 3rd) and nor do the malefics aspect him by opposition or a square aspect, you may then say that his brother is healthy [or safe]. Indeed if the malefics were to aspect him by opposition, or by a square aspect without reception, you may say that his brother lives and is well, but experiences distress and anxieties and great worries. If indeed they were to aspect him by the said aspects with reception, you may say that his brother experiences the aforesaid worries, but will be well liberated, and will escape them.

If indeed the benefics were to aspect him by a trine or sextile aspect, without reception, or by a square or opposition with reception, you may say that his brother finds himself well, and is living well in the land where he is. If however the benefics were to aspect him from a trine or sextile aspect with reception, say that his brother is well and is living well, and is prospering, indeed so that he is not lacking anything he needs for living.

If indeed he were in the 4th without the aspects of the malefics, he is trying to acquire money in the land in which he is.

---

[90] *Status.*

If indeed he were in the 5th and were joined with the Lord of the 5th, with reception (whether the Lord of the 5th were a benefic or not, provided that he were not impeded in a bad way), it signifies that his brother finds himself well, and rejoices and is happy with the people of that land in which he is. If indeed he (with whom the significator of the brother is joined) were a benefic, and it were a conjunction by body or from a trine or sextile aspect with reception, say that his brother is well and cheerful, and rejoices, and is happy with the men and women of the place in which he is, and enjoys eating, drinking, clothing, and is engaged in venereal cultivation,[91] and in all things in which men delight–if he is a man fit for such a thing, or who delights in such things (as are young men and those similar to young men). If indeed he were void in course in the 5th, or in corporal conjunction with the malefics, or in their square aspect or opposition without reception, and those malefics who impede him were likewise and themselves impeded, it signifies his bad disposition, and his bad condition, and the poor temperament of his body, because the 5th is the 3rd from the house of brothers.[92]

If indeed you were to find him in the other houses (which will not be taken up [here], as the 6th, 8th, and 12th are), with the significators mentioned above, tell him the same thing, but it will be less [good].

If however you were to find him in the 8th joined to the benefics by a trine or sextile aspect, say that his brother is not becoming really well, nor is he becoming so sick that he ought to have fear; but he has a bad [unbalanced] temperament.[93]

If however he were joined to malefics and were in the 6th, or were joined to the Lord of the 6th, you may say that his brother is taken ill. And you may say the same thing if the Lord of the 6th were in the third, unless the Lord of the third were well disposed, just as was said above. Then look to see if you were to find the brother of the querent to be taken ill, and see if

---

[91] I.e., sexual pleasure.
[92] I do not know why the 3rd from the 3rd would relate to these problems.
[93] Note the 8th is also 6th from the 3rd.

the Lord of the third is joined to the Lord of the 8th house, or enters into combustion: it signifies that he will die from this illness.

If indeed you were to find him in the 7th, say that he is in the land to which he has set out, he is not yet leaving from it, and he is staying in it like a foreigner; nor is he well disposed nor very badly, but finds himself to be both.

If he were in the 8th, he will fear for himself, and especially if he were combust or joined to the Lord of the 8th in the 8th, or joined to malefics impeding him in the 8th, because then it signifies his death.

If he were in the 9th, it signifies that he has set out from the land in which he first was, to another land farther away; or perhaps he gave himself to a certain religion, or in some other way takes on a clerical or religious life.

Indeed if he were in the 10th and were joined to the benefics by a trine or sextile aspect, and especially with reception, it signifies that he has acquired some office, or honor, or a dignity, in the land in which he is. If indeed he were joined to the malefics by a square aspect or by opposition, or they impede him in some other way, or he were combust in the 10th, his death may be feared.

If indeed he were in the 11th, joined to the benefics from a good aspect, or were joined with the Lord of the 11th, it signifies that he is with some friend of his, with whom he is having a good time, and is rejoicing, and he delights with him. If indeed they were malefics aspecting him, it signifies that he does not rejoice in the things he has, nor does it seem to him that he is in a good condition.

If indeed he were in the 12th, and were joined to benefics receiving him, and the benefic which received him were not impeded, it signifies that he has some mastery,[94] or conducts a business in horses and cows (whence he makes money), and leads his life in a praiseworthy way. If indeed that benefic were impeded or were joined to malefics impeding it, it signifies the bad disposition of the same, so that he is sick or badly disposed,

---

[94] *Magisterium.* I.e., a professional skill or office.

indeed so that if he is joined with the Lord of the 8th or were combust or entered combustion, it may be feared that he will die there.

If he were in the 1st, he rejoices and he will be made joyful by those loving him, and he is well disposed.

If he were in the 2nd, he does not rejoice in whatever station he has; it is possible that he is a captive or detained in another way, indeed so that he cannot leave the place in which he is, when he wants.[95]

If perhaps he were retrograde, he tries to return to his own place, and when he can.

And for the present let these statements about brothers suffice for you, because it would take a long time to speak about all the accidents of brothers. For if the querent had asked about a sick brother, I will tell you about this below in the treatment of illness.[96] If he had asked about a brother who is present and well, I will tell you those things which will be useful in the Treatise on nativities, in a discussion which will be just as long as will be necessary.

Besides, it is necessary that I tell you certain other things which likewise are able to be included in this chapter, which are these: of course if someone asks about his father, look to the 4th for the father; and tell him just as I told you about the brother in the 3rd house. And concerning the 5th [for the father], say what I said about the brother in the 4th house. And concerning the 6th for the father, say what I said about the 5th for the brother. And concerning the 7th for the father, say what I said about the 6th for the brother. And concerning the 8th for the father, say what I said about the 7th for the brother. And concerning the 9th for the father, say what I said about the 8th for the brother. And concerning the 10th for the father, say just as I said about the 9th for the brother. And concerning the 11th for the father, say what I said about the 10th for the brother. And concerning the 12th for the father, say what I said about the 11th for the brother. And concerning the 1st for the father, say what I said about the 12th for the brother. And concerning the 2nd for the father, say what I said about the 1st for the brother. And concerning the 3rd for the father, say what I said about the 2nd for the brother.[97]

---

[95] The 2nd is the 12th from the 3rd.

[96] See 6th House.

[97] Bonatti has worded this in an awkward way, but all he means to say is that one should treat the father's derived houses as one does with the brother. For instance, since the 4th is the

If he asks about his uncle, namely his father's brother, you will give the 5th to him and say about the 5th for the uncle just as I told you about the 3rd for the brother; and concerning the 6th for the uncle, just as I told you about the 4th for the brother;[98] and understand this for all houses.

If he asks about a slave or client, you will give the 6th to the slave, and say about the 6th for the servant, just as I said about the 3rd for the brother; and say about the 7th for the servant, just as I said about the 4th for the brother; and say about the 8th for the servant just as I said about the 5th for the brother; and so forth with all of them.

But I will not omit this: because even if any house may have its own 6th and 8th and 12th, still in any question at all the 6th [house] of the question and its Lord signify its illness.[99] The 8th of the question and its Lord signify[100] its death. The 12th and its Lord signify its deception [or capture]. Still, they are made diverse [through derived houses] in this.

---

father's 1st house, then for the father's 1st house you should say what you did for the brother in *his* 1st house (i.e., the 3rd). If you are interested in the father's money (his 2nd house, or the 5th), then say what you did for the brother in *his* 2nd house (i.e., the 4th).

[98] This cannot be right: the father's brother would be the 3rd from the 4th, i.e., the 6th.

[99] I.e., illness generally. In other words, the houses that result from treating the Ascendant as the 1st always have general applicability, even if the question calls for derived houses to be applied.

[100] Reading *significant* for *significat*.

ON THE FOURTH HOUSE

Chapter 1: On a home or inheritance which someone wishes to buy, or to have in some other way: whether the querent will possess it

If someone were concerned about some house, or some measure of land or a vineyard, or meadow, or olive orchard, or a forest, or about some inheritance, which he wished to buy, or otherwise wished to own it, and his question were absolute (so that he does not speak about land or a home or an inheritance of such-and-such a person), look at the Ascendant and its Lord, and the Moon (which signify the querent), and look at the fourth sign and its Lord (which are the significators of the quaesited thing).

If the Lord of the Ascendant or the Moon were in the fourth, or the Lord of the fourth were in the first, or one of them were corporally joined to the other [or] by a trine or sextile aspect, with reception, he will easily obtain the quaesited thing, and without complications or impediment. If indeed it were without reception, or they were joined together by a square aspect or from the opposition with perfect reception, the querent will attain the quaesited thing.

If however they were not joined together (whether by aspect or by body), but the Moon or another planet transferred the light between them, the querent will attain the quaesited thing through someone who interposes himself, and leads the matter to completion though his own wisdom and industry. If indeed that planet which is lighter, and who is joined to the other, goes retrograde before their conjunction is perfected degree by degree, the matter will be destroyed after the querent thought it was completed, and it will be annulled.[101] But if the matter were completed through the [planet] which interposed itself to perfect the matter, if it were the Moon which transferred the light, then see in which house she herself is, because the matter will be completed through the person which is signified by the house in which the Moon is. If however it was another planet that transferred the light between the Lord of the Ascendant and the Lord signifying the quaesited thing, see which house it is Lord of, because the matter will be perfected through that person: like if it were the Lord of the 3rd house, the matter will be completed through the querent's brother. Which if he did not have a brother, it will be perfected by one of his lesser blood relations. And if this were not so, it will be perfected by one of his neighbors. If it were the Lord of the 5th, the matter will be perfected by a child or by one of the

---

[101] This is "restraint" or *al-intikāth* (الإنتكاث). See Tr. 3, Part 2, Ch. 15.

people who are signified by the 5th house. If it were the Lord of the 6th, it is perfected through a slave or client or someone who is signified by the 6th house. And if it were the Lord of the 7th, it will be perfected through the wife or girlfriend or partner; which if he did not have a wife, it will be perfected by one of those who are signified by the 7th house.[102] And if it were the Lord of the 9th, through some religious person. And if it were the Lord of the 10th, it will be perfected through some magnate or leader. And if it were the Lord of the 11th, it will be perfected through some friend of the querent. And if it were the Lord of the 12th, it will be perfected through someone who pretends to be the querent's friend, when he is not. And if it were the Lord of the 2nd or 8th, it will be perfected by such a person that is not expected and of whom no mention will be made in the discussion.

If indeed the Lord of the 4th were not joined to the Lord of the Ascendant, nor the Lord of the Ascendant to the Lord of the 4th, nor the Moon; nor were there a planet which transferred light between them; or there were some planet which would prohibit their conjunction, the matter will not be perfected.

If however you wished to know who it will be who does not allow the matter to be perfected, see that planet which prohibits the conjunction between the Lord of the Ascendant or the Moon–whose house it is Lord of. Because the annulling of the matter will come to be through the person who is signified by that house.

Chapter 2: On the kinds of things bought, and their nature

If indeed the querent were to ask, as often happens, "See what kind of thing it is that I intend to buy or obtain; whether it is sterile or fruitful earth, or the foundation of the house is solid or cracked, or damaged in some other way; whether its laborers are good and loyal or not," look for this likewise from the Ascendant and its Lord: because then the Ascendant and its Lord signify[103] the laborers of the land or vineyard, and forest workers, and the inhabitants of a house.

And the sign of the 4th signifies the land or home or inheritance, and what kind it is, and what is in it; and the 7th signifies that which is in the land, namely its grain, and barley, other common grains, domesticated plants which tend to be grown in the garden, as are cabbage, fenugreek, parsley, borage [or borrago],

---

[102] No 8th house signification is given.
[103] Reading *significant* for *significat*.

spinach,[104] and the like, if it were in the season in which grains and domestic plants were in the fields or gardens; it can even signify vines like vine-arbors[105] and similar things.

If Jupiter were in the 7th, well disposed and of good condition, it signifies that in that land there is grain and plants which yield more useful seeds, and which are more edible for the usefulness of men. If Venus or Mercury or the Moon or the Sun were there, well disposed and of good condition, it signifies that in the land are herbs in which men delight, like roses and others producing odiferous fruits, and flowers whence garlands come, and the like. If however Jupiter or Venus or the others that where there, were impeded, there will be some of what I said, but not much.

While if it were Saturn, there will be rocks in that land, and heavy and deep things, and underground serpents impeding the success of the land.

If indeed Mars were there and he were well disposed and of good condition without impediment, there will be wild roses and *lambruscae*[106] (namely wild vines making fruits in hedgerows). Or perhaps it could be that there are vines producing the sort of wine that men get drunk from. If indeed he were badly disposed, there will be bramble-bushes,[107] *salvincae*,[108] and other kinds of poisonous needles that wound men.

The 10th from the Ascendant signifies the trees which are in [the land]. If Jupiter were in the 10th, free from impediments, well-disposed, it signifies that there will be copious trees, and that those trees produce good fruits and those from which men derive usefulness and wealth, like pears, apples, olives, cherries, figs, and the like. If however Venus were there, well disposed, it signifies odiferous and delicious fruits which are readily carried in the hand by youths, and even by others, like fragrant apples, juniper berries, oranges, and the like (and especially in hot regions). If indeed the Sun were there, free from impediments and otherwise well disposed, he signifies good fruits of great trees, such as nuts [especially almonds], pine nuts, and even apples and cherries and the like. If however Mars were there, free and well disposed, he signifies fruits of trees which are obtained with labor from their trees, and they have spines in

---

[104] *Bleta*. I also note that an English vegetable called "blet" is also known as "silver beet."
[105] *Perguleta*.
[106] This is probably related to *lambruscura*, paneling or wainscoting.
[107] *Rubi*. A *rubus* can also mean a blackberry bush, so perhaps there are berries despite the prickles?
[108] Unknown word, but its similarity to the root *salv-* (indicating health and preservation) suggests it might have been an ironic colloquial name for a poisonous plant.

their rinds, or other coverings. And the Sun and Mars can even signify domesticated vines or other fruits, such as chestnuts, medlar fruit,[109] cornel-cherries,
and the like. If however Saturn were there, free and well disposed, he signifies
that there will not be a great quantity of trees there, and there will be trees with
bitter tastes, such as pears and especially wild ones, and even sometimes sorb-
apples, acorns, nuts, and the like. If however Mercury or the Moon were there,
and in the kind of condition as was said about the others, they signify fruits of
many kinds, and diverse tastes, and diverse colors, and they signify them
according to what those to whom they are applied, signify.

Indeed if Jupiter were badly disposed, then there would be trees of little
usefulness, and even those which produce little fruit and easily lose their own
fruit. Likewise with Venus if she were badly disposed; however it could be that
the trees would be of the sort described above. If however Saturn were badly
disposed, there will be few wild trees, and whose fruits are hardly or never
edible by humans. The same must be understood regarding Mars and the Sun
for the trees they signify, as with those which Mercury and the Moon signified.
Likewise they will signify that which those to whom they will be applied, will
signify.

If however any of the aforesaid planets were retrograde, he who buys the
land will sell the fruits of those trees and will hardly preserve any of them for
himself, nor will he strive to have a part of them, except if Venus were the
significatrix (because then he will reserve for himself a part of those fruits, and
especially more of the delicious ones).

Chapter 3: On the quality of the laborers

If however you wished to know about the nature of the laborers of the land
or vineyard, or of the custodians of a meadow or forest, or what kinds of
tenants they are, look to the Ascendant and see if Jupiter were [there], direct, of
good condition–the laborers will be good and loyal; and they will be men of
middle age. And if he were oriental, there will be youths of good spirit; and if he
were occidental, they will already be beginning to grow old, or they will perhaps
be old men; however all will be of good spirit. And if Jupiter were direct, they
will remain laborers in their labor, and will be useful to the querent. And if he

---

[109] Reading *mespilae* for *nespilae*, with Hand.

were retrograde, they will leave their labor and the querent will lease the land to other laborers worse than them.

And if it were Venus instead of Jupiter, they will be good and loyal laborers; and almost in everything they will be just as those which are signified through Jupiter; except that Venus signifies younger people and those more delightful in the aforesaid qualities.

And if it were Saturn instead of Jupiter, these same laborers or tenants will be liars and thieves, even if they are old or decrepit men.

And if it were Mars instead of [Jupiter], the laborers will be thieves and liars, and they will be more openly angry than those which are signified through Saturn, and they will be *scarani*[110] and greater doers of evil than if it were merely [a matter of] thievery.

And if Mars or Saturn were direct, they will remain in their labor; if they do not, they will withdraw from it, and the labor will be leased to better laborers, or at length to better tenants.

Chapter 4: On the oldness and newness of things

If however you wished to know about the trees or the building, whether [the trees] were planted long ago or indeed recently, or whether the building was made recently, see if some planet were in the 10th: [for then] the building will not have been made either very long ago or recently; likewise with the trees, for they will not be very old nor very new.

If indeed no planet were there, see where the Lord of the 10th house is, [and] if he aspects the house from the place in which he is (or if he does not aspect it, but aspects a planet which aspects the 10th from its [own] place): the trees will be young, and the building built recently, indeed it is not old–and particularly if the Lord of the 10th were oriental. If however it were occidental, the trees will be old and the building old.

---

110 Unknown word, but paronyms of this word in modern Italian have to do with bad luck. In the second chapter on the 9th house, Bonatti groups *scarrani* with thieves and robbers.

If however [the Lord of the 10th] did not aspect the 10th, nor were he joined to some planet which aspects it, nor one which renders[111] his light to the 10th, and he were occidental, these same trees will be ancient and the building ancient. Then look likewise from the Lord of the 10th house if you wish to know what will happen to these trees or building: if it were direct (whether it were a benefic or malefic), the trees and building will remain in their condition. If it were retrograde, the trees will be torn down from the land, and likewise the building.

If indeed the Lord of the 10th did not aspect the 10th house, and were not in the 11th or in the 3rd or in the 5th or in the 9th from the Ascendant, the land will be without trees and without a building. And it will not be cultivated; even if were, [it will be] badly cultivated.

In addition, so that you may know whether there are seeds in it (namely wheat or other grains), if the season it right for it, look then to the Lord of the 7th house; if he were to aspect the 7th, there will be seed in it which the owner of the earth may hope to recover for his own use. If indeed it did not aspect it, there will not be useful seeds there.

Chapter 5: On the site[112] of the land

If however you wished to know what kind of site the land is, look to the 4th house, and see of which triplicity the sign is. Because if it were of the triplicity of Aries, the land will be mountainous, or there will be rocks in it; and it will be poorly disposed for tilling; and it will be poor [or barren] earth, and it will be cultivated and will need much manure and effort for it to be able to bear fruit.

If however the fourth sign were of the triplicity of Taurus, the land is flat, and fit to support tilling, and will be fertile.

And if the fourth sign were of the triplicity of Gemini, part of the land will be flat and part will be mountainous; and it will be neither very fruitful nor very sterile. Likewise if the fourth sign were the bicorporal sign of its triplicity, because it signifies mountainousness and flatness, [but] neither especially one nor the other.

If the 4th domicile were of the triplicity of Cancer, it will be marshy or *aquaesternium*[113] or water in another way, or near a watery place.

---

[111] This is Abū Ma'shar's "reflecting the light," or *al-radd al-nur*. See Tr. 3, Part 2, Ch. 11.
[112] *Situ.* This word refers to the kind of location and terrain; it can also refer to the soil; I will translate it as "site" in this chapter.

And if you wished, attend to the fourth and its partner:[114] which if they were fiery, it signifies arid, and rocky and mountainous [places].

And a certain person said that the 4th house and its Lord always signify an immovable thing to be bought, as are homes and land and the like. And he said that the 5th and its Lord signify its profit. And he said that if the thing were movable, and something which changes quickly, and crosses from the hand of one to another's, that the 7th and its Lord signify it, and the 8th and its Lord signify its profit.

Chapter 6: If renting the land or the house would be useful

And if someone wishing to rent the land or a house–or if he were a laborer who took up the land in the way of a laborer, or for a fixed right to the land for a given year (as often happens), or for a house in order to live in it–were to ask, and he wanted to know if it is good for him to hire it out, you will give the 1st and its Lord to him who rents the thing, and the 7th and its Lord him who leases it. And you will give the 10th for the usefulness which may follow from it, and you will give the 4th to the end of it which could follow from thence.

If the Lord of the Ascendant were in the Ascendant, or were to aspect by a trine or sextile aspect; or a benefic were there (whether it had dignity there or not); or the Part of Fortune (unimpeded), it signifies that the renter will rent the thing, hoping for good from it; and it will not pain him to have farmed it, and he will be delighted, and will rejoice in its farming.

If indeed a malefic were in the Ascendant, it will be one or the other of these: either if he had farmed it, it will pain him to have farmed it; or he will not farm it; or he wants to farm it so he may deceive the lessor.

Then, look to the 7th for him who leases the thing; if the Lord of the 7th were in it, or it were to aspect it from a trine or sextile aspect, or a benefic were there, not impeded in a bad way, the lessor will perfect that which is appropriate for the renter, and he will keep his promise to him, and he will be useful to him. If however a malefic were there (who was not the Lord of the 7th) the lessor will not keep what he had promised to the renter, and will try to deceive him, and will act fraudulently against him.

Then look at the 10th. If a benefic were in it or were to aspect from a trine or sextile aspect, the matter will be arranged and perfected. If indeed there were a

---

[113] Hand translates this word as "strewn with water."
[114] *Socium.* I do not know what this means in this context–perhaps the 10th?

malefic in it (who was not the Lord of the 10th) or who aspected [the 10th] by opposition or a square aspect, the renting will not be perfected; and it could be that dissent could arise over trees or buildings located on that land.

Then look at the 4th, and you will give it to the end of the matter. If a benefic were there or the Lord of the 4th were there, or aspected [the 4th] from a trine or sextile aspect, the end of the matter will be good and useful and praiseworthy. If indeed a malefic were there (who was not the Lord of the 4th) the end will be bad and the renter will derive loss and inconvenience from it.

ON THE FIFTH HOUSE

Chapter 1: Whether a man will have children by his wife or by another woman he talks about, or likewise should he ask about children in a similar way

If you were asked by some man whether he will have children by the wife he has (or by another woman); or if a woman were to ask whether she would have children by the husband she has (or by another): take the shadow immediately, and organize the figure according to the Ascendant and the remaining houses; and look at the Ascendant and its Lord and the Moon. And if you were to see the Lord of the Ascendant and the Moon (or one of them), joined to the Lord of the 5th (which is the house of children), say that he will have children; likewise if the Lord of the 5th were joined to the Lord of the Ascendant.

And if you did not find them joined together, see if any planet transfers light between the Lord of the Ascendant and the Lord of the 5th, because it signifies children (even if after a delay). Which if this were not so, see if the Lord of the Ascendant or the Moon were in the 5th house: say that he will have children. Likewise if the Lord of the 5th were in the Ascendant, say that he will have children; which if this were not so, see if the Lord of the Ascendant (or the Moon) and the Lord of the 5th are both joined to some other planet who is heavier than they; because he will collect the light of both, and will be the receiver of the disposition, and he will be the significator of children, whether they ought to live or not. And see if he himself is free from the impediments I told you about in the treatment of the impediments of the planets (namely that they are not retrograde, or combust, or cadent, and so on):[115] [in which case,] say that those children will live.

If indeed that heavier planet who is the receiver of the disposition, were impeded–namely retrograde or combust or cadent (whether from the angles or from the Ascendant) or besieged by the malefics–or if he had one of the aforesaid impediments, the children will not live long, nor will their father and mother be blessed[116] by them.

Then look to Jupiter, who naturally signifies children. If you were to find him in the Ascendant, or in the 3rd, or in the 5th, or in the 9th, or in the 11th, free

---

[115] See Tr. 5, the 6th Consideration.
[116] *Beati*, which also has connotations of being made fortunate: so it could simply mean they will not be blessed enough to have any, or perhaps that they will not be made fortunate by the ones they do have.

from all aforesaid impediments, say that the mother has either conceived or will conceive shortly, perhaps in the first copulation or shortly thereafter, indeed so that the matter seems to be either already done or in [the process of] becoming.[117] And if Venus were in the 5th, unimpeded, and there were another benefic there besides Jupiter or Venus, it signifies that the woman will be made pregnant soon.

If indeed Jupiter were impeded in the aforesaid places, say that the conception either has not taken place, or, if it has, it will not be completed, but the woman will miscarry or abort. Likewise if Venus were joined to Saturn or Mars, or were under the rays of the Sun, going toward corporal conjunction with the Sun, the woman is not pregnant, unless a benefic were in the 5th: because she would be better able to be pregnant, or will be soon, but her delivery will hardly be good. Which if Saturn or Mars (or another malefic, and especially the Tail of the Dragon, which signifies emptying) were in the 5th or were to aspect [the 5th] by opposition, it signifies that the woman will not be pregnant; and even from the square aspect the malefics appear to frustrate conception (if they were to aspect the 5th by a square aspect).

Chapter 2: When the question about a child is absolute

If indeed the question were absolute, so that a man or woman may say, "will he [or she] have children?" but does not say whether it concerns "this woman" or "this man," look then at the Ascendant and its Lord; and see if the Lord of the Ascendant were in the Ascendant, or if a benefic were there, well disposed, or in the 10th or in the 11th or in the 5th, and Jupiter (as was said) in the 3rd or 5th or 9th, or 11th: the querent will have children; but there will be some delay (though not a great one).

If however the Lord of the Ascendant were not in the 5th (which is the house of children), but were in the 4th, or were in the 7th, nor were he impeded by combustion or retrogradation, nor were he besieged by the two malefics, or joined corporally to one of the malefics which would impede him (namely to Saturn or Mars), or he were with the Tail; and Jupiter were in one of the places said above (the 3rd or 5th or 9th or 11th), the man or woman will have children, but there will be a greater delay in this than before.

---

[117] *Quod erit illud tanquam res quae videtur iam facta vel est in fieri.*

If indeed one of the malefics (namely Saturn or Mars or the Tail of the Dragon) were in the Ascendant, or aspected it from a square aspect or by opposition, and the Lord of the Ascendant were impeded by retrogradation or combustion or cadence,[118] or were in the 2nd or 6th or 8th, or the 12th,[119] and Jupiter were in a bad place (and specifically in the 8th) or if he were impeded in a bad way from retrogradation or combustion or cadence,[120] it signifies that the querent will have either no or few children; nor will he rejoice in them (which is to be blessed by them); and he will see their death. And see where the Moon is then: which if she herself or the Lord of the 5th were impeded, and one of them were impeded in the 6th, the querent will be saddened by reason of their illness; if it were in the 8th, by reason of their death; if in the 12th, by reason of their capture.

And see what sign was in any of the aforesaid houses, because the reason why the querent will be saddened on account of children will be from the part of the body ruled by that sign. If it were Aries, it will be by reason of the head; if it were Taurus, it will by reason of the neck; if Gemini, it will be the lungs or hands; if Cancer, by reason of the chest; if Leo, by reason of the stomach or the spine [or the back]; if Virgo, by reason of the belly and the parts adjacent to the navel; if Libra, by reason of the hips; if Scorpio, by reason of the private parts; if Sagittarius, by reason of the upper thighs; if Capricorn, by reason of the knees; if Aquarius, by reason of the legs; if Pisces, by reason of the feet.

And let this always be of concern to you: because if you were to find Jupiter or Venus or the Sun or the Moon or Mercury or the Head of the Dragon in the 5th, not impeded by evil impediments, do not give up hope of looking for children; because they all signify that the querent will have children. And if some benefic were not in the 5th, and you were to find one of the malefics there who has testimony there, the [chart for the] question is not completely evil. It signifies that he will have children, but they will not inherit their paternal or maternal goods; but rather it appears that [the parents] will have to see their [children's] death.

Throughout this whole time, look out for Jupiter if he were in an angle, because this signifies children, even if not many. If he were oriental in an angle,

---

[118] *Casu*. Usually this refers to being in fall or detriment; but Bonatti rarely includes this in his lists of the three or four standard impediments. Therefore I (like Hand, p. 63) tentatively call this cadence (which also has connotations of falling).
[119] Places "cadent from the Ascendant."
[120] *Casu*. See above note.

it signifies speed in having children. If he were occidental in an angle, it signifies slowness in having them; and that there will be some delay in it.

Chapter 3: Whether a woman is pregnant

Moreover, if someone is concerned whether a woman has conceived and carries a conception [i.e., an embryo] in her womb or not: look at the Lord of the Ascendant and the Moon (which signify the woman), or one of them; and look at the 5th and its Lord (which are the significators of the conception). If you were to find the Moon in the 5th, or you were to find the Lord of the 5th in the Ascendant, free from the malefics and the other aforesaid impediments, it signifies that the woman has conceived and has a conception in her womb. Likewise if the Lord of the Ascendant were to commit its own disposition to some planet in an angle. And it would be most secure and certain if he to whom the Lord of the Ascendant committed his disposition were received, or [the other planet] itself received the Lord of the Ascendant. Because then it signifies a conception.

Indeed if he to whom the Lord of the Ascendant were joined, and to whom he committed his disposition, were in a cadent house, it signifies that the woman had gotten an affliction, and that what seems to be a pregnancy, is more likely to be an illness than a conception; and if it is a conception, it will not come to a good end; and especially if the Ascendant were Aries or Cancer or Libra or Capricorn, or one of the malefics were in some angle; and more strongly so if the Tail were there (because it signifies abortion more so than the other malefics).

If indeed a heavy planet to which the Lord of the Ascendant committed its disposition, were in a good place from the Ascendant, and were not in conjunction with the malefics, but were free from impediments, and the Moon likewise were safe, it signifies that the conception will come to a good end, and that the birth will not be frustrated. Likewise if the Lord of the 5th (which is the significator of children), were in the Ascendant, free from the aforesaid impediments (namely that it were not retrograde, nor combust, nor joined to the malefics, and specifically corporally to the Tail, or to the other malefics by opposition or square aspect), it signifies conception. If indeed it were impeded by one of the aforesaid impediments, there will not be a conception; and if there were, it will be frustrated and terminated.[121]

Chapter 4: Whether a woman is pregnant or not

Sometimes women tend to doubt whether they are pregnant or not; and even their husbands, aspiring to have children, do not know whether or not it is so. And they are accustomed to inquiring about this from an astrologer, in order to be certain. Whence if a question were made to you by a woman about herself [as to] whether she is pregnant or not,[122] nor were the question about someone else, look to the Ascendant and its Lord; and see where the Lord of the Ascendant is, which if it were in an angle, free from the malefics and other impediments, it signifies that the woman is pregnant. Likewise if the Lord of the Ascendant were in the succeedent houses, or even in the cadents (provided it were received by a planet located in an angle). If indeed it were in a house cadent from the angle, or were it joined to a planet which did not receive it, or if [the other planet] did receive and were retrograde or combust or cadent, it signifies that the woman is not pregnant. Likewise if the Moon were impeded; but if the Moon were received by a planet which was free from the aforesaid impediments, she is pregnant. If indeed the Moon were not received, and the Lord of the Ascendant were impeded, she is not pregnant. And if the Lord of the Ascendant were in a good place, and aspected the Ascendant by a praise-worthy aspect, she is pregnant.

If perhaps a man were to ask about a woman, with her consent, the judgment will be the same.[123] If however the man asked of his own accord and for himself, but the woman was unaware [he was consulting an astrologer], you will consider the 7th and its Lord (by means of the above conditions), and you will judge by the Lord of the 7th according to what you judged for the Lord of the Ascendant; but with the Moon not being overlooked.

---

[121] *Delebitur.* This word has close associations with *aborisci*, so it is unclear whether Bonatti is suggesting a miscarriage, abortion, or both.
[122] Bonatti switches back and forth between saying the woman *is* pregnant, and *will be* pregnant. My understanding is that the woman is asking about a hypothetical pregnancy in the *present.* But it may be that these conditions will also hold if a woman says, "*Will I* get pregnant in the near future?"
[123] This is a key point: if one asks about another person who has given consent to consult the astrologer, that person is the true querent and is assigned the 1st house.

Chapter 5: If a woman who has conceived carries
one or more in her womb

And if you were concerned about a pregnant woman, or if someone were concerned whether she carried one or more, look for this from the Ascendant, and see if the Ascendant were Gemini or Virgo or Sagittarius or Pisces;[124] or if the Ascendant were any one of the other signs and had two good planets in it (or [they were] in the 5th): she has conceived two. If however the Head of the Dragon were there with them, say that she carries more than two in her womb, and it is possible she carries four. And if there are no planets in the Ascendant or the 5th, see if any of the planets aspects the Ascendant or the 5th, degree by degree, so that the aspect is not more than one degree ahead of the line of the Ascendant or of the 5th, or more than two behind.[125] Because however many planets aspected it, that many will have been conceived in the womb, even if all planets aspect those degrees; and see how many they were and how many aspected by trine or sextile aspect–that many from among them will make it to birth.[126] Indeed, however many aspect from the square or opposition, that many from among the conceived will suffer detriment.

And if you were to find the Sun and the Moon in one sign, but so that the Moon goes toward the Sun, and she is not more than 5° away from him behind, nor in front of him by more than two degrees,[127] you will judge the same if the Sun or the Moon is in Gemini, Virgo, Sagittarius, and Pisces. Because if the Ascendant were one of the fixed signs, or the movable ones, and likewise the 5th were of these signs, and the Sun and Moon were in fixed or movable signs, nor were there more planets in the Ascendant or in the 5th, or aspecting them,[128] as I said, you may know that the woman carries a single one, and not more.

Chapter 6: If a woman carries a male or female

And if [someone] were to ask whether a woman carries a male or female, look then to the Ascendant and [its] Lord, and the 5th and its Lord, and see if

---

124 The common or "double-bodied" signs.

125 I believe that by "ahead of," Bonatti means "in an earlier degree than the cusp's"; by "behind," he means "in a later degree than the cusp's." See my Introduction.

126 Literally, "will reach perfection" (*pervenient ad perfectionem*).

127 By "behind," Bonatti means "in an earlier degree than the Sun's, moving toward him"; by "in front of," he means "in a later degree than the Sun's, moving away from him."

128 *Vel eorum aspectus*, lit. "or of their aspect."

they are in Aries, or Gemini, or Leo, or Libra, or Sagittarius, or Aquarius:[129] it is a sign that she carries a male; if not, it seems that she carries a female. If indeed the Lord of the Ascendant were in a masculine sign, and the Lord of the 5th were in a feminine sign, or the Lord of the 5th in a masculine sign and the Lord of the Ascendant in a feminine sign, then have recourse to the Moon (who is the participator in every matter), and see if she herself were in a masculine sign and is conjoined to a planet who is in a masculine sign (then she will attest to him who was in the masculine sign); or if she were in a feminine sign, she will attest to him who was in a feminine sign (whether the Lord of the Ascendant were in a masculine sign, or the Lord of the 5th, or vice versa).

Likewise if the Moon were joined to a masculine planet, she will attest to him who was in a masculine sign; and if she were joined to a feminine planet, she will attest to him who was in a feminine sign. Likewise, if the Lord of the Ascendant or the Lord of the 5th were a masculine or feminine planet, the Moon will attest to him to whom her site [or location] is likened.

And may you know that Saturn, Jupiter and Mars and the Sun are always masculine, unless sometimes in certain cases (of which this is not so). And Venus is always feminine, unless sometimes in cases (of which this is not one). Mercury is said to be masculine when he is oriental in the world, so that he rises in the morning before the Sun; he is called feminine when he is occidental in the world, so that he sets after the Sun in the evening. Likewise, when he is joined to masculine planets he is masculine; and when joined to feminine planets he is feminine.

---

[129] I.e., the masculine signs.

ON THE SIXTH HOUSE

Chapter 1: Whether or not a sick person will be freed
from the illness in which he is held

If a question is made to you by some sick person, whether he will be freed from the illness in which he is held, first see who is the one who asks–namely, whether he himself is the sick person, or whether [he is] another person who asks on [the sick person's] behalf; and if it is his business to ask, or not; and if he asks from the consent of the sick person or of his own accord. Because if he himself asks with the consent of the sick person and with his permission, the 1st is given to him and the sick person. If however he asks of his own accord, the first is given to him, but to the sick person is given the one through which his person is signified: so if he asks for his brother, the 1st is given to the querent, the 3rd to the sick person; if for his father, the 1st is given to him, the 4th to the sick person. And understand this about the significations of all of the houses according to what was said above in the Treatise on the twelve houses.

You will even consider of what social condition the sick person is, namely whether he is a layperson or a cleric, or a religious person of another type; and whether he is among those who are put over a doctor, or over whom a doctor is put.[130] For on this matter there were many and contrasting opinions.[131]

You must even look to see the kind of illness, and its nature, for a brand-new illness is looked at differently than an old one. And I will tell you about the conditions [rank] of the sick and of the infirmities; and over what sick people a doctor should take charge, and which not; and in which cases; and which sick people are to be in command of a doctor, and which not, and in which cases, and how and when, according to the diverse opinions for judging sick people, if Jesus Christ our Lord would lend his grace to me at this juncture.

For certain people gave the Ascendant to the doctor, the 10th to the sick person, the 7th to the illness, the 4th to the art of medicine. And Sahl and his followers were of this opinion.[132] And so according to this [opinion][133] the

---

130 *Praeponuntur…praeponitur.* I believe the last clause really means, "who are in a doctor's care."
131 See below. This issue concerns which of the other houses will be assigned to the doctor and the treatment; but it does not affect the assignment of the house to the sick person.
132 See Sahl, *On Quest.*, 7th House, "If a sick person will get well or die."
133 In this paragraph Bonatti's use of the verb *praepono* (to set or put over/before) is equivocal. We are not only speaking of the order of angles from most important to least important, but we are also opposing the angles to each other (as when one might say the doctor in the 1st is "set over" the illness in the 7th). Bonatti's original sentence does not really make sense (nor

doctor was put before the sick person, the sick person before the infirmity, indeed the 7th [or infirmity] before the medicine. And likewise they put the doctor before the sick person, like if a question would arise about a sick person (with him and the doctor being ignorant), then the doctor is put before him. Because [if] either another [asks] for him from his willing [knowledge] (of whatever condition the sick person is), then the 1st is given to the sick person, the 10th to the doctor, the 7th to the infirmity, the 4th to the medical art. And in this case, the sick person is put before the doctor.[134]

But if someone of his own accord asks about a sick king, [the king] being ignorant, the 1st is given to the doctor, the 10th to the sick person [the king], the 7th to the infirmity, the 4th to the art of medicine. If however he asked in the same way about the Pope, or about some other cleric, the 1st is given to the doctor, the 9th to the sick person, the 7th to the infirmity, and the 3rd to the art of medicine.

Now however I will tell you the circumstances[135] of illness, for if you were to know the circumstances of illness, you would be able to judge them better and more securely regarding them. And even though the art of medicine is said to have been invented for the wealthy and great men, still the common man of the rustics has already embraced remedies; nor is it surprising, because they themselves, just like great men, are taken ill and try to be freed of it.

To speak of an illness as many years old or old, I reckon it as long-lived and of long standing, on account of it being a year old: because year-old illnesses are never cured easily, but rather with the greatest difficulty. But an illness that is

---

does it match Sahl's scheme) unless it is read solely in terms of the order or angles, as I have translated it here. The original reads: "And so according to this [opinion] the doctor is put before the sick person, the 7th the infirmity, indeed the 10th the medicine." Perhaps it is just a typesetting mistake.

[134] This is a somewhat vexed paragraph, and I have had to supply a couple of words. Bonatti is underscoring the need to determine who is represented by the 1st house (as he has done in previous chapters), and he is showing that Sahl's view only applies to certain querents. If the querent is a third party asking about the doctor and the sick person (without having been sent by them), then we follow Sahl's view and give the Ascendant to the doctor, the 10th to the patient, the 7th to the infirmity, and the 4th to the medicine. But if the patient has sent the querent to ask for him, then the patient becomes the true querent, and we give the Ascendant to the patient, the 10th to the doctor, the 7th to the infirmity, and the 4th to the medicine. The distinction implies that if an unrelated third party asks, then the real intention and act belongs to the doctor, who is making the healing of the patient (the 10th) his aim. But if the patient has sent the person who asks, then the intention and act belongs to the patient, who has a successful trip to the doctor (the 10th) as his aim. This distinction between querents is confirmed in the following paragraph.

[135] *Conditiones.* Bonatti is speaking of the history and condition of the illness (and the patient: see below).

not old, I consider to be not yet a year old. Whence if an illness is old (which is more than one year), of whatever circumstances the sick person is, you ought to give the 12th to the illness. If it is a new illness which is not a year old, you ought to give the 7th to it, if you give the 1st to the doctor–because the doctor is the enemy of the illness. And if you give the 10th to the sick person, you ought to give the 4th to the art of medicine, because even though the art of medicine cures the sick person, it is still his opposite: and an opposition indicates enmity. Whence the art of medicine is said to be the enemy of the infirmity, because in the medical arts are studied those things which are contrary to nature and which do not nourish it, but on the contrary sometimes exterminate it. If you give the 9th to the sick person, the 3rd is given to the art of medicine. If you give the 3rd to the sick person, as sometimes happens, the 9th is given to the art of medicine.

And you must consider whether the illness is universal or particular. Because if it is universal, you ought to judge universally about the whole body. If it is particular, you ought to judge according to that part of the body in which the illness thrives. But if you were inquiring how the houses are diversified signifying the infirmities[136] and doctors and sick people and the arts of medicine, since these houses ought to be the same or rather almost the same: I believe strongly that the reason could be provided to you, but it would be lengthy to explain it in detail, nor can everything be disputed everywhere; whence it is necessary for us to hold to the sayings of the philosophers, and to know that they did not say things without reason; so it behooves us to believe them and learn from them. Henceforth I will lay out for you the method of judging about a sick person whether he will be freed or not, notwithstanding that I want you first to know what Sahl said about this, and what his followers said, just as it ought to be understood.

Because when he said that the Ascendant signifies the doctor, he said this was the reason: because the illness is signified through the 7th, and the doctor is the enemy of the illness; whence, since the 1st is the enemy of the 7th (which signifies infirmity), the 1st is rightly given to the doctor, since he himself is the enemy of infirmity; and in this [manner] the doctor is signified by the 1st. Wherefore, insofar as the 1st house were made fortunate, so will the doctor's cure be useful for the sick person; and insofar as it were made unfortunate, the doctor's cure will be harmful to him.

---

136 Reading *infirmitates* for *domos*.

And therefore Sahl said that the 1st is given to the doctor, and this was because he said that the 10th is given to the sick person, for no other reason than because it is signified through the 10th whether the sick person is obedient to the doctor; because if he obeys well, [the treatment] will be some help to him; and this will be known through the planet which was found in the 10th. Wherefore if it were benefic, the sick person will be obedient, and that is the reason he will be better able to be cured.

He gave the 7th to the infirmity, because through the 7th will be known whether the illness will be short or long; for if a benefic were there he will be liberated quickly, and specifically if it has a dignity there. And if a malefic were there who was not well disposed, the illness will grow strong in the sick person.

The 4th is given to the medical art, because through the 4th is known whether or not the medical art will be effective for the sick person, insofar as it were well or badly disposed: for if there were a benefic there, the medicine will be powerful in the sick person; indeed if a malefic were there, who did not have a dignity (namely by domicile or exaltation or two of the other lesser dignities), the medical art will be more likely lead to harming the sick person than to be useful to him.

But by another means and a direct line,[137] so that it may be known whether the sick person might be liberated or not: the 1st and its Lord and the Moon are given to the sick person, and the 6th is given to the infirmity, if the infirmity were new (if it did not last longer than a year). If indeed the illness were of long standing (which he would have had for more than one year), the 12th is given to him, as was said. You even ought to see whether the significator of the sick person was of the planets which have friendship with the significator of the doctor (or of the medical art or the infirmity) by whichever house the doctor or sick person or the medical art or the illness are signified. Because if the significator of the doctor were from among those planets which love the significator of the sick person, the doctor will be useful to the sick person. If the significator of the medical art were likewise from among those who love the significator of the sick person, the medical practice of the doctor will be useful to him. Likewise, if the significator of the infirmity is from among them, the infirmity will cause less

---

137 *Linea.* This must simply mean, "in a more direct *way.*"

harm. But if the significator of the doctor were from among the enemies of the sick person, the doctor will not be helpful, nor his medical art, but rather he will be harmful and it will be the contrary for [the sick person]. And [the planet] who is from among the friends, will make things better;[138] and he who is from among the enemies, will harm, *et cetera*. And if all were from among the friends, everything will get better; and if all were from among the enemies, all will get worse.

And if the significator of the doctor, or the Moon, were joined with the Lord of the 7th, the illness will be come more aggressive. And if it were joined to the Lord of the sixth, it will be prolonged more than it seemed like it was supposed to be–but ultimately in this case the sick person will escape, and be liberated.

You will even consider whether the significator of the illness is in one of the azemene degrees, and were in the 12th, or the 8th, and one of the malefics aspected him: because it signifies that the sick person will not be liberated from the illness without there remaining some impediment in the limb deputed to that sign in which the azemene degree is. And it must be inquired there, from the sick person, or from the other person who knows how to judge for you, the length of the illness–because is the illness were of many years, the sick person will not be liberated quickly.

Chapter 2: On the sick person–whether he will escape

If some sick person were to ask of you whether he will be liberated from an infirmity or not, look at the Ascendant and its Lord, and the Moon (which are the significators of the querent), and see if the Lord of the Ascendant were in the angle of the Ascendant or in the angle of the Midheaven: it signifies his liberation, unless [the Lord] itself is impeded by the malefics from a square aspect or by opposition, or if it is combust, or if it is with the Tail of the Dragon in the same minute [of longitude], or going toward [the Tail], and there are less than 15' between it and the Tail, without the aspect of a benefic. For the aspect of a benefic breaks the Tail's malice by helping the Lord of the Ascendant, even if it were a square aspect (whether with reception or not).[139] But if it were by opposition with reception, likewise it will break [the Tail's] malice, unless [the benefic] itself were the Lord of the 8th house: because then he does not help,

---

[138] *Proderit*, lit. "advance."
[139] Note: it is not the aspect to the Tail that improves the situation, but the aspect to the *planet*.

but harms (whether he who is joined to the Lord of the Ascendant–or to whom the Lord of the Ascendant is joined–is a benefic or malefic). If however the Lord of the Ascendant were impeded, see then if the Moon were free from the malefics, and were in an angle, and aspected the Ascendant (if the Lord of the 8th neither aspected her, nor were joined to her corporally): it signifies the escape from the illness.

Look even at the Lord of the Ascendant or at the Moon, namely at the one through which you are working, and the one that is stronger in signification, to see if it were above the earth: because it is a sign of escape–and especially if it were to aspect the Ascendant, or is joined to a planet which aspects the Ascendant, and renders the light of the Lord of the Ascendant to the Moon or to the Ascendant (nor should the Lord of the Ascendant nor the Moon be joined to a planet appearing below the earth): then it signifies liberation, unless a bad cure or bad care makes for the contrary. Because by no means would a sick, but sane, person be able to treat himself poorly if he wished, saying "I will do what the astrologer says," by doing the opposite of what he should. Nevertheless, since you have discharged your duty, let him who thinks so assign the harm to himself through his own fault.

If however the Lord of the Ascendant or the Moon were below the earth (namely in the 2nd, or 3rd, or 4th, or 5th, or 6th) nor were it joined to any planet located above the earth, it signifies his death. If however a benefic planet (to which the Lord of the Ascendant or the Moon is joined), who signifies the escape of the sick person, were retrograde, it signifies the prolonging of the illness–and more strongly and emphatically if he were cadent from an angle–but [the sick person] will ultimately be liberated.

If indeed that planet to whom the Lord of the Ascendant or the Moon is joined, and to whom they commit their disposition, had entered into combustion, it signifies the death of the sick person. Moreover, if the Lord of the Ascendant were the significator (namely that he were the strong one, so that the signification [of the querent] were attributed to him more so than it was to the Moon), and he were joined to some malefic planet located below the earth, it signifies [the patient's] death. If however the Lord of the Ascendant were impeded, as was said, so that he could not be the significator of the sick person, but the signification went to the Moon, see even if she herself were above the earth; which if she were joined to a malefic planet located below the earth, it signifies the death of the sick person. Likewise if the Moon were joined to the Lord of the Ascendant, and he himself were fast in course, and were descending from his increase up to the middle of his eccentric, or from his further longitude to his first station (which happens to him when his argument is from 15° up to two signs and fifteen degrees),[140] then it signifies that the sick person will be liberated quickly, and strength will quickly return to his body). And if you were to find the Moon, or the Lord of the Ascendant, joined with Saturn, it signifies the prolongation of the illness, even if it were a new illness. If indeed it were of long-standing it signifies the prolongation of its long duration. And if the Lord of the Ascendant were below the earth, and the Moon were joined to a planet in the 3rd or 6th or 9th or 12th (which is cadent from the angle), it signifies the death of the sick person. Likewise if the Lord of the Ascendant were joined to the Lord of the 8th house, and the Moon were otherwise impeded, or the Moon were joined to the Lord of the 8th house and the Lord of the Ascendant were impeded, it signifies the death of the sick person. However, this should be attended to: that if the Lord of the Ascendant were received by the Lord of the 8th house, and the Lord of the Ascendant himself did not receive the Lord of the 8th, because it does not signify death, but it signifies a very fearful illness; but the sick person will not be put into danger unless by error. If however the Lord of the Ascendant or the Moon were to receive the Lord of the 8th house, it signifies death.

You will even see whether the significator of the sick person or the Moon is found in the 9th from the Ascendant of the question, because then it restores fear to him that by a simple error he could be endangered, because it seems that he will go to the grave. If however you were to find [the significator of the sick person or the Moon] in the 9th from the house through which he himself is signified, it signifies that it again gives him more fear. And if it were the Moon or another planet who transfers the light of the Lord of the Ascendant to the Lord of the 8th, it signifies the sick person's ultimate fear, and that the tiniest error in eating or his diet could put the sick person in danger, and it will hardly be that he will escape. But it *was* possible that he might escape by the best cure and best care, by those standing by as much as the sick person and even the doctor, and by the patient's obeying the doctor.

If however the Lord of the Ascendant were in the 8th, and were received by the Lord of the 8th (nor did [the Lord of the Ascendant] receive him), it signifies liberation after losing hope. But if the Lord of the Ascendant were to receive

---

140 I am unclear as to how this measurement comes into play (the "argument" is a concept from Ptolemaic astronomy, referring to an arc measured from the *awj* to the center of a planet's epicycle), but at any rate Bonatti means "from the middle of its direct course, until it slows down and reaches its first station."

[the Lord of the 8th], it signifies death. If however the Lord of the 8th were heavier than the Lord of the Ascendant, and the Lord of the Ascendant were joined to him with reception, indeed so that the Lord of the Ascendant received the Lord of the 8th, it signifies death. If however there were a conjoining of the Lord of the Ascendant with the Lord of the 8th, and that conjoining were by a trine or sextile aspect, even it signifies death (whether the Lord of the Ascendant received the Lord of the 8th or not). If the Lord of the Ascendant were in one of the angles, it signifies death,[141] but not immediately; but it signifies it when the Lord of the 8th arrives at the degree of the Ascendant. Which if were not then, it will be when the Lord of the 8th arrives at the degree in which the Lord of the Ascendant was (at the hour of the question); or, if the Lord of the Ascendant were [joined to] the Lord of the 8th, it will be when he reaches the degree in which the Lord of the 8th was (at the hour of the question).[142]

Likewise if the Moon or some other planet had transferred the virtue or light of the Lord of the Ascendant to the Lord of the house of death, and the Lord of the house of death were himself strong, or were in an angle, and the Lord of the Ascendant were cadent from an angle, or were in the disposition of his own domicile, or his own exaltation, it signifies death. But if it were not cadent from an angle, even if it were in opposition to his own domicile or exaltation, if it were received, it does not signify death.

And if the Lord of the 8th house were in the Ascendant, and the Lord of the Ascendant and the Moon were impeded, it signifies that the illness will be increased greatly, and the sick person will be in danger of death; but he will escape it, though barely, with good care and precautions, just as was said. Likewise if the Lord of the Ascendant and the Moon were impeded, and he to whom the Lord of the Ascendant (or the Moon) committed its own disposition, were impeded, it signifies death.

If indeed the sole receiver of the disposition (which is the heavy planet to whom the Lord of the Ascendant or the Moon is joined) were impeded, it signifies the prolongation of the illness, and this will happen because the sick person will have a relapse; moreover because he will not be cured, nor will he

---

141 Bonatti seems to be getting this and the previous sentence from Sahl, *On Quest.*, 6th House, "If an infirm person will get well or die." But the sentences are joined in Sahl: "Indeed if the Lord of the Ascendant were joined to the Lord of the 8th from a trine aspect, and the Lord of the Ascendant were in an angle, it will signify death when the Lord of the house of death arrives at the degree of the ascending sign." The rest of the sentence seems to be a combination of Sahl and either another authority or Bonatti's own elaboration.
142 I supplied "joined to" in brackets because without it the sentence does not make sense—and it thereby parallels the sentence before it.

follow the prescribed diet, and because he will adhere to the advice of stupid people, and those who counsel him badly. Likewise if the Lord of the Ascendant were below the earth, and were joined to the Lord of the 8th in the 4th, or were above the earth and were joined to the Lord of the 8th in the 8th, or from the 8th, it signifies death if the Lord of the Ascendant were to receive the Lord of the 8th. If however [the Lord of the Ascendant] did not receive [the Lord of the 8th], even if the Lord of the 8th were to receive the Lord of the Ascendant, the illness will be made much graver, and he will be in danger of death; however he will be liberated by the help shown to him. Likewise if the Lord of the Ascendant did not aspect the Lord of the 8th, nor he him, but one of the others were to transfer light between them, and the Lord of the Ascendant were cadent from the Ascendant, and the Lord of the 8th were in one of the angles (because his strength in the angles is very evil), it signifies the sick person will die from the illness.

And Sahl said[143] that if the Lord of the Ascendant were combust, and were one of the superiors, and were in front of the Sun by 13° or less, or after the Sun by 4° or less,[144] or if he were one of the inferiors and were in front of the Sun by 3° or less or were after the Sun by 14° or less,[145] it signifies the death of the sick person unless by chance the Lord of the Ascendant were received; because then [in the latter case] it signifies escape after losing hope; and perhaps he will appear to be when he is not, and it is possible that he will be believed to be dead and be buried alive.

If however the heavy planet to whom the Lord of the Ascendant commits its own virtue or disposition, were free from impediments (nor were it cadent from the angles nor from the Ascendant, nor did it commit the disposition which the Lord of the Ascendant committed to him, to another planet), and the Moon were likewise free from impediments, it signifies that the sick person will be liberated, even without a great cure by doctors.

---

[143] *Ibid.*, but Sahl's text is not so explicit and does not distinguish between the superiors and inferiors.

[144] By "in front of," Bonatti means "in a later zodiacal degree" than the Sun's; by "after" he means "in an earlier zodiacal degree" than the Sun's.

[145] Here I believe Bonatti is assuming direct motion, so "in front of" means (as usual) "in a later zodiacal degree" than the Sun's, i.e., going away from him in direct motion; "after" means "in an earlier zodiacal degree" than the Sun's, i.e., approaching him in direct motion.

And a certain man of the Cretans said that when the Part of Illness[146] was from the beginning of the Ascendant up to the end of the 4th house, it signifies the cause of the illness to be something in the past. When it is from the beginning of the 5th up to the end of the 8th, it signifies a cause in the present. When it is from the beginning of the 9th up to the end of the 12th, it signifies the cause is in the future.

Indeed for the nature of an illness, whether it is lasting or not, look to the Lord of the 6th, which is the house of infirmities, and see if it is[147] a fixed sign: the illness will be fixed, and will stay in its condition [or nature], and will not change to something else. If indeed it were a movable sign, the illness will change easily to something else. If indeed it were a common sign, the infirmities will be alleviated at one time, and aggravated at another.

To know whether the illness is of long standing or new, look at the Moon, and see from what planet she herself were separated. If for example she were separated from an oriental planet, the illness will be new. If indeed she were separated from an occidental planet, the illness is of long standing. If you were to find that the illness is of long standing using the conditions set out, consider the 12th, and judge concerning the illness by it, just as you judged above about a new illness through the Lord of the 6th house. Look likewise in [judging] liberation from the illness: because if the Moon is joined to an oriental planet, it signifies that the illness can be cured quickly. If indeed she were joined to an occidental planet, the illness will be cured slowly and with much difficulty. Which if she were joined to no planet, change her from the sign in which she is, to the next, and see to which planet she is first joined after exiting the sign in which she is, whether she is joined to an oriental or occidental planet, and judge regarding the speed or slowness of the liberation from the illness, according to the one to whom she is joined. And all of this comes to be best and fastest if some benefic were to aspect the Lord of the Ascendant (and the Lord of the Ascendant were not cadent from the Ascendant nor from an angle). Likewise, see lest one of the malefics is joined to the Lord of the Ascendant, or [the Lord] to [the malefic] corporally or from the opposition or a square aspect: because it makes him unfortunate, and rarely or never permits [the sick person] to escape

---

[146] Source unknown. For the Part of Illness in diurnal charts, take the distance (in the order of signs) from Saturn to Mars, and project from the degree of the Ascendant; in nocturnal charts, take the distance from Mars to Saturn, and project from the Ascendant.

[147] One would expect this to say, "if it [the Lord] is *in* a fixed sign." But the Latin suggests we are looking for the quadruplicity of the sixth sign itself; there may be a transcription error here.

the illness. If the malefic were to receive the Lord of the Ascendant, the sick person will escape the illness, and barely; if however it did not receive, he fears then that he will not escape, and will not be liberated.

Consider, too, the Moon: which if she were joined to a planet fast in course, and she herself were fast in course, it signifies that the sick person will be liberated quickly. If she were joined to a retrograde planet, it signifies the prolongation of the illness, and its lastingness. If however she were joined to a planet slow in course, it signifies the prolongation and aggravation of the illness, indeed so that the sick person will hardly escape it; and it seems more likely that he will die than that he will escape it.

Chapter 3: On critical days and good or bad crises in illnesses

Moreover, you ought to look at the place of the Moon at the hour of the question, or at the onset of the illness (if you were to have [the time of] its onset), and look ahead to where the Moon will be on the seventh day from the onset of the illness or the question, and likewise where she is on the fourteenth day, and where she will be on the twenty-first day; and where she will be on the twenty-eighth day. Because if she were well disposed on any of those days, the sick person will then be made better, and it will seem to be better for him, and the crisis will turn to the good, unless the malefics impede corporally or by opposition or a square aspect without reception. And if she were impeded on any one of those days, and badly disposed, it signifies that then the sick person will be made worse, and it will go worse for him, and particularly if she were then in conjunction with the Lord of the 6th house: because the sick person will be feared for. If indeed it were a malefic that impeded the Lord of the 8th, then the sick person will die.

Moreover, see on what day from among the other days (apart from those mentioned above) the Moon were joined to some benefic planet; on that day the sick person will be made better and he will rest, and it will be good for him. And it is from this that sometimes a crisis will come over the sick person for the good, on a day which it is not believed, and does not seem, like it ought to come to pass. And see in which of these days (apart from those mentioned above) the Moon will have come to the corporal conjunction of the malefics, or to their opposition, or a square aspect: because on that day the sick person will be made worse, and particularly if she were joined with the Lord of the 6th house. And if a crisis were to come, it will be more able to cause harm than health; and especially if it should happen that she were joined with the Lord of the 8th house; because then the crises can be more liable to cause death than life. And in this doctors are sometimes deceived, because when they have predicted a future crisis on a critical day according to the medical arts, the crisis comes to pass differently than they said: because it happened on account of the conjunction of the Moon with the planets on those days; whence doctors are vilified by the uneducated (because they fail in their prognostications), but are not to be censured.

But you will have to find the aforesaid days this way: because if you want to know the seventh day from the day of the illness, or from the day of the question, you must consider in what degree the Moon was at the hour of the question or the beginning of the illness; and add 90° on top of the others, and you will have the seventh day. Then project those 90° from the degree of the Moon, and in the sign in which the number were ended, there will be the Moon in that degree. Or if you were able to come up with it according to tables and the same place is found. Then see how and by whom she is aspected, and judge on the good or bad of the sick person according to the aspects of the benefic and malefic planets to the Moon.[148]

To find the fourteenth day from the day of the question or the beginning of the illness, you add 180° to the first position of the Moon, and project them from the degree in which she was, and where the number falls, there will be the place of the Moon on the fourteenth day from the day of the question or of the beginning of the illness. And then judge about the fourteenth day just as you judged about the seventh one above.

To find the twenty-first day, add 270° to the place of the Moon, and project from the aforesaid place of the Moon, and where the number falls, there will be the place of the Moon on the twenty-first day from the day of the question or of the beginning of the illness. Then look at the aspect of the planets to the Moon, and judge according to how you judged about the seventh day.

To find the twenty-eighth day, add 360° to the place of the Moon, and you will have the place of the Moon at the hour of the question or illness, and then judge as was said above about the seventh day.

And know this, because always on these days, whenever the Moon were to come to benefic planets, then the illness is alleviated, and whenever she were to come to the malefics, then it gets more serious.

---

[148] Bonatti seems to be recommending using exact degrees *as opposed to* just consulting an ephemeris ("according to tables").

Chapter 4: Whether an absent person will be taken ill[149]

And if someone is concerned about someone who is absent, or about anyone else, [as to] whether he is sick or not, see of what condition [or relationship] is he who asks, and he about whom it is asked; and judge according to this, namely whether he asks about his brother, or father, or child, or slave, or wife, or partner, or enemy, or a bishop or other religious person, or the king or another master of his, or a friend, or a hidden enemy. Because you will have to give the 1st to the querent; and to the quaesited, that [house] through which the quaesited [person] is signified. Look then to the Ascendant and its Lord, and give it to the querent; and you will give the Lord of the house through which the quaesited [person] is signified, and the Moon,[150] to the quaesited.

If the Lord of the house of the quaesited or the Moon were in an angle, not impeded by a malefic, it signifies his condition to be sound. The same [goes] if one of them were succeedent to an angle, free from the malefics and from all the other aforesaid impediments. If however the Lord of the quaesited [person] were in the 6th, or were joined corporally to its Lord (or in his opposition or square aspect), it signifies him to be sick, whether it were in the 6th house of the question, or in the 6th house from its own, or joined with its Lord. If indeed these aforesaid impediments were not present, say he has not been taken ill.

And the Master[151] said that if the Lord of the Ascendant and the Moon were void in course, you ought to see which of them has traveled through more degrees in the sign in which it is, and change it to the next sign which succeeds it; and look to see to whom it is joined first, to a benefic or a malefic; which if it is joined to a benefic who received it, it signifies liberation, unless that benefic is impeded by the aforesaid impediments, or is itself with the Lord of the 8th house—because then the death of the sick person is feared, and especially if the Lord of the Ascendant or the Moon were to receive the Lord of the 8th house; but not if he [the Lord of the 8th] received it, for then that signifies escape from the illness, almost after losing hope. It appears however that he ought to escape

---

[149] Bonatti has more information on the status of absent people in the section on the 7th House, Chs. 34-35.

[150] This reversal of the normal rule (that the Moon signifies the querent) seems to be based on the idea that the question concerns the absent person and *his/her* own intentions and actions, not those of the person who merely happens to ask the question without any particular intention of his own.

[151] This is undoubtedly from Māshā'allāh, an extrapolation from *OR*, Chs. 2 and 3.

unless an error of the doctor or the patient or those attending worked to the contrary, [as] by such an example below:

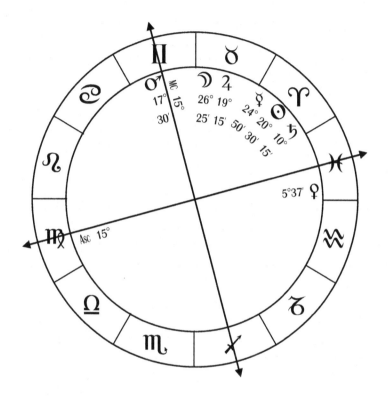

Figure 6: Question of a Sick Person

The question of a certain sick person.[152] The ascendant was Virgo, 15°; and the 10th house Gemini, 15°; and Mars in Gemini, 17° 30'; and the Moon in Taurus, 26° 25'; and Jupiter in Taurus, 19° 15'; the Sun in Aries, 20° 30'; Saturn in Aries, 10° 15'; Mercury in Aries, 24° 50'; Venus in Pisces, 5° 37'.[153]

---

[152] This chart is from Māshā'allāh (*OR*, ch. 3). According to Hand (*OR*, p. 68), it was cast for April 11, 791, at 12:40 UT.

[153] Both 1550 and 1491 give incorrect values for Mercury, the Sun, and Jupiter. I have used Māshā'allāh's values here, because the delineation of the figure only makes sense with them. I also note that this Ascendant-Midheaven combination would put the chart location around 20° N latitude, which includes middle portions of India, Oman, and a region of Arabia just south of Mecca.

And [Māshā'allāh] said that he examined the Ascendant and its Lord, and the Moon, and the rest of the planets and angles, and the other houses. And Mercury (who was the Lord of the Ascendant) was void in course, joined to no one; and the Moon was likewise void in course, joined to no one. Therefore the Lord of the Ascendant and the Moon signified, by the emptiness of their course, the prolongation of the infirmity and its seriousness. Whence he changed the Moon from the sign in which she was (namely from Taurus) to Gemini. And he changed the Moon and not the Lord of the Ascendant, for the reason that she herself had traveled through more degrees in the sign in which she was, than Mercury (the Lord of the Ascendant) had in his. And after she had entered Gemini, she was first joined to Venus (who was in Pisces) rather than to one of the other planets, and she committed her own disposition to her.[154] And Venus was joined to Jupiter, and received him by her domicile (namely from Taurus), and likewise Jupiter received Venus from his domicile (namely from Pisces). Nor did Jupiter commit his disposition to any other, because he was not being joined to Saturn [in this chart] (for he himself is not joined to any of the planets except for Saturn, who is heavier than him; the others are all joined to [Saturn, generally speaking], because they are lighter than him).[155]

And that conjoining which Venus was making with Jupiter by mutual reception, signified that the sick person ought to have been liberated from the illness. However, the infirmity would be in increase until the conjunction of Venus with Jupiter perfected, degree by degree, and she herself would have transited him by 1'. And it seemed that the illness was to be in increase for two days and 15 hours, by giving about one day for each single degree, and two hours for every 5', because there were 2° and 38' between their perfect conjunction [and their current position], from which time the sick person was to be relieved. And he said that it was the sick person who asked about his own condition, and his infirmity did not cease to get worse until the conjunction of Venus with Jupiter was complete, degree by degree. [But] immediately when Venus was separated from Jupiter by one minute, the sick person began to be better, and he began to rest, and his pain was diminished.

And this same philosopher said that if Venus had been joined to Mars and not Jupiter, that the sick person would have died, unless Mars (who was the

---

[154] Reading *illae* for *illi*, following Mash'allah's exposition.
[155] Bonatti is saying that "joining" takes more than a mere aspect: it is important to note who is joining to whom; and each planet can only join to others heavier than itself.

Lord of the 8th house[156]) had received Venus, and she himself had not received him–because if she herself had received Mars, it would have appeared that the sick person would have received death, and would have died; because Mars signifies the matter the question was about, namely death. Because it is always the case that when the Lord of the Ascendant or the Moon are both (or one of them) joined to the Lord of the quaesited matter, the matter about which the question was, is perfected, especially if reception intervenes. For the judgment of death is not wholly like the judgment of other things, because if the Lord of the Ascendant or the Moon is joined to the Lord of the 8th house without reception, it signifies death, unless the Lord of the 8th house receives the Lord of the Ascendant or the Moon, and neither the Lord of the Ascendant nor the Moon receives him. But if the Lord of the Ascendant or the Moon receives the Lord of the 8th, it signifies death, whether or not the Lord of the 8th receives the Lord of the Ascendant or the Moon. For death is not like other matters, because when death is signified, one does not look to see whether or not the matter changes after it happens; for none of the significators can change or destroy death after it arrives in actuality. But other matters are changed and destroyed, sometimes even after they were perfected.

But when the Lord of the Ascendant or the Moon are joined to the Lord of the quaesited matter, or the Lord of the quaesited matter is joined to the Lord of the Ascendant,[157] it signifies the effecting of the matter. But even if it were sometimes perfected as I have told you above, after the Lord of the quaesited matter is joined to a malefic (to whom he commits disposition) impeding him, the matter is destroyed after it has been perfected. But in [matters of] death it cannot happen that it is destroyed after it has been perfected, because it itself resolves every question; and its sentence is of the sort that it cannot be appealed. Concerning health however, or its liberation, it is not this way: because if some planet were to signify the liberation of the sick person, and afterwards it were joined to a malefic planet who impeded him and [the first planet] committed his disposition to [the malefic], the matter will be destroyed after it seems to be arranged, so that it (namely the liberation of the sick person) ought to perfect. Whence he who seems destined to be liberated, can die after it seems he ought to be able to escape, but he who is going to die cannot be revived after death, whatever the receiver of the disposition seems to signify afterwards.

---

[156] Reading *octavae* for Bonatti's *quartae* ("4th").
[157] Or the Moon?

You will even consider the Lord of the house signifying the sick person, [to see] in which part of the figure you find it (i.e., whether in the first quarter or in the second, or in the third or in the fourth), and operate through it. Which if you find him in the first quarter of the figure, it signifies he asks about an illness which already was. If however he is in the second quarter, it signifies he is asking about an illness which exists now. If indeed it were in the third quarter, it signifies he is asking about a future illness, or about its return (because it signifies he is about to relapse). But if it were in the last quarter, it signifies he is asking about a chronic illness, namely one which already was, and now is, and will be or is going to last (and all the more surely if he were joined with one of the Lords of the signs of one of the quarters, in his own quarter).

Chapter 5: Whether a slave would be freed from slavery or not

In the preceding chapter we spoke about a sick person, whether he would be freed from an illness or not. Now it remains to speak in this chapter about a slave, whether he will be freed from slavery or not. Nor [is this] useless, because slavery is wholly vicious compared with illness; for there is not an illness which can be said to be worse than that which afflicts always, everywhere, and indifferently and continuously. For illness is but intermittent, sometimes afflicting and sometimes in repose; [this is different from] slavery, for with it intermissions and repose do not intervene.

Whence if a question were posed to you for a slave, as if the slave said, "See if I will be liberated from slavery or not," then the 1st is given to the slave, and likewise the Lord of the Ascendant and the Moon; the 10th is given to his master, of whatever sort the master is—even if he is another low-class person.[158] Then look to the Lord of the Ascendant for the slave, and see if he himself is joined to the Lord of the 10th house, and it is a perfect conjunction (whether corporeal or by aspect, of whatever type the aspect is), whether with reception or without reception; and let the conjunction be complete degree by degree, and minute by minute: say that he will be freed from his slavery, and easily and soon.[159] If indeed the Lord of the Ascendant were separated from the Lord of the 10th house by one minute or by more, it signifies this, that he is already freed

---

[158] In other words, the 10th governs people who are masters *over the 1st*, not merely people who are elevated in an absolute sense (like kings and emperors).

[159] The meaning seems to be that an exact aspect with the Lord of the 10th can only separate from then on, hence it shows the slave leaving his master. Note that Bonatti does *not* mention applications as showing freedom, and he is careful to mention the aspect's exactness.

from slavery. If indeed it were not as I told you for the Lord of the Ascendant, look then to the significatrix (namely the Moon) and judge according to what I told you about the Lord of the Ascendant. If for example the situation I described to you does not exist for the Lord of the Ascendant or the Moon, namely that neither of them is separated from the Lord of the 10th house, look at them again, and if you were to find them (or one of them) joined with the Sun (as was said with the Lord of the 10th) or separated from him by the conditions set out before, you will judge the same about them with the Sun, that you judged with the Lord of the 10th.[160]

If indeed his question was determinate and not absolute, as if he said, "Will I be freed from the service of my master in which I am, or go out of his power, or not," then look at the Lord of the Ascendant, and see if he himself were cadent from an angle, and did not aspect the Ascendant, nor were he joined to a planet in an angle (nor [one] who aspected the Ascendant); or were in the 3rd, or in the 9th, or were joined to a planet in them: say that he will be freed from slavery, and will leave the power of his master. Which if this were not true of the Lord of the Ascendant, [but] were true of the Moon, you will judge the same.

If indeed the Lord of the Ascendant or the Moon were in the Ascendant or in the 10th or the 4th or the 7th, or one of them were joined to a planet in them, he will not be freed if the one to whom the Lord of the Ascendant or the Moon were joined, were direct. If indeed it were retrograde, it signifies liberation, but with slowness and the greatest labor, and complications and delays.

If however the Lord of the Ascendant were impeded in the Ascendant, or in the 10th, or 7th, or in the 4th by corporal conjunction to any malefic planet, or through its opposition or square aspect, or if it entered into combustion, he will not be freed from his slavery, unless by death, which dissolves all hindrances with a perverse solution!

---

[160] Bonatti is clearly saying that the Lord of the 10th signifies the master by rulership, and the Sun signifies him naturally (by "universal" signification).

Chapter 6: Whether a master would sell a slave

If for example at some point a slave–hoping that (or perhaps fearing lest) his master will sell him or in some other way give him over to someone else–were to ask, saying: "My master, at whose home I am, is good to me; [but will] the other person to whom I am about to go, be better to me?"[161] Look then to the Lord of the 1st house; which if he were joined to some planet who receives him from the sign in which [the Lord of the 1st] is (by domicile or exaltation or two of the other lesser dignities), nor were the Lord of the 7th received,[162] he with whom the slave is, and in whose power the slave is, is better for him. If indeed the Lord of the 7th were received,[163] he to whom he wishes to go, is better for him.

Moreover, consider the Lord of the Ascendant and the Moon, and see from whom one of them is separating; and see to whom [either the Lord of the Ascendant or the Moon] is joined. If it is separating from a benefic and is joined to a malefic, the one with whom he is, is better for him. If indeed it is separating from a malefic, and is joined to a benefic, he to whom he intends to go is better for him. If however one of them (namely the Lord of the Ascendant or the Moon) separates from a benefic and is joined to a benefic, both of them are good to him; but if the condition [or nature] of one benefic is better than the condition [or nature] of the other, judge according to it. If indeed it is separating from a malefic and joined to a malefic, both of them will be bad to him, in accordance with whichever one of them is [better or more badly] disposed.

And if you did not find that the Lord of the Ascendant or the Moon was joined to any planet, if either one were void in course, look at the sign in which it is (namely the Lord of the Ascendant or even the Moon), [to see] if it has greater dignity in it than in the 7th or in the 2nd (namely domicile or exaltation or bound or triplicity, or face): [then] the master with whom he is now, will be better for him. If indeed it were to have a greater dignity in the 2nd or the 7th than [it does] in the rising sign,[164] the other master is better to him than the first.

---

[161] The sentence is not written in a question-like way; but it is clear that this is how Bonatti intends it to be read. As usual, Bonatti's extraordinarily long clauses make his setup merge into his instructions, which makes literal translation awkward.

[162] By whom, the Lord of the 1st?

[163] By whom, the Lord of the 1st?

[164] Since by definition the Lord of the 1st has domicile in the 1st, it would have to be rather well dignified in the other sign. The Moon would have an easier time.

Chapter 7: On buying a slave, or any small animal, or a slave-girl

We have already discussed whether a slave would be freed from slavery or not. It remains in this chapter to speak about buying a slave (and when I speak about a slave, you can understand the same about any small animal which is not ridden); and this is signified by the 6th house.

Whence if someone were interested in a slave and wished to buy him, and were to pose the question to you whether or not the purchase of this slave he intends to buy will be completed or not: look at the Lord of the Ascendant and the significatrix (who is the Moon), which are the significators of the querent, and see if they both (or one of them) were joined to the Lord of the 6th house, or the Lord[165] of the 6th house to the Lord of the Ascendant, or if you were to find some planet who transfers light between the Lord of the Ascendant and the Lord of the 6th: tell him that he will acquire the slave about whom he asks (or the animal about which he asks, because it is signified by the 6th house). If indeed you did not find the Lord of the Ascendant (or the Moon) joined to the Lord of the 6th, or *vice versa*, nor did you find a planet who transfers light between them, he will not acquire the slave or animal about whom he asks.

If however it were a question about buying a slave-girl, Sarcinator said that you ought to then put the 12th for the slave-girl. Arastellus gave the 6th to a slave-girl, just as to a male slave. Arastellus's purpose concerned when there was mention of a slave-girl simply, just as in the chapter on slaves. Sarcinator's point was that just as a slave-girl is the wife of a slave (whom someone intends to buy), wherefore if the 6th signifies his slave, the opposite signifies the slave's wife, which is the 12th; and in this they both spoke well. Whence if a question arose about a slave-girl in the sense that she herself is of the class of slaves, you can give the 6th to her just as to a male slave. If it were inquired about her in the sense that she is the wife of the slave about whom the question is, you can give her the 12th. You can even give the 12th to someone for another reason, namely when someone seeks a slave-girl from someone, the 1st is given to the querent, the 7th is given to him from whom the slave-girl is sought, the 6th from the 7th (which is the 12th from the 1st) is given to the slave-girl of him from whom she is sought; and even through the same method you can give the 12th to a [male] slave.

Whence if a question to you came to be about a slave-girl and the question were absolute, just as I told you above about the freeing of a slave, then you

---

[165] Reading *dominus* for *dominum*.

give the 6th to her. If indeed the question were about a slave-girl in the sense that she is the wife of a slave, then you will give her the 12th. And if, in the first situation [i.e., in an absolute question] you were to find the Lord of the Ascendant, or the Moon, joined with the Lord of the 6th, or the Lord of the 6th with the Lord of the Ascendant, say that he will obtain the slave-girl he speaks of. If for example in the second situation [i.e., in a question about the wife of a particular slave] you were to find the Lord of the Ascendant or the Moon to be joined with the Lord of the 12th, or the Lord of the 12th with them, judge the same. Likewise if some planet transferred the light between them, it will signify the obtaining of the matter, just as I told you about the slave.

Chapter 8: Whether a master will obtain the goods of a slave or slave-girl

In this chapter it remains to state whether the goods of a slave will make their way into the hands of his master or not. For a certain slave of a certain man was discharged from service; he whose slave it was asked whether he was going to obtain the leftover possessions of the slave. See if such a question should come to you: you ought then to look at the Lord of the Ascendant and the Moon, and see if they both (or one or the other of them) are joined to the Lord of the 7th house, which signifies the substance of the slave (because it is the 2nd from the 6th, which signifies slaves, and [so] the 7th their substance). Say that the master will acquire the quaesited substance, namely that which belonged to his slave. And say the same if the Lord of the 7th were joined to the Lord of the 1st house. Likewise if the Lord of the Ascendant or the Moon were in the 7th, or if the Lord of the 7th were in the Ascendant or even in the 2nd–but this is not secure, because if the Lord of the 2nd were then impeded, or the Lord of the 7th received him but the Lord of the 2nd did not receive him, the master could suffer detriment in his own substance, by reason of recovering the substance of the slave. Likewise if some planet transfers light between the Lord of the Ascendant and the Lord of the 7th, the master will obtain the substance of the slave by means of someone who introduces himself into the matter.

ON THE SEVENTH HOUSE

Chapter 1: On marriage,[166] whether it is perfected or not; and if it were perfected, how it will be; and if it were not perfected, what will impede it so that it does not perfect

If a question were made to you concerning a marriage, whether it would be perfected, or not; and if it ought to be perfected and you would wish to know by what means it will be perfected; and if it ought not to be perfected, and you wished to know the reason that will impede it so that it does not perfect. Look then at the Ascendant and its Lord and the Moon (who are the significators of the querent), and the 7th and its Lord (which are the significators of the quaesited). Because a woman can just as well ask about a man, as a man can about a woman. And see how and in what way they aspect each other. If for example the Lord of the Ascendant or the Moon were joined corporally to the Lord of the 7th, if it were a man who asks, he will obtain the woman; and if it were a woman who asks, she will obtain the man; and the marriage will be perfected.

If indeed they aspected each other by a trine or a sextile aspect, the marriage will likewise be perfected, whether with reception or without reception, be it an aspect or corporal conjunction. If indeed the aspect were from the opposition, it will not be perfected unless reception intervenes (neither will there be hope of it). If indeed the aspect were a square with reception, it will be perfected, even if there is some delay in it. If however it were [by a square aspect and] without reception, there will be hope that it perfects, and it will be believed firmly that it will perfect; but it will not perfect, unless perhaps (as sometimes happens) [by means of] those who have it in their power such that they can make it happen (such as are the friends of the querent), so that they would make the union, then perhaps the matter can be perfected, but barely. By the same token if the Lord

---

[166] Throughout this section there is an apparent ambiguity both in the terminology and customs of marriage. *Coniugium* refers more to the physical relatedness of a marriage union; *matrimonium* and *connubium* refer more to the social/spiritual institution. Bonatti uses all of these, but seems to use them as equivalents. Moreover, not everyone got married by the Church or even the civil authorities at the time of Bonatti's writing–so is the issue whether they simply say "I do" (which anyone can do), or whether the marriage is accompanied by an official ceremony, or what? Of course, today we recognize civil marriages, religious marriage, common-law marriage, domestic partnerships, civil unions, same-sex marriage (in some countries); so perhaps the ambiguity is universal. I will translate all of Bonatti's terms as "marriage."

of the 7th were joined to the Lord of the Ascendant according to the aforesaid conjunctions.

Likewise if even the Lord of the 7th were in the Ascendant, the marriage will be completed with ease, and without trouble, and the desire of the woman [for the marriage] will be stronger than that of the man, if a man asks; if indeed a woman asks, the desire of the man [for the marriage] will be stronger than that of the woman.

If however the significators did not aspect each other, but there will be some planet who transfers the light between them, the matter will come to be through the agency of certain people who introduce themselves into the matter; and see of which house the planet who transfers the light between them is Lord, because the matter will come to be through what is signified by that house. And if it were a masculine planet, it will be a man; and if it were feminine, it will be a woman. Then look to the planet who transfers the light or disposition between the Lord of the Ascendant and the Lord of the 7th, or to whom they (namely the Lord of the Ascendant, or the Moon, [and] the Lord of the 7th) commit their disposition:[167] if it is free from impediments, so that it is neither retrograde nor combust nor cadent from the angles or from the Ascendant, nor is besieged by the malefics, nor in their opposition nor their square aspect without reception–if it were like this, say that the matter will be perfected and will endure.

If a benefic were the receiver of the disposition or the transferor of light, and it were free from the aforesaid impediments, the marriage will endure in a good, and tranquil, and useful, and benign state. If indeed it were a malefic, then even if it were found to be free from the aforesaid impediments, and even if it signified the perfection of the marriage, and its durability, still there will be many contentions and altercations and fights between them, even if not always. And there will be whisperings, more so from the side of the one whose significator is malefic (whether the man's or the woman's, if the significator is malefic). And perhaps a divorce [or separation] will take place[168] between them by reason of those whisperings. If indeed the receiver of the disposition or the transferor of the light were unfortunate and malefic, the matter will be destroyed after it is believed and thought to be arranged; and it will be destroyed by an evil destruction, indeed so that evil wills will rise up from it, and contentions and enmities. If indeed it were benefic and were impeded by the aforesaid

---

[167] This must refer to the collection of light.

[168] *Celebrabitur.* I am not certain why Bonatti uses this positive term ("will be celebrated"), but perhaps he simply means there will be an official proceeding.

impediments (or by some one of them), understand in any event that the matter will not be perfected, even after it is thought to be arranged; but contentions and enmities will not arise from it. And if people were to whisper, [the whisperings] will not be durable, but rather perhaps both parties will back off from their proposal, by complete and common consent.

Chapter 2: What it will be that impedes the marriage

If indeed you wished to the know the reason why the destruction appears after the marriage was thought to be arranged, look then to see who is the malefic who impedes the receiving of the disposition of the significators of the man and woman.

If it were the Lord of the 2nd house, it will be by reason of the querent's substance, because it may be that he[169] will tell the other side that he is a pauper.

If it were the Lord of the 3rd, it will be by reason of the querent's brothers. And if he had no brothers, it will be through one of those things which are signified by the 3rd house.

And if it were the Lord of the 4th, it will be by reason of the parents or through one of those things which are signified by the 4th house.

And if it were the Lord of the 5th, it will be by reason of children, because perhaps it is said that the querent already has children, and that matter will continue to be the reason;[170] and if he had no children, it will be because he is not able to have children; just as sometimes there are those who cannot beget children, and women who do not conceive, or who have passed the age of conceiving; or because the woman had another man; or it will be because of one of those things which are signified through the 5th house.

---

[169] The querent. For simplicity's sake I will treat the querent as a male in this section.
[170] The text reads, "it is said that the querent *will have* [*habebit*] children" but I am not certain why Bonatti thinks it would be impediment. I have translated it as *habuerit*, so that perhaps the impediment is due to the question of which children will be heirs.

And if it were the Lord of the 6th, it will be by reason of the querent's illness; which if he does not have an illness, it will be through one of those things which are signified through the 6th house.

And if it were the Lord of the 8th, it will be by reason of the cutting off[171] of the woman's dowry; or perhaps because the querent will die before the marriage may be perfected–which you will be able to discern if the Lord of the Ascendant is impeded by the Lord of the 8th house, or were joined to him (or *vice versa*),[172] and they receive each other, just as will be said in the chapter where death is considered; or it will be through one of those things which are signified through the 8th house.

And if it were the Lord of the 9th, it will be by reason of some religious person, or perhaps because at some time the querent was a religious person, or will assume the custom [or routine] of some religion; or it will be by one of those things which are signified through the 9th house.[173]

And if it were the Lord of the 10th, it will be by reason of the king or an authority, or some great noble, or some lay office which will have come to the querent, or through one of those things which are signified through the 10th house.

And if it were the Lord of the 11th, it will be by reason of some friend who disturbs the matter, or through one of those things which are signified through the 11th house.

And if it were the Lord of the 12th, it will be by reason of the quaesited's illness or because she is of low birth, or through one of those things which are signified through the 12th house.

And if the planet who transferred the light between the Lord of the Ascendant and the Lord of the 7th, were naturally malefic, there will be detriment and

---

[171] *Discretionis.*

[172] Lit., "or himself to him." I have translated this is *vice versa* so as to avoid the awkward gender phrasing.

[173] By "religious," Bonatti does not mean just anyone with religious faith, but someone with an official status in some religious organization.

destruction from the side of those who introduce themselves into the matter, and who seem to want to perfect it.

Chapter 3: How they will act together

Even though I touched on it somewhat for you above about how the husband and wife will comport themselves toward one another if the marriage were perfected, still I will tell you this much more about this same topic; nor is it a matter which seems ought to be downplayed. And it is that you should look to see if the Lord of the Ascendant were joined to the Lord of the 7th, or the Lord of the 7th to the Lord of the Ascendant by a trine aspect, and with reception: they will always live as one while they endure, both in a good and peaceful condition and agreement, which will not be disturbed by any means; and one will always want what the other wants. If indeed the conjunction were by a trine aspect without reception, or by a sextile with reception, it will be practically the same; however there will sometimes be certain light contentions or altercations between them, but neither will worry about it, nor will it darken their hearts.

Even if the conjunction were by a sextile aspect without reception, or by a square with reception, it signifies concord and a good condition between them, but there will be more discord and contentions between them (but they will not last a long time). And if the Moon were joined to a planet in whose domicile or exaltation she were in, it will be the same.

Indeed if the aspect were by opposition, it signifies a multitude of discords, and contention between them, more and more often, and of long duration, and they will rarely act well together. And likewise if they were joined corporally in one sign, so that there were fewer degrees between them than there are in the quantity of one of their orbs (namely of the one with the smaller orb).

After this, look at the Lord of the Ascendant and the Lord of the 7th to see which of them were heavier or were in an angle: because that one whose significator it is, will rule. Thus if the significator of the husband were in an angle, or were heavier, and the significator of the woman were cadent from an angle and lighter, the husband will rule the woman, and especially if the woman's significator were joined to the husband's significator. Indeed if the husband's significator were cadent and were lighter, and were joined to the woman's significator, the woman will rule the man and will be in charge over him. If indeed one of them were not in an angle, nor were one joined to the other, that one will predominate whose significator is heavier; and whichever one of them were seeking the conjunction of the other or were cadent, and the other were in an angle or succeedent to an angle, that one will be subject to the other, whether it is the significator of the man or the significator of the woman; that one [will be weaker] unless one of the planets cuts off[174] their light, or prohibits their conjunction, just as was said in the Treatise on the prohibition of conjunction or light.

Likewise if the Sun were impeded, the condition of the man is made weaker. If indeed Venus were impeded, it impedes and weakens the condition of the woman. If however the Moon were impeded, it will signify the impediment and worsening[175] of the man and woman. Even if they both want to rejoice and treat each other well, they will not be able to, and will both be made very unfortunate. Likewise if the Moon were impeded and aspected the Ascendant, or one of the malefics were in the Ascendant, there will be contentions and discord between them, which will befall them from the side of the querent. If indeed the malefic were in the 7th, they will befall them from the side of the quaesited; and the occasion of contention and discords will be by means of the occasions of the significators of that house of which the malefic (who is in the Ascendant or in the 7th) is Lord; like if he were Lord of the 2nd house, it will be by reason of substance; if he were the Lord of the 3rd it will be by reason of brothers; and understand this about all the other houses, according to the particular content of whichever one it is.

Chapter 4: About a woman, whether she is spoiled or a virgin, or has a lover or someone else whom she loves apart from the husband (if she were married), or apart from her lover (if she has one)

If perhaps someone wanting to contract marriage with some woman were suspicious that she is not a virgin. Because possibly some people told him bad things about her, just as oftentimes tends to happen, either by reason of jealousy or to disturb the marriage so that it is not completed; or perhaps [there was] someone who wanted something lewd from her that she did not want to do

---

174 *Abscindat.* This refers to one or more of Abū Ma'shar's versions of "cutting the light" or *qaT' al-nūr* in *Abbr.* III.46, also described in al-Qabīsī (III.24). See Tr. 3, Part 2, Chs. 12, 18.

175 *Deteriorationem.* This is the word Bonatti uses for a condition of the Moon (Tr. 5, the 4th Consideration), following Sahl. The Arabic term ("retreat") refers to being cadent. Although Bonatti does not mention this condition of the Moon, perhaps he is implicitly drawing a connection between the weakness of the Moon (by cadence) and the weakness of the marriage.

with him; and [the querent] wants to be informed about this, and came to you to pose the question whether the woman is a virgin or not.

You will then consider the Ascendant and its Lord, and the significatrix (which is the Moon, although [the querent] does not have a house in this case, nor a planet as a significator), and see if both were in angles and fixed signs: tell him that the woman is a virgin, indeed that no stain of corruption is in her. And if something evil is said about her, he should not believe those who say it, because they are all lying, and nothing filthy can be found out about her, not even if she were tempted by someone.

Indeed if the Lord of the Ascendant and the Moon were in fixed signs, and the angles were movable signs, she has been tempted but did not yield to the words of the tempters. If however the Moon were joined to Saturn or Jupiter or Mars or the Sun, corporally or by aspect, so that there were 5° or less between them, she is tempted by someone who bears the look of that planet to whom she is joined. If indeed the Moon were joined to Venus or Mercury, she is tempted by some woman on behalf of another man, but neither cares about nor yields to her words, but holds the temptress in derision. If indeed the Moon were separated from the aforesaid planets by 3', the woman is angry with the temptress or the other tempters, and they have stopped their temptation of her.

If indeed the angles were fixed signs, and the Lord of the Ascendant and the Moon were in movable or common signs (but the common ones introduce less than the movable ones), she was tempted and is yet tempted; and at some time endured what was said to her by the temptress women; but she did not yield to them, but persevered in her virginity.

If however the Lord of the Ascendant or the Moon were in movable signs, or they were both in common ones and the Moon were joined with one of the aforesaid masculine planets, someone who bears the look of the planet to whom the Moon is joined, has already hugged and kissed her, and he has touched the woman's private parts, and has even put his own member up against them; and the thing happened only up to the point of believing himself to have known her;[176] and she herself was deceived, indeed so that her virginity came to an end; however she did not believe herself to have lost it, because for her part she did not commit the shameful thing willingly; and thus what was done was the reason for her bad image. And such things of this type tend to happen when

---

[176] *Et fuit res tantum ante quod credidit ille se cognovisse eam.* In other words, he stopped "before" (*ante*) the point of actual intercourse.

men have much privacy[177] with women, or frequent them much, or sometimes at large banquets, or by going to pleasure-gardens, or when women go off to parties that are long-lasting or remote from the city, and so on.

If however the Moon were with the Head of the Dragon, the deed happened by touching but was not consummated, nor did she lose her virginity by this means. If indeed it were the Tail instead of the Head, neither in the past, nor now, nor in the future will she be judged free of reproach. And the same can be said about Mars if he were there instead of the Head, except that Mars does not impose so much malice onto the woman as the Tail does. If indeed the Moon were joined to Venus by the aforesaid conditions concerning the signs and angles, it does not seem she completed the deed; nor did she persevere in it; and it seems to be something else about her, because she appears to love girls and to rub herself with them, and sodomize with them, and accomplishes her shameful act against nature. While if the Moon were impeded in the last face of Gemini, the woman has already corrupted herself with her own hands, and has deflowered herself.[178] If however she were impeded in the last bound[179] of this stated sign, it signifies that the woman perseveres in this evilness. And if the Ascendant were a movable or common sign, or the Lord of the Ascendant and the Moon were in movable or common signs, the woman's virginity has already been taken earnestly and with her being willing; and even if she were not willing, she has still been deflowered. And if the Ascendant were a fixed sign and the Lord of the Ascendant were in a fixed sign (even if the Moon were in a movable or common sign), or the Moon were in a fixed sign (even if the Lord of the Ascendant were in a movable sign, or if the Ascendant were a movable or common sign), the woman has not lost her virginity; it could be, perhaps, that someone has put his member against the woman's private parts by force, and ejaculated there, but still has not corrupted her. And if the Lord of the Ascendant or the Moon were combust in a movable sign, the woman was oppressed and her virginity was taken by force. And if she were combust in a fixed sign, she was oppressed and someone wanted to corrupt her, nor however did she submit to being corrupted. And if the Moon were in the Ascendant with Saturn, and the Ascendant were a fixed or common sign, she is not actually deflowered, but someone has abused her through a wicked, sodomitical deed. And if you

---

[177] *Domesticitatem.*

[178] Gemini rules the arms and hands; but why the last face of Gemini (the Sun's)? In traditional texts on sexuality, it is considered bad for Venus and/or the Moon to be in Mercury's domiciles.

[179] Ruled by Saturn, according to the Egyptian bounds.

were to find the Lord of the Ascendant or the Moon in the 5th, or the Lord of the 5th in the Ascendant, or you were to find them joined corporally in one sign, it appears that the woman has already conceived [in the past]. And if they were separated from one another by 3° or less, it seems that the woman has already given birth.

Indeed, if the Moon were impeded by Mars, and Mars were in a square aspect with Venus, indeed so that the aspect has already completed, such that Venus is separated from Mars by 1' or more, and Venus were then in Cancer or Scorpio or Pisces, or Mars were in Aries or its triplicity and in a square aspect to this same Venus (so long as she herself is separated from him as I said), say she is a virgin and not corrupted; nevertheless you can excuse the woman, if you wish, through this method, even if perhaps you find her to be deflowered through one of the aforesaid means, because she does not believe herself to be deflowered; because if you found her to be a true virgin, say that nothing bad can be said about her. But if you were to find her to be deceived in the way I said, such that her virginity was taken by hand or in another way (because sometimes a woman is corrupted, and her virginity is lost solely by the touch of her hands or another's, or by the titillation of the fingers, provided that she has an orgasm[180]), for this reason you may say that even if she herself laughed or had fun with someone else, she was not, however, known [sexually] by some man, whatever may be said about her; and thus the woman will remain excused [of guilt] in the eyes of the one who asks you; because if you tell him the whole truth, perhaps he will consider her corrupted and that she has gone with a man.

Chapter 5: If a woman is doing it with someone besides her husband

If someone jealous of his wife's touch (worrying lest she is doing something bad with another man) were to come to you with this question, look in this case at the Ascendant and its Lord and the Moon, and the planet from which she herself is separating (which are the significators of the querent); and the 7th and its Lord and the planet to which the Moon is joined (which are the significators of the woman). And see to whom the Moon or the Lord of the 7th is joined; because if the Lord of the 7th and the Moon are joined to the Lord of the Ascendant, whether with reception or without reception (so long as it is not

---

[180] *Dummodo ipsa spermatizet.* I am fairly confident about this translation. Bonatti's verb *spermatizo* comes from the Gr. *spermatizō*, "to conceive," but earlier he used it to describe male ejaculation (and uses a different verb for conceiving).

joined to another, closer one by aspect or conjunction), say the woman is not to be blamed, whatever may be said about her.

If indeed the Lord of the 7th or the Moon or either of them were joined to the [primary] Lord of the triplicity of the Ascendant ([or] to the second or third [Lords]), or one of them were joined to the Lord of the 7th and the Lord of the 7th or the Moon were separating from the Lord of the Ascendant, it seems that the woman has someone else whom she loves besides her husband. If however the Lord of the 7th were void in course, the woman does not have a lover, nor is she to be blamed. If however you were to find the Lord of the 7th, or the Moon, or both, separated from another planet (not including the Lord of the Ascendant), and the separation was not by more than 3°, the woman loved another man besides [the querent], but sent him away afterwards. If indeed the Lord of the 7th were with the Head of the Dragon without a conjunction of another,[181] say the woman is not to be blamed; if indeed it were with the Tail without a conjunction of another, she seems blameworthy, and in the past, and now, and in the future she will be able to be blamed.

Then look to see if the Lord of the 7th or the Moon were joined to some [planet] with Mars,[182] and the Head of the Dragon were there: it appears that the woman has a lover whom she herself loves and who is intimate with her. And if the Tail were with Mars, while being joined with the Lord of the 7th or the Moon, as I said, the malice is decreased; and even if perhaps the woman loves someone who bears the look of Mars, still he has not joined with her in marriage.[183] And if Mars were conjoined with the Lord of the 7th or with the Moon in one sign, without the Tail, the woman has a lover in an area not very far from her own house. And if he were in the same degree, it seems then that the lover is in the home, or is a member of the man's family. And if the Moon (or the Lord of the 7th) were separated from Mars, or he from it, the woman has a lover, and maybe that she had him before she had her husband; but one has already dismissed the other, nor do they have a way to do it together.

If for example Mars were the Lord of the 7th, or the Moon were the Lord of the 7th in Aries or Scorpio, and Mars were to aspect one of them with the

---

[181] *Alterius.* This means that the Lord of the 7th or the Moon is joined *only* to the Head of the Dragon. In the following paragraph he considers a combination of the Lord, the Head/Tail, and Mars.
[182] I have added "[planet]" to make the sentence grammatical, but my sense from the paragraph is that this should read, "were joined with Mars," and no third planet is meant.
[183] *Non iunxit eam sub iugo suo,* lit., "He has not joined her under his own yoke."

reception of either[184] (namely that Mars should receive), she loved him a long time ago, but not enough for him to have done the deed with her. If indeed Mars were not received by the Lord of the 7th nor by the Moon (even if they themselves were in the aforesaid signs, and received by Mars), the woman loves someone else, and he whom she loved, loves her. But he did not do the deed with her. And if the occasion presented itself, she would well consent to him.

If however the Moon or the Lord of the 7th were joined to Jupiter without reception, the woman loves a certain noble man, greater and nobler than her (or a bishop or other prelate, or perhaps a judge), and she loves him yet, but he does not love her. If indeed mutual reception were between them, then she loves him and he her; nor does she remain on account of something else that prevents the deed from happening, unless because the opportunity is not there.[185] If however the Lord of the 7th or the Moon were conjoined with Mercury, it seems the woman loves some literate youth, or money-changer, or merchant, who seems to be younger and more handsome and elegant than her husband. If indeed the Lord of the 7th or the Moon were joined to Venus with reception, from any aspect, or even by a trine or a sextile, whether with reception or without reception, the woman does not care for men, but mixes with women and uses them improperly. If however the Lord of the 9th or Jupiter were to aspect Venus, or Venus and the Lord of the 7th committed their disposition to him, she will be punished for having perpetrated such foul and wicked deeds, and she will dismiss them; and perhaps that she will assume a religious life because of it, and because of her shame. If however it were Saturn instead of Venus, the woman loves a certain man who bears the looks of Saturn, or a certain old man, or a certain religious figure clothed in black or dull vestments; and especially if Saturn were the Lord of the 9th, or were in the 9th, or were under the rays of the Sun. If however it were the Sun instead of Venus, namely so that he aspected the Lord of the 7th or the Moon, she loves and has loved some magnate from among those who are as though fit [for a] kingdom; if with reception, he did the deed with her; if without reception, he does not care about her. If however multiple planets aspected the Lord of the 7th at the same time, especially if it were Saturn and Mercury, more than one person has done the deed with her, nor has she so far been chastened by this fact.

---

[184] *Cum eorum receptione utriusque, scilicet quod Mars recipiat.* This does not seem to make sense. If the Moon were the Lady of the 7th in Aries, then who is the other "of them" that Mars could receive? This passage is not in Sahl nor in al-Rijāl.

[185] *Nec stat propter aliud quod res non perficitur, nisi quia commoditas non adest.*

If however someone asks about a woman who is not his wife nor his lover, [then] according to the aforesaid conditions you will give the Ascendant to the woman just as you give her the 7th, unless she were a woman who had a determinate house, like a sister or daughter or others which are assigned to her, to whom you will give the houses attributed to them. However, you ought to pay attention to this: because in the aforesaid deeds that are not completed, reception signifies they will be consummated in the future;[186] a lack of reception, not.

Chapter 6: If a conceived child is said to be his

Which if he (or perhaps someone else) has doubts about his wife–just as often happens when merchants go off to travel, or who go to the region of the cities, or on campaigns, or to similar places, and sometimes find their wives or girlfriends pregnant when they come back–and they fear lest they are not pregnant by them, and one of them asks of you whether the conceived child is legitimate or a bastard, look to the Lord of the Ascendant and the Moon (who are the significators of the querent) and the fifth sign and its Lord (which are the significators of the child). If they were aspecting each other by a trine or sextile aspect (whether with reception or without reception), the conceived child will be legitimate. If indeed they were aspecting each other from a square aspect or an opposition with mutual and perfect reception, or the Lord of the Ascendant or the Moon were in the house of children, or the Lord of the 5th domicile were in the Ascendant without the aspect of the malefics, or they were benefics aspecting the house of children or its Lord, the conceived [fetus] or child (if it is already born) will be legitimate.

Which if it were not so, see if the malefics or Saturn or Mercury or Mars were to aspect the house of children or its Lord: it will be a child conceived or born in disgrace, and the conceived [fetus] will be exposed.[187]

Chapter 7: If someone wanted to take a wife who is corrupted

And if someone wanted to take a wife who is corrupted (perhaps because it will be said of her that she has children), as sometimes is the case when woman

---

[186] *Complementum futurum.*
[187] *Sparedon,* from Gr. *sparganon,* "swaddling clothes" or "objects left with an exposed child."

are widows, or other corrupt women do it with other [men] in secret, and conceive, and give birth, and cause their concealed children to be nourished, and send them away to orphanages[188] or to other religious places, and the men sometimes grumble that this is the case (whence some are scared to accept such wives on account of the scandal); or perhaps for other reasons, and he comes to you to ask whether the woman has a child. Sahl said[189] that you ought to look to see if Venus were in Aquarius or in Leo, and Mercury were with her: [for then] the woman has never given birth, nor has she conceived. If indeed Venus and Mercury were both in Taurus or in Scorpio, he said that the woman has a child. Likewise if Mars (and Venus and the Moon, or so much as one of them) were with Mars in Gemini or Virgo or Pisces, the woman has a child. If indeed the aforesaid planets were in Sagittarius, they signify the woman's barrenness, both past, present, and future; and if she were discovered to have given birth thus far, the child will die, nor will it outlive her. And if Saturn and Mars were in Aries or in Cancer, or Libra or Capricorn, the woman will be saddened because of the child, and it was born of a lover, not her husband, and neither did she observe faithfulness with her husband. But if Jupiter and Venus were in the aforesaid signs, namely Aries, Cancer, Libra or Capricorn, the child and the conceived child will be that of her own husband without the stain of wickedness.

Chapter 8: Whether a woman who has left or was expelled from the home would return or not

This particular chapter is subordinate to the one above, so that it can be correctly comprehended under it; and it is in accordance with the fact that very often it tends to happen that men expel women from the home, sometimes with cause, sometimes without cause; or the women disappear from their husbands' homes by themselves, or even with cause or through fear lest the men beat them, or for some other reason. And suppose a woman who left the home (in which she was living with a husband or perhaps a lover) were to come to you, and poses the question whether she would return to the house or not.

Look then to the Lord of the 7th (which is the Ascendant of the woman in this case, because the 7th is given to an expelled person),[190] and see if it aspects

---

188 *Hospitalia.*

189 *On Quest.*, 7th House, "Whether a woman might [already] have a child or not."

190 This is a very interesting point that parallels Bonatti's assigning of houses to people far from home or on journeys (see below). Again, it highlights the importance of understanding

the Ascendant, indeed so that no other planet aspects the Ascendant as well as it does: say that the woman will return to the home of which she speaks. You may understand the same about the Moon.

If the Lord of the 7th did not aspect the Ascendant, but he were to aspect another planet (which is not impeded) which aspects the Ascendant,[191] the woman will return to the home with the interposition of some person who introduces himself into the situation, and [that person] will bring her into harmony with the husband. Which if none of these were the case, look then to the Sun (who is naturally the significator of a husband) and Venus (who is naturally the significatrix of the woman). And if the Sun were then above the earth, and Venus [were below the earth and][192] were to aspect the Ascendant by a praiseworthy aspect, namely by trine or sextile, the woman will return readily to the home in question, and without great clamor or rumors. And if the Sun were below the earth and Venus were above the earth, and she likewise aspected [the Ascendant] by a praiseworthy aspect, the woman will return to the home, but with obstacles, and delay and complications, and with duress and rumors; and it will be known by many people before she returns.

Moreover, look to see if the Moon were increasing in her light, that is, from her first appearance from under the rays of the Sun, up until the completion of her second dichotomy:[193] the woman will return to the home, but with slowness and duress. If indeed the Moon were decreasing in light, so that she was already in her third dichotomy and transited the combust degrees, up until she approached the rays of the Sun (not, however, so that she were next to the rays of the Sun so that she did not appear), the woman will return to the home in question, shortly and without much duress, and without much complication and without rumors.

Moreover, see if Venus were occidental and retrograde, returning toward the Sun: the woman will return to the home of her own accord, and by her own will, fearing lest her husband vex her and punish her for having vanished. If indeed Venus were retrograde, and she were already appearing from under the rays of the Sun, the man will regret having expelled the woman from the house, and he will rejoice over her return; but he will not regret having beaten her, nor for having made himself disagreeable; however the woman will return angry just

---

what sort of person is asking the question. In this case, the woman is not merely a querent—she is someone put out of doors and wanting to return to her home (the 1st).

[191] There are echoes of Māshā'allāh here.

[192] I have added this phrase because it mirrors the situation later in the paragraph.

[193] *Dicotomitatis.* By "dichotomy," Bonatti means the endpoint of a lunar quarter.

as she left in anger; and she will regret having returned to the home, just as she regretted having left; and [what is] more, she will not have good will toward the husband.

Chapter 9: On a lawsuit or controversy which exists between some people: who will win, or who will lose, or if they will settle prior to the suit or not

Regarding a lawsuit or controversy which exists between people, or which is ready to become one between two sides, if someone who ought to win wishes to be assured by you, and posed a question to you about it, look at the Ascendant in the hour in which you were asked by him who posed the question to you, and its Lord, and the significatrix (namely the Moon) for the querent; and the 7th and its Lord for the adversary; and see if the Lord of the Ascendant or the Moon were joined with the Lord of the 7th (or he with one of them), by a trine or sextile aspect with mutual reception: they will come to an agreement that is above board, without the intercession of another. If however one received the other, and the received did not receive the receiver, they will come to an agreement without litigation, but not without the intercession of another; and those who intercede will be, usually, from the side of him whose significator receives the other. And if they were joined by a square aspect, or by opposition with reception, or by trine or sextile without reception, they will come to an agreement, but they will litigate first; and the agreement will always come from the side of him whose significator is less heavy, and who commits his disposition to the other;[194] and better than this is if each significator were to receive the other. If the light one were joined to the heavy one, and did not receive him, but the heavy one received the lighter, it signifies that the receiver wishes to come to agreement, even if the light one does not wish to (nor will he stand firm with him[195]); and all the more so if the aspect were a trine or a sextile, and if they were joined corporally in one sign, indeed so that their conjunction were not impeded by another, whether with reception or without reception: they will even come to agreement without the intercession of another.

After this, look at the significator of the king or authority or judge (which is the Lord of the 10th house) to see if it aspected one of the significators (namely

---

[194] This is another indication that an applying planet who signifies something will commit disposition automatically to the significator to whom he applies.
[195] *Nec stabit per eum.*

the Lord of the Ascendant or the Lord of the 7th) or were joined corporally to him; or if the Lord of the Ascendant wished to be joined with the Lord of the 7th (or he with him), and the Lord of the 10th house cut off their conjunction: they will not come to agreement, unless they first go to court in person before the judge; and this will be from the side of the judge or authority, who does not permit them to agree, and perhaps makes them go to court in order to extort something from it.

Then look at the Moon, and see if she transfers light between the Lord of the Ascendant and the Lord of the 7th (and if the Moon did not transfer light between them, see if another planet transfers the light between them). Because if it were so, someone will intercede who will reconcile them, even if they have already begun to litigate.

After this, look at the Lord of the Ascendant (who signifies the querent), and the Lord of the 7th (who signifies the adversary), and see which of them were stronger: because he whose significator were stronger, ought[196] to win. For he who is in an angle will be stronger, and especially if he were in one of his own dignities, and in the dignity of greater quantity; and the one of them who had the greatest number of strengths, will be stronger by that much, and especially if he were received in the place he were located (because he will be stronger in himself, and will have allies who will help him).[197] And if they ought to be reconciled, as I said, the reconciliation will be initiated from the side of the lighter planet, and who commits its disposition to the other: for if the Lord of the Ascendant were lighter, and the Lord of the 7th heavier, it will come from the side of the querent; indeed if the Lord of the Ascendant were heavier, and the Lord of the 7th were lighter, the agreement will be initiated by the adversary. And the planet which is cadent from an angle, is said to be weaker, unless another planet (who is in a strong place and receives him) supports him.

Moreover, it is necessary to look and see whether the Lord of the 7th is in the Ascendant: because then it signifies that the Lord of the Ascendant (namely the querent) will win totally and the adversary will lose. And if the Lord of the Ascendant were in the 7th, it signifies that the adversary will win and the querent will lose. For whichever of the significators is found in the house of the other, a conquered person is signified. And this does not only happen in litigations or monetary pursuits, but it even happens in battles and wars: because always,

---

[196] *Debebit.* Bonatti is not commenting on who has the better moral or legal claim, but making a descriptive statement about who will actually win. You may understand the same when this phrase appears again below.
[197] Here reception confers allies.

when the significator of either one is found in the house of the other, it is said to be already conquered, and is like a conquered person.[198]

After this, you must see whether the Lord of the Ascendant or the Lord of the 7th is retrograde: because if the Lord of the Ascendant were retrograde, it signifies the weakness of the querent, and that he himself will not be firm in pressing the suit, and that he will refuse [to speak] the truth to his adversary, and will not confess it, nor will he believe himself to have legal right.[199] If indeed the Lord of the 7th were retrograde, it signifies weakness on the part of the adversary, and that he himself will flee the lawsuit insofar as he can, and will refuse [to speak] the truth, nor will he believe himself to have a good case. Look even at the significator of the judge (whether he is a king, or authority, or judge who must pass judgment between them), who will be the Lord of the 10th, to see whether he aspects the significators of the suit or not; which if he were to aspect them, and were direct, he will proceed according to the rule of law in the case, and he himself tries to make it short and decide quickly. If however he were retrograde, it signifies that the judge or king or authority does not proceed according to the rule of law in the case, nor will he be concerned to decide it, but rather it will be prolonged more than it ought to be prolonged by law. The same must be said about the prolongation of the case if the Lord of the Ascendant were separated from the Lord of the 7th, or if the Lord of the 7th were separated from the Lord of the Ascendant.

Moreover, see if the Lord of the Ascendant were joined with the Sun or with the Moon, or one of them were joined to him, so that another does not impede their conjunction (provided that the conjunction of the Sun is not corporal, because it would signify [the Lord's] impediment–unless the planet is in *kasmīmī*, because then it would become strong), or if the Lord of the Ascendant were in the domicile of one of the luminaries, or if the Sun or the Moon were in the Ascendant: because if this were so, it signifies the strength of the querent. If indeed the Lord of the 7th were so disposed, as I said concerning the Lord of the Ascendant, it signifies the strength of the adversary.

And look to see if the Lord of the Ascendant were joined to the Lord of the 10th house: the querent applies for help from the judge, or from him who ought to know about the case; and perhaps that he tries to corrupt him so that he passes sentence in his favor. And if the Lord of the 10th house were to receive

---

[198] There is a slight ambiguity as to whether one Lord has to be in the other's *domicile* (the sign), or whether being in his *house* (by quadrant houses).

[199] *Ius.* Bonatti seems to be mixing several types of moral weakness and defensive action in this paragraph.

the Lord of the 2nd from the Ascendant, the judge seeks the querent's money. And if the Lord of the 10th[200] were to receive the Lord of the Ascendant, the judge will acquiesce in the pleadings of the querent; without that, however, he will not. And likewise, see if the Lord of the 10th house were lighter than the Lord of the Ascendant, and were joined to him: the judge or authority will do what the querent wants, even if the querent does not ask him. If however the Lord of the 7th were joined to the Lord of the 10th house, the adversary seeks help from the judge or authority. Because if the Lord of the 10th were to receive the Lord of the 7th, the judge will acquiesce in the pleadings of the adversary, and will lower himself to be corrupted, and will show the meanness of his spirit;[201] otherwise not. But if he were to receive the Lord of the 8th, he will accept the adversary's money. But if the significator of the judge (namely the Lord of the 10th) were lighter than the Lord of the 7th, and were joined to him, then the judge or authority will strive to provide the good of the adversary, even without his asking.

After you were to see the disposition and condition of both significators (namely that of the Lord of the Ascendant and the Lord of the 7th), and if you were to see they do not want to reconcile, nor does it seem to you that they will be reconciled, but rather it seems they want to go to court, see then if the Lord of the 10th house is joined to one of the significators (namely to the Lord of the Ascendant or the Lord of the 7th), or if one of them is joined to him, indeed so that another planet does not impede their conjunction: because the judge or decision-maker will be favorable to him with whose significator he is joined. That is, if he is joined to the significator of the 1st, it is favorable to the querent; if he is joined with the significator of the 7th, it will be favorable to the adversary. If he is joined to none of the significators, he will be favorable to neither of them, but he will proceed solely according to what is handed down by law.

If indeed he were joined to both of them with reception, as sometimes happens, the judge will settle between them and he will reconcile them together, whether they want to or not.

Then look at the Lord of the 10th house (which is that of the decision-maker), and see if some planet is in it. If it were its Lord, the judge will decide the case as cautiously and quickly as he can, honorably, unless it is Saturn. If indeed [the planet in the 10th] were the Lord of the bound or triplicity or face, he will decide the case, but he will not be particular about [or concerned with]

---

[200] Omitting *secundi*.
[201] Reading *animiculum* for *aminiculum*.

passing sentence.[202] If however there were a planet in the 10th which did not have dignity there, nor were it received by the Lord of the 10th, it signifies that the parties will not remain content with the judge or the sentence, because both will fear him, and will agree on another judge, and will stand by his judgment. And even see if Saturn were the significator of the judge and were in the 10th: the judge does not judge according to law [or justice], nor according to how he ought to. If then Jupiter or the Sun or Mercury or Venus or the Moon were joined to him by any aspect except by opposition, or if he were void in course, something bad is said about the judge, but what is said will be overcome quickly, and the judge will not be defamed because of it. If indeed [one of these planets] were joined to him by opposition, evil will be said about the judge by reason of an unjust judgment, and it will last a long time. If indeed Mars were to aspect Saturn from the opposition or a square aspect, then of whatever condition Mars were, the judge or authority will be defamed from thence. If however Mars were of bad condition, he will be defamed by a scandalous event, unless Saturn were then in Capricorn (because then Mars holds back some of his malice, especially if he were of good condition).

If perhaps you were to find that the parties do not remain content with the earlier judge, but establish *fidialium*,[203] just as was said, see if some planet is in the 10th: because through it you will be able to know the nature of the judge whom the parties arrange among themselves.

Because if Jupiter were there, the judge for whom they arrange is good and benevolent, just and benign; and in no way will he permit himself to be corrupted, whether by money or pleading, but he proceeds only in the path of truth.

If indeed it were Mars, the judge will be false, easily angered, unreliable [unfaithful], not loving justice, and who is quickly moved and changed from proposal to proposal, indeed so that the most recent error will be worse than the previous one, and they will regret having chosen such a judge.

---

[202] *Sollicitus in sententiando.* I take this to mean that he will not be eager to pass sentence, he being more interested in reconciliation.

[203] Unknown word; but *fides* and its paronyms pertain to trust; so perhaps this simply refers to them coming to a good-faith agreement about arranging for a new judge, or perhaps declaring that they will abide by the judgment of the new judge.

If it were the Sun, the judge will be of good soul; however, he will lower himself to be influenced by the pleading of friends, and turns himself toward them and gives them his ears, and [gives them] the hope of doing what they want; but ultimately he will judge rightly.

And if it were Venus there, the judge will be just and of good opinion, but will not be very profound in the law; yet he will judge in good faith.

And if Mercury were in the 10th, the judge will be of good abilities and acute, and quickly seeing the issue at stake. But he will judge in accordance as he is applied to the planets: if to the benefics, justly; if to the malefics, unjustly; if he is applied to none, he will judge according to the evidence he found.

(And in all of the aforesaid situations, the Lord of the Ascendant and the Lord of the 7th, and all of the aforesaid significators are considered, *without* the participation of the Moon, even if she participates in all things by nature; however something is removed from her.)[204]

If however the Moon were in the 10th, the judge will be fickle and unstable, and he will judge in accordance as things appear to him, not considering much that is according to law [or just], neither caring about what he judges nor what may be said about his judgment, good or bad.

You will even consider a certain secret, which I do not remember ever having found in the sayings of the ancients (however, I have attempted it and I have found it to be accurate): namely, that you consider the place of the Lord of the Ascendant and the place of the Lord of the 2nd, and subtract the lesser from the greater; and what is left over will be the remainder of the Lord of the 1st and the Lord of the 2nd. Then consider the place of the Lord of the 7th and the place of the Lord of the 8th, and subtract the lesser from the greater; and what is left over, will be the remainder of the Lord of the 7th and the Lord of the 8th. And take these two remainders, and subtract what is lesser from the greater, and keep this third remainder.

---

[204] *Derogatur ea aliquid*, reading *ea* for *ei*. I am not sure what this last phrase is supposed to contribute.

Then take the place of the Lord of the 9th and place of the Lord of the 12th, and subtract the lesser from the greater, and this will be the remainder of the Lord of the 9th and the Lord of the 12th; and take it and the third remainder, and subtract the lesser from the greater, and that which is left over will be the Part signifying the help and strength of the querent or quaesited:[205] add, from above, the degree of the ascending sign, and project from the Ascendant just as you do for the Part of Fortune if it were in the day; if however it were in the night, project from the nadir.[206]

And see in whose domicile or exaltation or bound or triplicity its number came to an end: because the planet which is the Lord of that place, or is stronger and more powerful in it, will be the one sought, namely the helper of him whose significator it aspects more or better, minute by minute–or who were closer to that place, provided that it had some dignity in it; and who renders him stronger; and all the more if it were with reception. Which if both the remainders were equal, the signified thing will be in the Ascendant in the day; at night, in the nadir. And if you were to do this, always prefer the Lord [by domicile]; which if he were impeded, operate through the Lord of the exaltation; but if he were impeded, operate through the Lord of the bound; which if it were impeded, operate finally through the Lord of the triplicity. Wherefore the planet on whose side this were to fall (of the several places stated), or who were to aspect him more, or who were closer to him, having dignity there, will be the one signifying the reason why, and how, the said things come to be, and whence they happen.

But if the Lord of the 1st and the Lord of the 2nd are the same, its place will be as[207] the remainder of the Lord of the 1st and the Lord of the 2nd. If indeed the Lord of the 7th and the Lord of the 8th are the same, its place will be as[208] the remainder of the Lord of the 7th and the Lord of the 8th. Subtract then the lesser from the greater, and do as was said concerning the remainder of the Lord of the 1st and of the 2nd, and concerning the remainder of the Lord of the 7th and the Lord of the 8th. What has been said in lawsuits, you may understand the same in combats and wars, and in all controversies.

---

[205] The reason to use the 12th and the 9th seems to be related to the implied reason why the 9th is considered in matters of prisoners: the 9th is the 10th from the 12th, suggesting those who have authority over the prisoner. Is the idea that the querent is worried about being thrown in prison?

[206] I.e., the 7th house cusp. Bonatti uses "nadir" functionally, so the 7th is the nadir of the 1st, just as the 4th is the nadir of the 10th.

[207] *Tamquam.*

[208] *Tamquam.*

Chapter 10: On buying and selling

If someone wishing to buy something poses a question to you about the matter, whether he will obtain the thing or not, then look at the Lord of the Ascendant (who is the significator of the querent), and likewise the Moon (who is not to be omitted); and look at the Lord of the 7th, who is the significator of the one selling as well as of the thing to be sold in an absolute sense, unless the thing to be sold is made determinate.

And see if the Lord of the Ascendant or the Moon is joined with the Lord of the 7th, or the Lord of the 7th with the Lord of the Ascendant: the querent will obtain the thing he asks about, and without great delay or complications; and the perfection of the purchase or sale will come from the side of him whose significator is lighter. So if the Lord of the Ascendant were lighter, it would come from the side of the querent. If the Lord of the 7th were lighter, it would come from the side of the seller.

If indeed the aforesaid significators were not joined from some conjunction or aspect, see if the Moon or some other planet were to transfer their light between them: because if it were so, it signifies that some person introduces himself into the matter, and the thing will be perfected in that way. Even if the transfer of light came to be from one planet to the [other] seven planets, so long as the light were led back to the Lord of the Ascendant, or at the very least to the Ascendant, the matter about which the question [was asked] will be perfected.[209]

If however the question were determinate, see what the querent is asking about: because if he were to ask about buying a slave, or about one of those things which are signified by the house of slaves, you will give the 1st to the querent, the 6th to the quaesited thing. If he asks about a horse or cow or about one of those things which are signified through the 12th house, you will give the 1st to the querent, the 12th to the quaesited thing. If it were asked about buying a city or about a house or castle, the 1st is given to the querent, the 4th to the quaesited thing. And so you are able to understand about anything for sale through the house through which it is signified.

Then see if the Lord of the 7th were in the 1st: the seller pesters the buyer to buy the thing, and the desire of the seller will be greater than that of the buyer.

---

[209] Again, Bonatti is drawing on the doctrine of Māshā'allāh, that it does not matter through how many planets the light must be transferred, so long as it finally reaches its destination.

If however the Lord of the 1st were in the 7th, the buyer pesters the seller to sell him the thing, and the desire of the buyer is greater than that of the seller.

Moreover, see if one of the benefic planets (namely Jupiter or Venus) were in the 1st: the purchase will be completed without labor and without complications and without delay, nor will the buyer strive to deceive the seller. If indeed the Sun were there, and he were not joined corporally to one of the planets, it will be the same. And if Mercury or the Moon were there, and one of them were not in the aspect of any malefic, it signifies the same thing as the Sun. If however Saturn or Mars were there, or the Sun, [and] were joined to one of them corporally, or Mercury or the Moon [were there and] in some aspect of one of the malefics, it will signify that the matter will hardly be able to be perfected; and if it were perfected, it will come to be with difficulty and complications and tardiness, and the buyer will strive to deceive the seller, and will strive to commit fraud if he can, nor will he stand by him.[210] If however one of the aforesaid benefics were in the 7th just like I said, it signifies goodness on the part of the seller, just as I told you about the 1st on the part of the buyer. If indeed one of the aforesaid malefics were there, it signifies malice on the part of the seller, just as I told you about the buyer.

Then see if the Moon were separated from some planet, and were joined to another immediately, and without any distance: namely when she is separated from one, and were joined immediately to another, degree by degree (or as much as 5° or less fell between her and him to whom she is joined): it appears that he who sells the thing will not let go of it, but had it on a hereditary basis, or in some other way without buying it. And Sahl said[211] that if it was an object which the seller let go of, he has not yet paid off its price to the one who had sold it to him. And he said that if the Moon were separated from some [planet], and were not yet joined to another, that there will be a delay and tardiness and complications and litigation or an agreeable settlement. And he said that if the planet from which the Moon is separated were entering into combustion, that he who sells the thing will never get it back, but will die first. Moreover, may you see if the planet from whom the Moon is separating, is free from impediments, and itself aspects the Lord of the sign through which the sold item is signified by a trine or sextile aspect: it signifies that the seller repurchases the thing, or in some way will yet get it back.

---

[210] *Nec stabit per eum*, i.e., remain faithful to the deal.
[211] *On Quest.*, 7th House, "A question on a purchase or sale: what will be so concerning it."

Chapter 11: Whether a thief (or another who flees) will be found or not, or if he will return of his own will

If someone at sometime were to flee from somebody, just as when a slave or slave-girl or another servant flees; or if perhaps there were someone who had been a guest, and something drew him away and he left; or perhaps it is a wife who likewise flees and [the querent] wants to find her, and he poses the question whether or not she will return to him, and in what direction she flees: look at the Ascendant and its Lord, and the Sun, and give them to the querent; [give] the 7th and its Lord to him who flees (and the Moon, which naturally signifies every fleeing thing because of her quick movement). Then look to see if the Lord of the first is joined anywhere with the Lord of the 7th, or if the Lord of the first were in the 7th: it signifies that he will find him, if he well desires to pursue him, and applies himself well by inquiring into him. And if the Lord of the 7th were joined to the Lord of the 1st, or the Lord of the 7th were in the 1st, or were joined with a retrograde planet, it does not seem that he will have to put much work into finding the one who flees, because it will be one of the following two:[212] for either he will return of his own will, and his own free movement, or if he were to seek him out, he will find him before he has gone very far from the house in which he is staying.

And likewise, see the Moon (who signifies the one who flees). If she were separated then from the Lord of the 1st, and joined immediately to the Lord of the 7th, it signifies that someone who has news about the one who flees, will come to the querent and tell him where the one who flees is. And if the Moon were separated from the Lord of the 7th, and were joined to the Lord of the 1st, he will regret having fled, but he fears being sent back, whence he sends someone to him who seeks him, in order to ensure safety for him from [the querent], and thus he will return without other inquiries by the querent.

Then see if the Lord of the 7th were joined to some malefic planet in an angle, or a malefic were joined to him: it signifies that he who flees will be caught, if the querent wished to pursue him well. And indeed if they (the Lord of the 7th and the malefic who impedes him) were not both in an angle, but just one of them were in an angle: the fugitive will not be caught so that he would be put into prison, but he will be found and detained without imprisonment. If indeed the Lord of the 1st were to aspect the malefic who impedes the Lord of

---

212 *Alterum duorum erit.*

the 7th, the querent will find him who flees being held in the power of someone to whom [the querent] ought to give money before he gives [the fugitive] to [the querent]. Likewise if a malefic were in the 9th, it signifies the impediment of the fugitive in his journey, and that he will be caught. But if it were a benefic in the 9th, he will not be caught, nor can he be caught, unless the benefic were heavily impeded.

Then look to see if the Sun and the Moon (or at least one of them) were joined to the Lord of the 7th, or aspected him from any aspect: because the fugitive will not be able to hide, indeed not so that he is not found. Likewise even if the Lord of the 7th enters combustion or is already combust, it signifies that the fugitive will be found, even if he were to hide himself. And if the Lord of the 1st (or one of the malefics) were to aspect him then, he will be caught and dragged off as one conquered. Indeed, if the Lord of the 7th were joined to some benefic by body or aspect (whether he is under the rays [of the Sun] or not), the fugitive will [not] be caught even if he were found, except in one case: namely, if the benefic were retrograde or combust or entering under the rays of the Sun: because then it cannot defend him from being caught.

Then look to see if the Lord of the 7th were joined with a stationary planet (in whichever station it was, namely the first or the second), and were in an angle or in one succeeding an angle: it signifies that the fugitive does not know to flee, and does not know which course to take, namely whether to flee or not; and indeed he will remain in some place until he is found and caught. But the [kinds of] captures that come to pass do differ, when the planet is stationary. Which if it were in its first station, then the querent will catch the fugitive, or another will capture him and will give him to [the querent]. If however it were in its second station, the fugitive will be caught, and perhaps he will be caught while in flight, and incarcerated and prosecuted, but he will flee again from the prison, or from his fetters; however it hardly seems that he escapes so that he will not be caught again.

And Sahl said[213] that if the planet to whom the Lord of the 7th is joined, were direct, the fugitive will be caught, but will not be sent back to prison; however, he will be returned to the querent or to him who seeks him, and neither will he incarcerate him over it.

Moreover, if the Moon were waxing in light and number, the fugitive will be pursued for a long time before he is caught, and his capture or discovery will be

---

[213] This seems to be from *On Quest.*, 7th House, "A question about a fugitive [with] substance or another lost thing: if it would be found."

greatly prolonged. If indeed she were in waning light, and number, he will be discovered quickly and with little labor.

In order to know in which direction the fugitive is going, look at the significatrix of the fugitive (which is the Moon), and see where she herself is then: which if she is in the Ascendant, or between the Ascendant and the 4th, it signifies that he will flee in the direction of the east. If she were in the 1st exactly, in the east. If in the 2nd, [he is in] the east, turning a little toward the north. Again, if in the 3rd, turning more again towards the north. If however the Moon were in the 10th, it signifies that he will flee toward the south. If in the 11th, toward the south, but turning toward the east; if in the 12th, turning more again toward the east. If she were in the 7th, it signifies that the fugitive goes toward the west. If in the 8th he goes to the west, turning toward the south; if in the 9th, turning more again towards the south. And if she were in the 4th, it signifies that the fugitive flees toward the north. And if she were in the 5th, he goes toward the north, turning toward the west; and if she were in the 6th, turning more again toward the west.

And you could even add or take away from your work, insofar as you were to see the Moon or the Lord of the 7th to be in a direction or sign [that is] eastern, southern, western, or northern. If indeed the one who flees were a thief, and the querent or follower or pursuer wants him, to the extent that he is a thief it will be the same judgment in all cases and all things as for other fugitives; and by that much worse, if the planet with whom the Lord of the 7th is joined, had entered then into combustion, because it signifies that the thief will die by reason of his capture (if he were captured). And if the planet with which the Lord of the 7th is joined, when it enters into combustion, were joined to some malefic, it signifies that the thief will be found by a kind of discovery that will not be useful to him who finds him. Because he will find him dead, perhaps having died terribly: perhaps he finds him hanged or decapitated or burned, or perhaps his body is mutilated. For if Mars were in the 7th and the Lord of the 7th were impeded in the 10th, he will be hanged; if indeed the Moon were under the rays of the Sun, and were otherwise impeded by Mars, he will be burned; and if Mars were in the Ascendant while he impeded the Lord of the 7th or the Moon, he will be decapitated. If however it were Saturn who impeded the Lord of the 7th or the Moon, and he were under the earth, he will be submerged and suffocated in water; if he were above the earth, he will be hit and beaten with sticks, indeed so that it will be the reason he dies, or nearly so, indeed so broken to pieces he cannot escape. And if then the Moon were joined with the Lord of the sign in which she was, or with the Lord of the 8th house, the querent will obtain the goods of the thief, even if the thief were dead.

It was said concerning a fugitive or a thief (and of one like them), that one must look in this place. If the fugitive (as sometimes happens), asked you: "Is it good for me to return to the place from which I fled, or not," you must then look at the Moon. If she were separated from a benefic and joined to a malefic, it will be better for him to return to the place whence he fled. If indeed she were separated from a malefic, and joined to a benefic, it will be worse for him to return, and flight will be better for him. If however she were separated from the benefics, and joined to benefics, [then] if the benefic from whom she is separated is better disposed (even if both are good), it is better to return (and *vice versa*). If indeed she were separated from a malefic, and joined to a malefic, either way is bad for him. But if the malefic from whom the Moon is separated is more badly disposed, it is worse for him to return (*and vice versa*).[214]

Chapter 12: On stolen goods, whether they will be recovered, or the querent will obtain them or not

If someone were to approach you about a theft that has been committed, posing a question as to whether an object of the stolen property will be recovered or not, and you wish to look into the matter for him, look at the 1st and its Lord at the hour of the question, and the significatrix (namely the Moon), who are the significators of the querent; and the 7th and its Lord for the thief, because the thief is signified by the Lord of the 7th. If for example you were to find him in the 7th, it signifies that the querent can find the thief, if he wishes well to look for him, and to labor and strain in this matter, i.e., to find him. Indeed if you wished to know whether he will recover the stolen thing, look at the 2nd from the Ascendant to see if it were joined to the Lord of the 8th and received him (because [the Lord of the 8th] signifies the substance of the thief): the querent will obtain the stolen thing, or the goods of the thief, indeed so that he is recompensed for the theft committed. You may say the same about the Lord of the 1st, if it were joined to the Lord of the 8th and received him. If however the Lord of the 2nd from the Ascendant (which signifies the substance of the querent and even the stolen thing itself) were combust, it signifies that the thief has broken the stolen object up, and consumed and dissipated and

---

[214] This is very much like the 9th house question about which land to go to (see Tr. 6, Part 2, 9th House, Ch. 7).

destroyed it. Whence even if the querent were to find the thief, he will not find the stolen object.[215] If the Lord of the 2nd were going out of combustion, the querent will find a part of the stolen goods, but he will not find all of them, and he will hardly or never find more than half of them.

Then look to see if the Lord of the 7th were in the 1st, or were joined to the Lord of the 1st: the thief will regret having stolen the thing, and he will return it to the one it belonged to. Then look to see if the Lord of the first were joined to some planet located in the 10th or in the 1st, or at least in the 7th: because if it were so, the querent will find the thief, even without extensive investigation. And if the Lord of the first were joined to a planet cadent from an angle, which did not aspect the Ascendant, it signifies that the thief has already departed from the land, and has distanced himself so much that there is no hope of finding him. But if the planet that is cadent from an angle (to whom the Lord of the first is joined) were to aspect the Ascendant, it signifies the discovery of the thief as if after losing all hope, even if with much watching and extensive investigation.

Moreover, if you were to find the Lord of the 7th combust, and the Lord of the first aspected him, it signifies the discovery of the thief when he does not believe he will be found. Likewise if the Moon were to transfer light between the Lord of the first and the Lord of the 7th, it signifies the discovery of the thief. And if the Lord of the first did not aspect [the Lord of the 7th], and he himself (namely, the significator of the thief) were under the rays, he will still be found, but not easily. If however the Lord of the 1st and the Lord of the 2nd were both joined to the Lord of the 10th, the authorities or governor will compel the thief to return the stolen thing to the querent, or to him whose it is; or the thief will return it out of fear, lest he be dragged before the authorities or the governor of that land in which he is detained. If however the Lord of the 1st were joined only to the Lord of the 10th, the querent will threaten the thief through the authorities, and will strive to scare him into returning the thing to him; nor will the thief fear the threats very much; however the authorities, or the governor, will help the owner of the thing against the thief.

If indeed the Lord of the 7th were joined with the Lord of the 10th, even without the conjunction of the Lord of the 1st, the authorities or governor will not exercise their office well against the thief that he may restore what was stolen; but on the contrary they will help him. And if the Lord of the 8th (which signifies the substance of the thief) were joined to the Lord of the 11th (which

---

[215] Omitting the redundant and confusing *furtum seu.*

signifies the money of the authorities), it signifies that the civil authority will accept money from the thief and will help him. If however the Lord of the 2nd were joined to the Lord of the 11th, it signifies that the civil authority will accept money from the querent, in order to proceed against the thief, and it will proceed for this reason. If for example the Lord of the 7th were joined to the Lord of the 3rd or to the Lord of the 9th, or if it were in the 3rd or the 9th, it signifies that the thief has left that region; or if he were in the 3rd, then he is on a journey to exit the region, and has already approached neighboring regions. If he is joined to the Lord of the 3rd, he has already left the region completely. If he is in the 9th, or joined to the Lord of the 9th, he has already distanced himself much from that region, in the direction which I told you above when inquiring about a fugitive. If however the Lord of the 7th were in one of the angles, the thief has not yet left the land or region. And if you were to find that the thief has left the land or region, see whether the malefic or benefic planets are joined to the Lord of the 7th, because if the malefics are joined to him or if he himself is malefic, it will go badly for him on the journey of his flight. Wherefore if it were Mars, he will happen upon highway robbers, who will take from him what he carries, and who will strike him, and perhaps they will shed his blood. If it were Saturn, he will encounter thieves who will steal what he carries.

And if the significator of the thief were combust in any of the aforesaid houses (namely in the 3rd or the 9th), and were of the superior planets, and were before the Sun, or were of the inferiors and were after the Sun,[216] or were of the inferiors and were before the Sun while retrograde, it signifies that labor and sadness and distress and illness will happen to him on the road, which will be the occasion for the taking away and losing of what he carries. Likewise if the Moon were joined to the malefics, it signifies the taking away of substance. If indeed the benefics were joined to her, and they themselves were free from impediments, it signifies that it will go well for him in his flight, and on his journey, unless the benefic which is joined to the Lord of the 7th were impeded by retrogradation or fall or combustion (because it signifies the loss of what the fugitive carries with him). Nevertheless, if the benefic were impeded, and joined to another benefic who is in the 1st or in the 10th, nor is impeded, it signifies that he who pursues the thief, will take away the substance of the thief: because [the thief] will throw it down when he sees [the pursuer] going after him–but it will not promise he is caught.

---

[216] That is, if a superior is in a later degree than the Sun (with the Sun approaching it), or an inferior is in an earlier degree than the Sun (with it approaching the Sun).

And likewise if then the Sun or Moon were to aspect the significator of the thief or the significator of his substance, by a trine or sextile aspect, it signifies that the querent will recover the stolen goods. The same must be said if the Sun or Moon were in the 1st or in the 10th. Likewise if the Sun and Moon were to aspect each other by a trine or sextile aspect. If however they were to aspect each other from the opposition or from a square aspect, the discovery of the lost thing is signified, but the querent could find the thing at last only after losing hope. And the discovery of the stolen goods or other lost things will be after the Sun and the Moon are separated from the Part of Fortune, or they or one of them were joined corporally to it. And see how many degrees there are between the luminary which is closer to the Part of Fortune: that is, if the Part of Fortune were in an angle, the discovery will be within so many days as there are degrees separating the luminary from the Part of Fortune, or within that many weeks. And if it were in a succeedent, it will be within so many weeks or months. And if it were cadent, it will be within so many months or years. And a discovery which is through the signification of the Sun hurries [to be accomplished] more than that which is through the signification of the Moon. And that which is through the signification of the Moon is delayed more than that which is through the signification of the Sun. If indeed you did not find that the Sun or Moon aspect the 1st, nor do they aspect each other by any aspect, nor does one of them aspect the Part of Fortune, it signifies that the thief will not be found, nor will he be exposed, forever; nor will the thievery or the stolen object be recovered, by any means, nor by any labor, nor by any investigation which may come to be through the querent or through anyone on his behalf.

Chapter 13: Whether a lost object will be found

And if someone at some point were to ask you in an absolute sense about a missing or stolen object, and perhaps makes mention of it in terms of a theft, and perhaps not; but he says, "See about a certain thing of mine I lost, whether I will recover it or not," and you wished to look for him (whether the thing was stolen or not, or otherwise missing): then you ought to see if the Lord of the first, and the significatrix[217] (namely the Moon), were both joined to the Lord of the 2nd (who is the significator of substance) from the Ascendant: it signifies the discovery of the lost thing, quickly and with little labor. If however only one of

---

[217] Reading *significatricem* for *significatorem*.

them (namely the Lord of the 1st or the Moon) were joined to the Lord of the 2nd, it signifies the finding of the thing that was taken, but not easily like when both aspect [it]. Indeed if not one of them were joined to the Lord of the 2nd, nor him to [either one of them], see then if some planet transfers the light of one of them to the other: it signifies likewise that he will find the thing about which he asks. And if there were not a planet who transferred the light between them, but there is one who is heavier than the Lord of the 1st and the Lord of the 2nd, to whom both are joined, and he himself receives the light of both,[218] it signifies the finding of the quaesited thing. Likewise if even the Lord of the 2nd (which takes care of substance) were in the 2nd, or were to aspect it by a trine or sextile aspect, it signifies the finding of the missing thing, but with delay and complications, and concern and the agitation of the querent. And if you did not find the Lord of the 2nd in the 2nd, but there were another planet in the 2nd, and the Lord of the 2nd were joined to it or it to him (whether the conjunction were by body or aspect), it signifies the discovery of the quaesited thing. If however the Lord of the 2nd were not in the 2nd, nor were there a planet there whom he aspected, nor did it aspect him by trine or sextile aspect, it signifies the loss of the quaesited thing, and that it will not be recovered.

Moreover, if you were to find the Lord of the 8th from the Ascendant joined to the Lord of the 7th, he will not recover the lost thing, because it signifies that he who has the thing (whether he is a thief or someone else to whom the thing has come) has appropriated it for himself. And you will say the same if the Lord of the 7th were joined to the Lord of the 2nd, or he to it, without the conjunction of the Lord of the Ascendant or the Moon; just as if the Lord of the 1st or the Moon were to aspect them while they were joined to each other in this way, they signify the recovery of the quaesited thing, even with litigation and controversy. And if the Lord of the 8th is joined to the Lord of the 2nd, it signifies that the querent will recover the missing thing: because the conjunction of the Lord of the 8th signifies that the substance of the thief (or of him who has the querent's object) will go over to the substance of the querent and come to be his just as it was thus far. And if there were litigation from it, the querent will obtain and recover it. And if the same object were not recovered, he will have gotten the goods of the thief or of another adversary, to the extent that his thing was worth, and recompenses himself for the lost thing, and especially and most assuredly if the Lord of the 1st then aspected the Lord of the 8th or the 2nd.

---

[218] I.e., by collection of light. But it is unclear here whether Bonatti means "receive" in the technical sense of "reception."

And if then the Lord of the 10th house were to aspect, it signifies that the authorities or the judge or governor takes the things, and they wind up in his hands, and thence there will be hope that he will do what to him seems must be done. If however the Lord of the 8th house was being joined then to the Lord of the 10th house, it signifies that the thief or adversary will give money to the authorities or to the governor, so that [the authority] does not harm him, but [that] it would be better to help him. Then look around and see if the Lord of the 2nd were not joined to the Lord of the 1st, nor to the Lord of the 8th: it signifies that the thing about which the question was, is wholly lost, and that the rest of it will not be recovered, but rather it is as though it will be considered to have no value.

Then look to see if the Lord of the 2nd were joined with the Lord of the 3rd, or with the Lord of the 9th, or with any planet appearing in them, or if he himself were in them: it signifies that he who has stolen the thing or substance, or he with whom it ends up, carried it out of the country to another land. Then see if the Sun and the Moon were both below the earth at the hour of the question, or at the hour when the thing was carried off:[219] it signifies that the thing will not be recovered by any means, nor could it be recovered; nor is the thief known, nor is the lost thing known, nor is it known who has it. Then look to see if the Lord of the Ascendant and the Moon were both in the Ascendant, and the Sun were to aspect them from a trine or sextile aspect: it signifies that the thing asked about will be recovered on the very day in which it was taken or missing. Indeed if the Sun were to aspect from a square aspect, it will be found that week. If however he were to aspect from the opposition, it will be found in that month, and will be returned to its owner. Understand the same about any thing which is lost or taken in any matter whatsoever.

Chapter 14: If the thief or the one holding the lost object is a family member, or of what condition he is

Which if the querent is suspicious as to whether the thief (or he who has the quaesited thing) is a family member, or from what [people] he is, and he wished to know this from you: see if the Sun and Moon both, at one and the same time, aspect the Ascendant, or the Lord of the Ascendant were in the Ascendant, or were joined to some [planet][220] corporally, or with the Lord of the 7th, or if the

---

[219] Omitting an extra *non*.
[220] Bonatti does not specify what planet; but he may mean one of the luminaries.

Sun and the Moon were in their own domiciles, or they were in the domiciles of the Lord of the Ascendant, and they aspected the Ascendant or its Lord; or the Lord of the Ascendant were removed from the degree of the cusp of the Ascendant; and another planet were with him in the same sign (so that it is closer to the degree of the Ascendant): it signifies that the thief (or he who has the lost thing) is a family member. If indeed what I told you were not true of both luminaries, but were true of only one of them, he will be of the family members of the household, but will be a domestic and born in the house in which the lost or stolen object is. And if the Sun and Moon were in their own triplicities, the thief will be of those who are of interest to the owner of the thing by some kinship, but do not live in the house with him. If however the luminaries were in their own bounds or faces, the thief will not be among the inhabitants of the house, but he is familiar to[221] the inhabitants of the house, and more familiar to others than to the master of the house[hold], but is still known to him. And he himself enjoys companionship with them frequently, indeed so that it is believed that he is a blood relation of the people in the house. If however the luminaries were to aspect the Ascendant, and they did not aspect the 7th, the thief did not enter the house at any other time, but entered first when the quaesited substance was stolen. But if one of the luminaries were in a common sign, it signifies that the thief had already entered the house at another time, but it was not in order to steal; and those in the house knew when the thief entered that other time.

If indeed the significator of the thief (which is the Lord of the 7th from the Ascendant) were in the 3rd from the 1st (which is the 9th from the 7th), it signifies that the thief is not from that land, but from another far away from it. If the significator of the thief were in the 12th from the Ascendant (which is the 6th from its own house), the thief will be a slave. And it if were in the 9th from the 7th (which is the 3rd from the Ascendant), the thief is a religious person. And if it were in the 4th from the Ascendant (which is the 10th from the 7th), he even had duties with the king. And if he were in the 11th (which is the 5th from the 7th), he was among those familiar to the king, or the authorities or other magnates, namely from among those who are fit for a kingdom.

And if it were in one of its own domiciles, it will be a man who is used to having what is his, but is now indigent, and is ashamed of having to work in order to earn money. And if it were in its own exaltation, it signifies that the

---

[221] This could mean that he is a family member of someone in the household, although usually *familiaris* already means someone connected to the household.

thief is a noble, but on account of poverty he thinks to steal, because he is ashamed to beg or work in some other way to get what he needs. And if it were in one of the lesser dignities (namely bound or triplicity or face), he will not be very famous in that town, but will be famous in the area or neighborhood in which he lives.

Indeed after you learned that he is of the querent's family, or the inhabitants of his house, Sahl says[222] that if the Sun were the significator of the thief, that he will be the father of the querent. If indeed the Moon were the significatrix, it will be the querent's mother. And if it were Venus, it will be his wife; and if it were Saturn, it will be his slave or a foreigner. And if it were Jupiter, he will be more noble than everyone who is in the household, and about whom there is no suspicion that he is a thief. And if it were Mars, it will be his son or daughter or brother. And if it were Mercury, it will be among his close friends.

Then, Sahl said[223] that if the significator of the thief were peregrine, that you are to look at the Part of Fortune, to see if it is free from the malefics: before this time, the thief has not stolen anything; likewise if the Lord of the Ascendant were free from the malefics. And if Mars were separated from the Lord of the 7th, he was known to be a thief by them. Then he said that if Saturn were to aspect the Moon or the Ascendant, the thief stole with cleverness and ingenuity. And if Jupiter were the significator of the thief, he did not enter in order to steal, but he entered by reason of some other business, and the theft just happened, and he stole. And he said if Mars were the significator of the thief, he did not reach the stolen goods until he penetrated the house or dug under the wall of the house in which the substance was; or broke the bars on the doors or the gate, or found a key. And if Venus were the significatrix, it signifies friend-ship, security too, and his audacity among them while he entered into conversation, taking on the image and likeness of a visiting friend, and thus he stole from them. And if the significator were Mercury, the thief entered the house with ingenuity and cleverness or by some other art. And he said that when the Sun and Moon aspected the Ascendant, the thief will be among the inhabitants of the household. And if the significator of the thief were a benefic, he will be free; and if it were malefic, he will be a slave.

On the age of the thief. And he said if Venus were the significatrix of the thief, he will a youth or a girl; and Mercury is of a younger age than Venus. And if Mars were the significator of the thief, he will be a young man fully grown

---

[222] From *On Quest.*, 7th House, "If indeed you knew that the thief is of the household."
[223] *Ibid.*

from the completion of youth more than Saturn,[224] that is more than a youth. Jupiter indeed is older than Mars. And if it were Saturn, he will be an old, decrepit man. If however it were oriental, he will be of mature age. And if the Moon were the significatrix, and were in the beginning of the [lunar] month, it will be a youth. And if it were in the middle of the month, he will be of middle age, that is a complete man. And if it were in the end of the month, he will be an old man. If indeed the Sun were the significator and he were between the Ascendant and the Midheaven, the thief will be the age of a youth; and indeed you will not stop increasing the age until you arrive at the angle of the earth,[225] because that place is the end of life.

Chapter 15: On the location of the stolen goods

And if you were asked, or you wished to know on your own, in what place the stolen goods are being stashed or hidden, consider then the 4th house, which signifies all hidden things, and see what sign is on the 4th house.

Because if it were Aries or Leo or Sagittarius, the goods will be hidden in a stable or in another place where animals live. If it were in Aries, it will be in a place of small, domesticated animals which are eaten, like sheep, pigs, and the like. If it were Leo, in a place of domesticated animals that bite but are not eaten, like dogs; or animals that live in the forest as though it were their home,[226] like wolves, lions, and the like. If it were Sagittarius, it will be in a place of animals that are ridden, like in the stables of horses.

And if it were Taurus or Virgo or Capricorn, it will be in a horses' stable or in another place in which large animals are kept, which are eaten and slaughtered, as are cows, and the like. And if it were Virgo or Capricorn, it will be in a place where horses, donkeys, mules, or camels (and the like) live, which are not slaughtered or which are not eaten. And Virgo even signifies grain and especially things below the earth, like pits; or near the earth, as are root vegetables[227] and similar things in which grains are

---

[224] *Plus Saturno.* I do not know what to make of this phrase, which also appears in Sahl.
[225] I.e., the IC.
[226] *Tanquam domestica.*
[227] *Vegetes archae.*

stored. And likewise Capricorn signifies a place of goats or sheep to-gether, and the like.

And if it were Gemini, or Libra, or Aquarius, it will be in a house. If it were Gemini, it will be in a partition or wall of the house. And if the place of the 4th house were Libra, the stolen thing will be near the roof of the house. And if it were Aquarius, it will be next to the door, or above the door of the house, or above the gate in high places.

And if it were Cancer or Scorpio or Pisces, the place of the stolen goods will be near water. If it were Cancer, it will be near a well, or standing water, or a cistern. If it were Scorpio, it will be near a place in which filthy water is kept or let out. If it were Pisces, it will be a place which always remains moistened, as it were.

Moreover, Sahl said[228] that if you found that the stolen goods were in the house and you wished to know their location in the house, look at the Lord of the 4th and a planet which was in that same place. If it were Saturn, it will be in the latrine of the house, and in a place far away and deep. And if it were Jupiter, it signifies a place in a forest, or of prayers.[229] And Mars signifies the kitchen and a place of fire. And the Sun signifies a locked space in the house, and a place where the master of the house relaxes. Venus signifies a place where a woman relaxes. And Mercury a place with a painted building and the library, or the place of the *annona*,[230] and especially in Virgo. And if it were the Moon, it will be within a pit or cistern or place for washing. And he said, know that when the benefics are in the 4th from the Ascendant, the stolen goods will be in a

---

[228] *On Quest.*, 7th House, "A question about the place in which the stolen goods are."

[229] *Nemoris oratorium.* A *nemus* is either woodland or a consecrated grove; I am treating these words as though they had a comma between them.

[230] This should probably be understood as "provisions" in this context. *Annona* cannot be translated exactly. It was a state-run system of food collection and distribution (levied from farmers or through tribute), existing alongside private transactions. In the medieval period it came to be used primarily for supplying the military. Since it was a system and not a single object, one can refer to its cost or value, the means of subsistence itself (i.e., grain, oil), and how much the collection yielded. In modern terms it seems to mean something between "taxes" and the "cost of living" in the broadest sense. Bonatti (especially in Tr. 8, where he relies on Abū Ma'shar) uses it in three main ways: (a) its "severity" or that it is "oppressed," which seems to refer to the burden to farmers and tribute-payers; (b) its quantity: "abundance," "increased," "multiplication," "overflowing," "scarcity," "reduced," "decreased"; (c) its status as a crop vis-à-vis the weather–i.e., whether it is "saved" or its "salvation" is indicated, or whether it is "devastated."

clean and good place, and they have already been given to some noble person. And if the malefics were there, it will be in a horrid and fetid place, and they have already been given to some ignoble person.

On the number of stolen goods, if they are one or more

And if you wished to know whether it was one or more things that were stolen, Sahl said[231] that you ought to look at the signs which are between the Moon and Mercury, [to see] whether they are even or odd.[232] Because if they are even, the thing is going to be made of many things which are bound together, or which are more than one thing. If indeed there were uneven signs between them, it will be one thing.

Chapter 16: If one who is suspected of being a thief, is one or not

And if at some time some man were accused (as often happens) of being a thief, or were he caught or otherwise detained on such an occasion, so that it is said that he is a thief, and you wished to know whether he should be held culpable or not (if the question is put to you about it, or you have taken the hour by yourself): look at the Ascendant and its Lord, and the Moon (which has much to do in this), and consider [the Moon] first. First of all because if she were joined to benefics (whether they received her or not), he will not be the thief. If indeed she were joined to malefics, he will be the thief (whether she is received or not).

If indeed the Lord of the Ascendant were in an angle, nor were he joined to a planet cadent from an angle, it signifies that what is said about [the man] is true. If indeed the Lord of the Ascendant were in an angle, and he were joined to a planet cadent from an angle (who did not receive him), something bad was said about him at some time [in the past], but it was not true. And if the Lord of the Ascendant (because in this case the Ascendant is given to the thief) were in a cadent house, nor were he joined to a planet in an angle who received him, what is said about the detained man is false. If however the Ascendant were a movable sign, what is said about him will be false, and all the more strongly if

---

231 *On Quest.*, 7th House, "A question whether the stolen goods are one or more."
232 *Imparia.*

some malefic planet then aspected the Ascendant, and more so than this if the Tail of the Dragon were there.[233]

And even if you were to find the Moon to be void in course, declare the man to be wholly non-culpable. Likewise if the Moon were joined to a cadent planet (whether she were received by that cadent planet or not). If indeed the four angles were fixed signs, what is said about him is true, and he is the thief. And if the Moon were joined to a planet in an angle, it signifies likewise that what is said about the detained man is true; and especially if she (or the planet to whom she is joined) were in the 10th house; and even if she were in an angle and were impeded, it signifies the falsity of the way he presents himself.

And if you wished to know whether he has stolen something apart from the incident of which he is accused, see which of the significators (namely the Lord of the Ascendant or the Moon) is stronger–because in such a case the 1st and its Lord and the Moon are given to him about which one suspects the evil.[234] And see which of them is stronger, and see if it is separated from some malefic (whether or not it is joined [at that the moment] to a benefic or a malefic): it signifies that he has already stolen something before. And if it were not separated from a malefic, but were separated from the Lord of the 2nd, which is the house of substance (whether [the Lord of the 2nd] were a benefic or malefic), it signifies that he has already stolen something on another occasion. And if the Lord of the 2nd were a benefic, he did not go through with the theft; but if it were malefic, he went through with the theft. If indeed he were separated from a malefic, he went through with the theft. If indeed he were separated from the benefics (whether he were joined [at that moment] to benefics or not), he has never stolen anything up to now, unless the benefic is the Lord of the 2nd from the Ascendant: because then it signifies that he has already stolen something at some time; and even stronger than this if the Lord of the Ascendant were joined to some malefic after separation from the Lord of the 2nd.

Chapter 17: What kinds of things are those which were stolen

If you wished to know what kinds of things they are which were stolen, look at the Ascendant and the Moon, and see where [the Moon] is, namely in which

---

[233] Reading *fuerit* for *iuerit*.
[234] I.e., the suspected thief, as was said above.

sign and in which degree of that sign, and see in which planet's bound that degree were to fall.[235]

Which if it were in the bound of Saturn, and he were in the Ascendant or in the 10th in an earthy sign, the thing will be of those which pertain to the preparation[236] of the earth, which are materials of iron (as are plough-shares, harnesses, tilling devices,[237] and the like). If indeed Saturn were in the 7th or the 4th, they will be other iron tools with which heavy work is done (like cutting rocks, and the like); or it will be an iron bar, or one of the aforesaid objects [but made of] lead; or it will be lead or copper, and the like; and likewise if he were cadent from the Ascendant and the other angles. And if the Sun or Moon were to aspect him, then they will be iron weapons,[238] heavy, shiny, polished, with some rust, and the like. If indeed Saturn were not there, but were cadent from the Ascendant, so that he did not aspect it, nor did the Sun or the Moon aspect [him], and especially if he were in Aries, it signifies that the stolen thing is of little value, and is of those things which pertain to keepers of pens;[239] or they are low-quality arms, and of little strength, like old knives and swords and the like, which tend to shed blood, and the like. If however Saturn were in Gemini, the thing will be of diverse materials and types; nor however will it seem that they are expensive unless some other planet aspects Saturn. For if Jupiter were to aspect him from the 1st or from the 10th house, it signifies that part of the stolen goods are gold, the others are things of low quality. And if Jupiter were in the 7th or the 4th, and were to aspect Saturn, part of the stolen goods will be silver, others will be poor and of little value.

If indeed the degree in which the Moon were, belonged to the bound of Jupiter, one must then see who and how he aspects her. Because if she were in Aries or in another fiery sign, and Jupiter were to aspect her from the [1st] house or from the 10th, it will be a work of gold or made out of gold. If the Sun were to aspect her it will be raw gold, that is, unworked.

---

[235] The following seems to pertain to a rule that Lilly claims does not work (*Christian Astrology* II, p. 331).

[236] *Aptationem.*

[237] Lit., "double-toothed movers" (*motoria bidentia*).

[238] Of the sort suitable for hand-to-hand combat.

[239] *Archimandritas.* See Tr. 3, Part 1, Ch. 3.

If some one of them[240] were to aspect her from the 7th or the 4th, it will be silver or an object made out of silver. Which if Venus were to aspect Jupiter from any aspect, and Jupiter were in his own bound, they will be very dear [or expensive] things, as are pearls and other precious stones. If indeed Jupiter were in Taurus or in another earthy sign, it signifies that the stolen thing is a vestment of theirs, and noble. If however he were in Gemini or in another airy sign, the thing will be an animal, like a horse, mule, cow, and the like. If however Jupiter were in Cancer or in some watery sign, it will be something taken from the water, such as pearls and the like.

And Sahl said[241] that if the Moon were in the bound of Mars, the thing has already passed through fire, or in some way fire has touched it.

If indeed the Moon were to aspect Venus, dye has already been used on it. And if the Moon were in the bound of Venus in Aries, or in [Aries's] triplicity, it will be gold or silver. And if she were in Taurus and its triplicity, or in Cancer and its triplicity, it will be a vestment that is ornate or *abonasim*[242] (which is a kind of precious silk vestment of various colors and made with diverse pictures [or paintings]). And he said that you may know the goodness and beauty of the thing from the place of Venus in the signs. Which if she were in Gemini and its triplicity, it will not be a thing [made] from the substance of animals. And he said that if Venus were going out from under the rays of the Sun, it will be a new thing. If indeed she were retrograde, or at the end of her course, or of diminished number, it will be an old thing, and already hardened.[243]

And he said that if it were in the bound of Mercury, they will be books. And if she were in Aries and its triplicity, they will be coins taken from a purse or another vessel that is bound by red leather. And he said that if she were in Gemini and its triplicity, they will be coins themselves.

---

[240] Of Jupiter and the Sun?
[241] *On Quest.*, 7th House, "On a taken or stolen thing: what it is and of what manner of object."
[242] This may refer to the island of Abon, one of the Spice Islands.
[243] *Indurata.*

See likewise in what sign the Moon is; which if she were in Aries, it signifies that the stolen thing is of those which are carried on one's head. Wherefore if they were arms, they will be helmets of steel or painted leather. And if they were not arms, and they were of those things which pertain to women, they will be wreaths of flowers, and bracelets,[244] and other ornaments for the head which pertain to the adornment of women.

And if she were in Taurus, they will be precious things like necklaces, and other ornaments by which the neck is decorated.

And she were in Gemini, they will be ornaments of the arms and hands, or rings, and the like. And if Mercury then aspected her, they will be coins or other treasure that is painted, in which there are figures of sculpted figures of humans. And if Mercury did not aspect her, they will be things of painted leather on which there are likewise [human] figures depicted.

And if the Moon were in Cancer, it will be a thing taken out of the water, or it will be a thing which is naturally moist.

And if she were in Leo, it will be a thing worked with gold, or it will be burnished iron or yellow copper ore [or brass made from it]. And if the Sun were to aspect her, it will be gold without pictures.

If however she were in Virgo, they will be vestments worked with intaglios. And if Mercury were to aspect her it will be something minted in which there is a sculpted figure of a human.

And if she were in Libra, they will be balances. And if Venus were to aspect her, it will be a thing which is made[245] for the ornamentation of women, and smells like the types of things sent to one.

And if the Moon were in Scorpio, it will be copper [or a similar ore] or worked from yellow copper ore, or of gilded copper, and it is burnished or splendid. And if Mars were to aspect her, it signifies that it is raw gold or silver.

---

[244] *Viriae*, although bracelets do not go on the head.
[245] Reading *facitur* for *facit*.

And if she were in Sagittarius, it will be of varied or a variety of colors or diverse substances, joined in one, which are of greater appearance than value. If however Jupiter were to aspect the Moon it will be a thing (as I said) that is varied, but it will be precious.

And if she were in Capricorn, they will be vile things, and found in vile places. And if Saturn then were to aspect the Moon it will be a thing of little value, as though similar to the earth or made from earth,[246] and it could be copper or bronze.

And if the Moon were in Aquarius, it will be a thing which is extracted from some animal, just like a certain stone called *grapaldina*, which is said to be taken from the head of an old *ruspi*.[247] And if Jupiter were to aspect her, it will be worked gold or silver, or formerly extracted from a mineral. If however the Sun were to aspect the Moon it will be raw gold; and if Mercury or Venus were to aspect her, it will be silver; if indeed the Sun and Mercury were to aspect her at the same time, they will be coins rolled up in some leather purse or money-bag, and the like.

And if she were in Pisces, it will be haircloth[248] or silk, or made of haircloth or silk. If Jupiter aspected her, they will be precious things taken from the water, like pearls, amber [or ambergris], and the like.

From what houses the stolen goods may be sought

A certain modern [writer] said you will consider of what manner the lost or stolen goods are, because they are not all sought from one house, but from diverse ones according to the diversity of the objects. For there were some, as he himself said, who wished to say that any stolen thing was to be sought from the 10th house–but it is not so, since things are sought according to what are signified by the houses. For he said if the thing were stolen from the household members of someone, it is sought from the 2nd. And if it were his brother or

---

[246] Bonatti must mean things made of clay or earthenware, which would be of little value.
[247] In Catalan, a *grapaldina* is a stone said to be taken from the head of a toad (Cat. *gripau*). I do not know what a *ruspus* is, but it may be related to a venomous toad (Lat. *rubeta*).
[248] *Seta*, lit. "horse hair," as used for bristles. The word used for silk later in the sentence (*sericum*) is a generic word which can also be used to describe damask or velvet.

sister, or another one of his kin, it is sought from the 3rd. And if it were his father or father-in-law, it is sought from the 4th. And if it were the son, or other pleasing things, as are women's girdles or belts, or something similar, it is sought from the 5th. And if it were arms or a cuirass, or some small animal, it is sought from the 6th. And if it were a wife or lover, it is sought from the 7th. And if it were something of the dowry or the money of the dowry, or something deposited for safekeeping, it is sought from the 8th. And if it were a cleric or religious person, it is sought from the 9th. And if it were the tax revenue of the king or of some community [or society], it is sought from the 11th. And if it were a large animal or someone incarcerated, it is sought from the 12th. If however it were gold coins or books or grain or oil or the like, they are sought from the 10th. And this [is] according to the peculiarity of the aforesaid houses and their Lords. Likewise however, whatever type of thing, if it is of the goods sought, it can be sought from the 2nd and its Lord.

Chapter 18: The figure of the thief[249]

Abū Ma'shar gave a long discussion on what is said above, on the quality of the stolen goods;[250] but I do not put much energy into it, because what is said above by Sahl is enough. And I added what seems to me ought to be added, indeed so that it could suffice for you. Because there is not great utility in it;[251] but it would seem better to have the opinion of such a person who knows something.[252] Whence, in order to avoid great prolixity, it seems better to me to relate what can be said about the form of the thief and his quality. And it is that you look at the 7th house, which signifies the thief. And see in which of the many faces is the degree of the 7th house, because through it one can know the form or quality of the thief.

> For if the house signifying the thief were the first face of Aries, it signifies that the thief is a man of brown color, and when he steals he is dressed in clothes pertaining more to the color white, than to another color. And if it were the second face of Aries, it signifies that the thief is a woman who then had clothing pertaining more to the color red than to another. And if

---

[249] These descriptions are versions of the images of the zodiacal faces, of which there are many variants.
[250] I do not know what work of Abū Ma'shar's Bonatti is referring to.
[251] Lilly may have gotten his opinion of the above rules from this comment.
[252] *Sed potius aliqualis fama, ut videatur quis aliquid scire.*

it were its third face, it signifies that the thief has a pallid color and has red (or sort of red) hair.

And if it were the first face of Taurus, it signifies two men, one having a narrow face and having promptitude;[253] and the other dressed poorly. And if it were the second face of Taurus, it likewise signifies a man dressed badly and cheaply, and having a key in his hand. And if it were its third face, it signifies that there were three thieves, of which one knows how to drive away serpents, and the like; and another is an archer.

And if it were the first face of Gemini, it signifies that the thief tends to carry a rod or staff in his hand, and has one lackey with him. And if it were the second face of Gemini, it signifies that the thief knows how to play the pipes and use musical instruments, and has one with him who is stooped. And if it were its third face, it signifies that the thief is among those who gladly bear arms, even if not pressed by necessity, but so that he would seem armed.

And if it were the first face of Cancer, it signifies that the thief is a well-dressed man with beautiful, fitted clothes, and with him is a young girl. And if it were the second face of Cancer, it signifies that it is a young girl, who readily carries a wreath of flowers, who is not a virgin, and has with her another girl who is a virgin. And if it were its third face, it signifies that it was one man and one woman who stole.

And if it were the first face of Leo, it signifies that it is a man who wears short [or ripped] clothing and who readily has wild animals, like wolves, hawks, and the like. And if it were the second face of Leo, it signifies that there were two thieves, of which one readily carries a young roe-deer on his head, and the other carries and has his hands more elevated than other men do. And if it were its third face, it signifies that the thief is a man who often carries a small rod in his hand, and has an ugly face, and always looks as though he is sad.

---

[253] *Promptitudinem.* I am not quite sure what Bonatti means by this. Perhaps it is a misread for paronyms of *pomp-* (like *pompositatem*), which refer to grand displays–since the second man is dressed poorly, perhaps the first man is dressed well.

And if it were the first face of Virgo, it signifies that the thief was[254] a certain girl who looks as though she is good, and of whom no one would suspect anything. And if it were the second face of Virgo, it signifies that the thief is a brown man who was dressed in leather clothing, or leather was stitched with his clothing, and he had long hair, or even is accustomed to having long hair. And if it were its third face, it signifies that the thief was a certain white woman who does not hear well.

And if it were the first face of Libra, it signifies that the thief was one man who knew how to play musical instruments, and especially the pipes, and it seems as though he is always angry. And if it were the second face of Libra, it signifies that there were two thieves who live with others, nor do they have their own houses; and they often both go forth angry. And if it were its third face, it signifies that there were two men, of which one is an archer and the other is a man who knows only poorly how to serve, as though he is lazy; and he is poorly dressed.

And if it were the first face of Scorpio, it signifies that the thief is a woman of beautiful stature and a beautiful face. And if it were the second face of Scorpio, it signifies that it was beggars, one man and one woman, and dressed poorly. And if it were its third face, it signifies that the thief was one who goes stooped over his knees, nor does he stand well on them.

And if it were the first face of Sagittarius, it signifies that the thief is an ugly, and deformed, and stinking man. And if it were the second face of Sagittarius, it signifies that the thief was a certain woman dressed well. And if it were its third face, it signifies that the thief was a jaundiced man, having a gray face.

And if it were the first face of Capricorn, it signifies that the thief was a black man or having brown color, and a woman of full age. And if it were the second face of Capricorn, it signifies that the thieves were two women of full age. And if it were its third face, it signifies that it was one brown woman, and very shrewd.

---

[254] Reading *fuit* or *fuerit* for *furatur et* .

And if it were the first face of Aquarius, it signifies that the thief is of full youth. And if it were the second face of Aquarius, it signifies that it is a man having a beard or a long chin. And if it were its third face, it signifies that it is a man of brown color who is often angry.

And if it were the first face of Pisces, it signifies that the thief is a man who wears beautiful and good clothes. And if it were the second face of Pisces, it signifies that the thief is a woman of good stature and a beautiful face. And if it were its third face, it signifies that it was a poor man, dressed badly.

On the figure of the thief from the signs of the 7th house

You could say something in addition about the figure of the thief:

Because if the 7th house (which signifies the thief) were Capricorn or Aquarius, it signifies that the thief is a black or brown man as we might say; and he can have a mixture of saffron with blackness; and he is heavy in his gait, and rubs one foot against the other when he goes, or brings them together, and he casts his eyes down to the earth when walking; and he is thin or not very fleshy, and he is stooped, having small eyes, and the skin of his body is rough; and prominent veins, having a thin beard; and his lips are not very thick, nor very thin; and he has many hairs on his body, and his eyebrows are joined together.

If however the 7th house were Sagittarius or Pisces, it signifies that the thief is a white man having eyes that are not deeply black, but large, and with a large pupil; short and uneven nostrils; and that he is bald, having a blackness in one tooth, of fine stature, compliant and of good spirit (except that he was deceptive in this), a thin beard and curly blond hair.

If however the 7th house were Aries or Scorpio, it signifies that the thief is a red man, having reddish hair, orange eyes, a horrible and narrow gaze, a round face, bold, having a sign or mole on his foot.

If however the 7th house were Leo, it signifies that the thief is a man who has a color that is not truly black, nor really orange, nor really red: but his color has a certain whitishness not very far from blackness, in some way tinged with a blush of red; and he is a man of fine stature, and has wavy hair and blonde eyes, with a little orange.

And if the 7th house were Cancer, it signifies that the thief is a man having a white color mixed with red, eyebrows joined in the middle, eyes that are not truly black but rather black, a round face and fine stature.

If however the 7th house were Taurus or Libra, it signifies that the thief is a man having a color like white, but not truly white, leaning in some sense toward black; a beautiful form, beautiful hair, a face that is not round, a jaw that is not very long, beautiful eyes, darkness of the eyes, somewhat too large, but not so that they are unbecoming, somewhat widely apart, and he displays benevolence as though to everyone.

If for example the 7th house were Gemini or Virgo, it signifies that the thief is a man having a color similar to black: that is, not truly white, not truly swarthy, having a high forehead, long nose, long face, a thin beard, thin or little hair, beautiful eyes, not totally black; and long fingers on the hands.

And these statements about the figures of thieves should suffice for you.

Chapter 19: On contracting a partnership between two people, and their participation

If someone wishing to contract a partnership were to take it upon himself[255] to ask you whether it would be useful to him or not, and posed a question to you about it, and after this you wished to satisfy yourself of the hour of the question, you will give the 1st house to [the querent, and the 7th to] him whose partnership the querent wishes to have;[256] also make the Moon a participator of both. From the 10th house one may know what[257] will happen to him from the partnership he intends to contract. To what end the partnership will come to,

---

[255] *Procuratus fuerit.*

[256] There is a scribal error or lacuna here which I have corrected. The text reads that the 1st should be given to the potential partner, but that would contradict both the standard traditional practice of giving the 1st to the querent, and Bonatti's explicit statement below that the 1st goes to the querent and the 7th to the partner/partnership.

[257] Reading *quod* for *qui.*

you will know from the 4th house and from the planet to which the Moon were then joined (even if, however, the Moon were more on the side of the querent than on the side of the quaesited, still the planet to whom she herself is joined, signifies it for both of them; but less for the querent than for him with whom he intends to contract the partnership). Indeed the planet from which she then were separating or was separated, does more for the querent than it does for the quaesited.

And consider then in the hour of the question, if the Lord of the 1st (which is the significator of the querent) and the Moon were in Aries or Cancer or Libra or Capricorn, without perfect reception by domicile, or exaltation, or two lesser dignities together: it signifies that in the partnership there will be discord and disturbance, and it will be rectified afterwards and the partnership will endure, but there will not really be a good stability, nor will it be very useful nor very lucrative.

If however they were in Taurus or Leo or Scorpio or Aquarius, the partnership will be durable and stable; nor however will it be very lucrative, and when they buy something they will not sell it quickly, but rather it will remain with them more than what customarily ought to be.

If indeed they were in Gemini or Virgo or Sagittarius or Pisces, it signifies that the partnership will be useful and good and lucrative, and that pretty often there will be a steady flow of what is bought and sold,[258] and that they will easily and quickly sell their merchandise, and it will be safe and legal between them, and there will be a good feeling and good faith, nor will there be fraud between them.

And if one significator (namely of the 1st house, or the Moon) were in a movable sign and the other in a fixed or common one, or *vice versa*, it will be what I told you about, but not totally, rather less.

And if the malefics were to aspect the significators (namely the Lord of the Ascendant and the Lord of the 7th), their partnership will be bad, and one will employ falsity against the other, and deception, and they will not behave well, one toward the other. Whence, look to see where there were malefics impeding the significators (the Lord of the 1st and the Lord of the 7th), because that which is signified by the house in which the impeding malefics were, will be the reason why discord will come between the partners. What is signified by each individual house has already been repeated—it is enough for you to know this much.

---

[258] *Saepius reiterabit suum emere atque suum vendere.* Lit., "it will repeat its buying and selling."

And see if one of the malefics were in the 1st (whether it impeded the Lord of the 1st or 7th or not): it signifies that discord and fraud or deception and injury and malice will come from the side of the querent. If indeed one of the malefics were in the 7th, it signifies then that it will come from the side of him with whom the querent intends to contract the partnership, or with whom he has contracted it, if the partnership is [already] created (and perhaps the question were posed, what will come of a partnership that is already contracted).

Moreover, see likewise if the Moon is separating from one benefic and is joined to another: the partnership will begin well, and likewise it will end with esteem, whether they make money or not. If indeed she were separated from a benefic and were joined to a malefic, they begin well and readily, but they will end it badly and with litigation and discord (unless the malefic is well disposed, and received the Moon by perfect reception, just as I told you above). If indeed she were separated from some malefic, and were joined to a benefic,[259] they begin it readily but will end it well and with esteem. If however the Moon were besieged, namely so that she were separated from one malefic and were joined to the other malefic, it signifies that they will begin badly and will persevere in it badly, and will end it badly with quarrels and discord. And you may understand all of this whether they make money or not.

Having looked at this, wherefore if the Moon were joined to the Lord of the domicile in which she was (since he will receive her from his domicile), then it would not impede. And always consider this, because if the Moon were joined to the Lord of the domicile in which she were, the partnership will be ended well and on the level, and with the esteem of both partners, and money, indeed so that each of them remains content and believes himself to have done well in the partnership. If however she were not joined to the Lord of her own domicile, nor to any benefic from a good aspect, one of the partners will suspect evil of the other, and the other of him; and they will be separated for this reason. And if the malefic planets were below the earth, Sahl said[260] that they will be separated because of the bad opinions they have about each other.

Then look to the 10th house, and see which planet is in it. Because if the benefics were in it (because it is the significator of the being of the partnership), say that it signifies good and money about which they will rejoice, and they will say they did well. If however the malefics were in it, their money will be

---

[259] The text contains an error, reading "and were joined to a benefic to a malefic" (*et iuncta fuerit fortunae malae*). Since the partnership is supposed to end well, I have omitted the *malae*.
[260] *On Quest.*, 7th House, "A question on the partnership of two people, and what its end will be."

diminished, or rather as though they will not earn wealth in the arrangement of their partnership, but some situation will intervene which will dissolve all connection, namely by means of death (which dissolves all). And this can be known in this way, namely if the Moon were joined to the Lord of the house in which she is, and both were joined again to a malefic planet, or were joined to the Lord of the house of death: they will not be separated except by death.

Chapter 20: When people go to some man, whether he will be found or not

If someone about to set out to find someone, were to ask you whether he will find him or not, and you wished to look for him concerning such a question, see what kind of person it is to whom he intends to go—namely, whether it is the king or a prelate or other religious person, or whether he is another individual.

If it were the king, see if the Lord of the 10th house were in the 10th or the 1st or the 7th or the 4th: because it signifies that the king is in the place in which the man intends to find him. If indeed the Lord of the 10th were in the 3rd, and the journey were of one day (which is called a short journey), or it were in the 9th and the journey were of multiple days (which is called a long journey), it signifies the he will find him on the road, if the Lord of the Ascendant and the Lord of the 10th house were joined together. If however it were in the 11th or the 2nd or 5th or 8th, it signifies that he is not in the place in which the querent intends [to go], but he will not be far from that place: he will be able to find him through his inquiries. If however the Lord of the 10th house were in the 6th or 12th, he will not find him (nor in the 3rd or 9th), without a conjunction or aspect.

If however it were a cleric about whom [it] is asked, and he were in the aforesaid places, he will find him just as was said regarding the king.[261]

If however it were some other individual layman, look then at the Lord of the 7th. Which if he were in the 7th or the 10th or the 1st or the 4th, he will find him in the place in which he believes [him to be], unless he himself were joined to a planet cadent from an angle: because then he will not find him immediately, unless first he first would ask about finding him. If however the Lord of the 7th were in the 8th or 11th or 2nd or 5th, he will not find him in that place, but near there, not very far from the assumed location. If however he were in the 9th or 12th or 3rd or 6th, he will not find him in the place in which he believes [him to

---

261 Presumably we would look at the Lord of the 9th in such cases.

be], nor near there, and especially if the Lord of the 7th were in the 6th or 12th. If indeed it were in the 3rd or the 9th, and the Lord of the 7th and the Lord of the 3rd or 9th were joined together by body or by a noted aspect, it signifies that he will find him or happen upon him on the road.

Chapter 21: Regarding someone wishing to go on a military exercise or to war, or to start a battle, whether he is a duke or another, whoever he is, whether he will conquer or not

If there were a battle between some people, or it is hoped there will be one (as often happens), and one of them were to come to you and wanted to be informed by you [as to] what could happen to him as a result (whether he were a king, or emperor, or marquis, or duke, or having a state office, or an authority, or any other layperson or cleric who rules over the laity, and who ought to lead an army–whether he is noble or common or a rustic), provided that he is the conductor of the war or of one the parts of a battle)–he is called the commander of this army or battle, whether it was put together for such purposes for himself or for another.[262] And [suppose] he wanted to start some battle, or to go with the army against someone. And [if] he posed you a question concerning these matters, or he posed it on behalf of someone who is very concerned about it, and it was not the emperor or the king on behalf of whom it is asked, give the 1st to him, and its Lord, and see from what planet the Moon separates, and give it likewise to the querent. And you will give the 7th, and its Lord, and the planet to whom the Moon is then joined, to the adversary.

If however it were [on behalf of] the emperor or an authority or regent, and he were to ask about the matters of the empire or kingdom or the city which he rules, you will give him the 10th, and to his enemy you will give the 4th. If indeed he were to ask about his own, particular affairs which were not affairs of the empire or the kingdom or the city, you will give him the 1st and his enemy the 7th, and in all other things you will judge for him just as for any other individual person.

If indeed the Moon were not separated from any planet, nor were she joined to one, Sahl said[263] that then the Moon is not to be admitted that work.[264]

---

[262] I believe Bonatti means, "Whether the commander himself has decided to go to battle for his own interests, or has been ordered by another."

[263] *On Quest.*, 7th House, "On a general advancing toward war, or another concerned person, if he asks for him."

And you should see if the Lord of the 1st were joined to the Lord of the 7th, or the other to him, by a trine or sextile aspect with perfect reception, namely so that one of them receives the other: it signifies that there will be peace between them before the fighting. If indeed it were joined by a square aspect or the opposition (even if they received each other), or by a trine or sextile aspect without reception, they will not be pacified unless first they engage in battle or contend together. But after they have contended or engaged together, they will reconcile amongst themselves and the start of the peace or the peace arrangement will come from the side whose significator is lighter.

And you ought to know that the superior planets (namely Saturn, Jupiter and Mars) are stronger in combats and battles than the inferiors (namely the Sun, Venus, Mercury, and the Moon), and more stable and constant on account of the slowness of their motion–and because the inferiors apply to them, and they do not apply to the inferiors. Whence, if you can do it in your inceptions[265] for wars or battles, always make it so that you have one of the superior planets as a significator, just as will be said elsewhere. However, if you cannot have a superior, take from the inferiors as best you can: because it is good for you to have an inferior in a good state, rather than an unfortunate or impeded superior.

After this, consider, from what you saw, the peacemakers themselves: if either significator (namely the Lord of the Ascendant and the Lord of the 7th) were direct, the peace or concord which they make together will be good and firm, and especially if there were a trine or sextile aspect. If indeed either were retrograde, the peace will be false and it will be neither good nor durable, but it will be more with an evil inclination and guile, and one will try to deceive the other. Indeed, if one were direct and the other retrograde, he whose significator were retrograde will try to deceive the other, and will move with evil intentions and guile against the other.

And see in which place he were from the one whom he will try to deceive: because if he were in the 2nd from the 1st,[266] after they are reconciled, and because one will confide in the other, he will take his substance away from him.

---

[264] I.e., the Moon will not have the significations just listed (using Sahl's *immittas* for Bonatti's *mittenda*).
[265] Elections.
[266] Bonatti means to reckon by derived houses from the 1st or 7th house, whichever signifies the deceived. See the paragraph below on the 8th house.

And if he were in the 3rd, first he will deceive him on account of his brother, because he will take his brother away from him and hold him to extort something from him; or perhaps he will come to an agreement with his brother and make it so that he will injure [the deceived one] or send him out of the country into exile. Which if he did not have a brother, he will deceive him for some other reasons which are signified by the 3rd house.

If he were in the 4th, he will capture him and hold him in an underground and hidden prison, until he takes away from him what he wants; or he will take the kingdom, or a city, or castle, or villa, or house or other estate away from him, in proportion to the dispute between them.

If he were in the 5th, he will do the same to him with his child or because of the child, as was said with the brother or because of the brother (or one of those things which are signified by the 5th house).

If he were in the 6th, he will hold and incarcerate him in order to take away his slaves or other small animals (like his flocks, pigs, goats, dogs, hawks, and the like).

If he were in the 8th (because the 7th does not fall under this topic, except like the 1st) he will put him in prison and he will make him die in it, or in some other way will kill him.

And if he were in the 9th, he will send him on a long journey, and will make him suffer punishments there.

And if he were in the 10th, he will give him over into the hands of the authorities or another great man in order to hurt him; or perhaps he will incarcerate him in some castle or in some tower or other elevated place.

And if he were in the 11th, he will hand him over to some soldier or ally of the king or an authority, or to another magnate, in order to extort something from him, or he hands him over to one of his friends for the same reason, or in order guard him.

And if he were in the 12th, he will hold him and detain him in a remote prison, and by saying nice words to him, he will treat him as badly as he can in the detention,[267] and will hold him for a long time, indeed so that he despairs, nor believes he can ever escape, or so that he takes horses, cows, camels, and the other large animals away from him.

And note that the 4th signifies the prison [itself]. The 7th signifies incarceration or incarcerating. The 8th signifies the act of incarcerating. The 10th signifies him who is already incarcerated.[268]

Then, look at the Lord of the 7th (who signifies him who is incarcerated):[269] if he were retrograde, it signifies that he will flee from the prison. Look then to whom he himself is first joined in his retrogradation: because if he is joined to a benefic, it signifies good for him in his flight. Then look to see if you do not see that they will make peace or will be pacified. And see if the Lord of the 1st were separated from the Lord of the 7th, or *vice versa*: it signifies that the battle or litigation or contention or discord will be of long duration, nor does it seem that it will be completed in a short time. And if the Lord of the 1st were joined to the three superior planets, and were in the 1st or in the 10th or were at least received in the 4th (unless he who were to receive is the Lord of the 7th or the 8th)–nevertheless the 4th is below the 10th, and below the 1st [270]–it signifies that he who asks will conquer and win over the enemy, unless he is combust or has entered then into combustion. If indeed the Lord of the 7th were [itself] one of the three superior planets, and were in the 7th or the 4th, or were received in the 10th (but the 10th is below the 4th)–unless he who receives him is the Lord of the 1st or 2nd–it signifies that the enemy will conquer and win over the querent, unless he is combust, or entered then into combustion: because then he is debilitated, and no strength resides in him.

Consider even this already, concerning the significators (namely the Lord of the 1st and the Lord of the 7th): because even though the cadence of the Lord of the Ascendant from the Ascendant[271] is a great weakness, still, if he himself

---

267 *Dicendo sibi bona verba, faciet ei quam peius facere poterit ex districtione.*
268 This statement contradicts parts of Bonatti's earlier statement that the 4th signifies the act of capturing, the 8th the act of incarcerating, and the 12th the place of the prison and the prisoner himself.
269 Presuming that the enemy is the one incarcerated.
270 "Below" (*infra*) refers to power with respect to the house in question. The 4th is below the 10th in power with respect to the querent (1st house); but the 10th is below the 4th from the perspective of the adversary, since the 4th is the 10th from the 7th.
271 *Casus*, i.e., cadent from the Ascendant (in the 12th, 2nd, 8th, 6th).

were of the superior planets, it will be a strength for him against his enemies on account of his superiority; and for the adversary it will be a weakness on account of his inferiority, because the Lord of the 7th will be of the inferiors,[272] which are not strong in matters of war like the superiors are. Whence, therefore, you ought not to say to the querent that he will succumb, unless you have seen first to whom the Lord of the 7th is joined: because even if the Lord of the 1st (who is of the superiors) is cadent from an angle, and the Lord of the 7th (who is of the inferiors) is in an angle, still the Lord of the 1st is not less strong in this than the Lord of the 7th, unless the Lord of the 7th is joined to some planet who strengthens him. For if the Lord of the 7th is joined with some planet who is in a strong place (namely in an angle), and [the other planet] received [the Lord of the 7th], then the Lord of the 7th is strengthened, and you can say to the querent that he will succumb and will be conquered by his adversary or enemy. For if the Lord of the 7th were joined to a planet who did not receive him, he therefore will not be strengthened to the extent that the querent will succumb for this reason.

And *vice versa*, say of the Lord of the 7th (if he were of the superiors) what I said about the Lord of the 1st. Because if the Lord of the 7th (when he is of the superiors) were cadent from his angle (namely from the 7th), you will not judge victory for the querent over the adversary, even if the Lord of the 1st (who is of the inferiors) is in an angle, unless he himself were joined to another planet who is in an angle, [and] who receives him. For if he were so received, he will thence be strengthened to the extent that you could judge victory for him over his enemy, if the Lord of the 7th were cadent from an angle, even if he himself were a superior.[273]

If for example you were to find the Lord of the 1st strong in an angle, even if he were joined to some planet cadent from an angle which signified his impediment, nevertheless however he will be strong, because the strength which he has from the angle, is stronger than is the weakness which the planet cadent from an angle, brings to him. And this will endure for him as long as he is in his place and degree which was the angle, or until he is elongated from it by 15°, unless first a conjunction[274] were completed between him and the planet cadent

---

[272] I.e., because most of the signs ruled by a superior (Aries, Scorpio, Sagittarius, Capricorn, Pisces) are opposite signs ruled by inferiors (Libra, Taurus, Gemini, Cancer, Virgo). Aquarius and Leo are excepted since the Sun is not an inferior, though it would probably be better to have Saturn as the significator (via Aquarius) than the Sun (via Leo), in terms of superiority.
[273] I have made this one sentence instead of two as in the original.
[274] Remember that a "conjunction" generally speaking, includes aspects.

from the angle who impedes him. But whenever a conjunction is completed between him and the cadent planet, degree by degree, immediately he is weakened, and after that it is feared lest the querent succumb, even if from the beginning it were to go well for him; and the enemy will be strengthened, even if it were to go badly for him from the beginning.

You will judge the same way about the Lord of the 7th which you judged about the Lord of the 1st: namely if you were to find the Lord of the 7th strong in an angle, even if he were joined to a planet cadent from an angle (which signifies his impediment), nevertheless however he will be strong then, because the strength which he has from his appearing in an angle is greater than would be the weakness which he would have from the conjunction of a planet cadent from an angle (who impedes him), until he himself were in that place and that degree which was then the angle, or up until he were elongated from it by 15°– unless a conjunction between him and the cadent planet (who impedes him) were first completed degree by degree. But whenever the conjunction were completed, he is immediately weakened, and it appears that the enemy will have to succumb, even if from the beginning it had seemed to go well for him; and the querent will be strengthened, even if it seems from the beginning that it would go inauspiciously for him.

And [Sahl] said the same: say about the Lord of the 1st and the Lord of the 7th, if he entered into combustion, as you said when the conjunction of one of them with a malefic planet cadent from the angle and impeding him, is perfected.[275] If however the Lord of the 1st or the 7th were not joined with some planet in the sign in which he were, see with whom he will first be joined when he enters the next sign, after his exit from the sign in which he is: because if he is joined to one of the superior planets by a trine or sextile aspect with reception, and with him being in a strong place (namely in an angle or one succeeding an angle), or were joined to benefics from a trine or sextile aspect (and without reception), or from a square aspect or the opposition with reception, it signifies that he whose significator he is, will conquer and win everything, just as he wanted: and all things will go favorably for him (whether he were the Lord of the 1st or the Lord of the 7th). If indeed the conjunction were from a square aspect or the opposition with reception, and the receiver were in a strong place

---

[275] Bonatti seems to be elaborating from the following passage: "And if he were changed from that same place, he is weakened and will not cease to be weak until he (that is, the Lord of the 7th) is impeded by the malefics, or he is combust–and then the enemy will die" (*On Quest.*, 7th House, "On a duke advancing on to war; or when another concerned person asks for him").

(as I said); or from a trine or sextile aspect without reception, things will go as though semi-favorably, but not perfectly. If however the conjunction were from a square or opposition without reception, and the malefic were cadent or combust, or entered into combustion, it signifies that all things will go adversely for him in the end of the matter, however the beginning might have been.

And Sahl said[276] that when you change the significator into the following sign, that you should not judge by the strength of the inferior planets, unless by the goodness of their place from the Ascendant, and by their freedom from impeding planets, and by the help of other planets toward them.[277] Moreover, you ought to know that the significators (namely the Lord of the 1st and the Lord of the 7th) can have strengths and weaknesses relative to their position in a place. And they are these: because if the Lord of the 7th were in the 1st, it is the greatest weakness, and for the Lord of the 1st it is the greatest strength, because it signifies that the querent conquers the enemy, nor will he have a defense against the querent. It seems the same can be said in elections, just as happened to us when we rode against Valbona[278]: for the Ascendant [of the electional figure] was Taurus, and Mars was in the Ascendant: for we conquered all those wishing to stand against us.[279]

If however the Lord of the 1st were in the 7th, which is the greatest weakness to him and the greatest strength for the enemy, it signifies that the enemy will conquer the querent. And Sahl said:[280] and those things which I told you will come to be more strongly if one of the significators were to aspect the one who was in his own house; that is, if the Lord of the 1st were to aspect the Lord of the 7th [when the Lord of the 7th is] in the 1st, the querent will overtake the

---

[276] *Ibid.*

[277] In this passage, Sahl first implicitly brings up the doctrine that the superior planets will tend to win over inferior planets. He points out that if the Lord of the 1st is a cadent superior and the Lord of the 7th an angular inferior, one should not assume that the angularity of the inferior will make him win; rather, one should see if another angular planet receives the inferior (in which case he *will* beat the angular superior). Only after speaking of changing a planet from one sign to another does he say, "And you would not judge by the strengths of the inferior planets except through the goodness of its place from the Ascendant, and through its liberation from the impeding planets; and through the aid of the higher planets with respect to it." But he does not say that essential dignities count for nothing (as Bonatti's statement above might imply).

[278] Valbona castle is a 13th Century castle in the Veneto province of northeastern Italy, near Padua. It still stands today and is a popular tourist destination. Bonatti must be referring to defeating either those at the castle itself, or else people fighting on behalf of its owner. See Bonatti's biography in the Introduction for the likely time this battle took place.

[279] Mars would have been the Lord of the 7th, and signified the enemy.

[280] *Ibid.*

enemy, and conquer him. And if the Lord of the 7th aspected the Lord of the 1st [when the Lord of the 1st is] in the 7th, the enemy will overtake the querent, and conquer him.[281]

Likewise look to see lest the Lord of the 1st falls in the 8th: because if it were thus, or if the Lord of the 1st were conjoined to the Lord of the 8th, it will cause fear in the querent—or the Lord of the 8th were joined to the Lord of the 1st, it signifies then the death of the querent. And if the Lord of the 7th were in the 2nd from the 1st, or were joined to its Lord, or [the Lord of the 2nd] to him, it will cause fear in the enemy, and signifies his death, and especially if the Lord of the 2nd were impeded by one of the aforesaid impediments by which a planet is impeded; because the 2nd from the 1st is the 8th from the 7th, just as the 2nd from the 7th is the 8th from the 1st. And you may say the same about the Lord of the 8th if he were impeded, because then it signifies death, indeed so that he will hardly or never escape it, unless he who were the lighter of the two were received by the heavier, and the lighter one himself did not receive the heavier, or *vice versa*: because if each receives and is received, it signifies death. If indeed one received and the other did not receive, it does not impose the necessity of dying, even if however it threatens death.

Then consider if the Lord of the 1st is joined to the Lord of the 10th, or it to him, and in addition to this the Lord of the 1st were in the 10th: it signifies that if the battle or combat were in the district or kingdom of him who asks, that he himself will be strong, or rather stronger, than all who come against him; and that he himself will conquer them all (unless perhaps there is an innumerable multitude), and he will capture the adversary or enemy who contends with him; and better and more strongly than that, if he who were heavier (namely the Lord of the 1st or the Lord of the 10th) were in the angle (namely in the 1st or 10th), or in one succeedent to that angle (namely in the 2nd or 11th): because it signifies then that he will not be able to be conquered, nor will there be someone strong [enough] to be able to have men against him in his district or kingdom.

If however it were in the district of another, he will conquer the enemy by the aforesaid conditions; but, however, he will not be so strong, because he could lose his possessions, and even men; however, the common belief and rumor will be that he will have won; but he will not be able to [win] against such a multitude as he could in his own district; but he could conquer against an equal [number] or against one stronger than him by one-fourth or one-third.

---

[281] In this case, the aspect shows the Lord has *control* over the affairs of his own house and his enemies' being lodged there.

If however the Lord of the 7th were in the 4th (which is its 10th), or were joined to the Lord of the 4th, or the Lord of the 4th were joined to him, and the heavier of them were in the angle (namely in the 7th or the 4th), or in those succeedent to the angles (namely in the 5th or the 8th), it signifies that the enemy will not be conquered, and nothing can be done against him if the combat were in the district of the enemy. If however the combat were in the district of the querent, it may be feared lest the querent lose his district or kingdom.

And Sahl said[282] if one of the significators were joined to some planet in an angle or to the Lord of an angle, and better yet if [the significator] himself were in an angle, because it signifies the strength of that significator. And he said, if one of the significators were in an angle, free from the malefics, and were in a movable sign, it signifies death for him, soon after the attainment [of his goal]. Likewise, look to see if you see the Lord of the 7th in the 1st and the Lord of the 1st did not aspect him, or [the Lord of the 7th] were in the 12th,[283] it signifies the flight of the enemy.[284] If indeed the Lord of the 1st were to aspect him, [the Lord of the 1st] will conquer [the Lord of the 7th]. And if for example [the Lord of the 7th] were retrograde, it signifies his flight and the conquering and breaking apart of his side. If indeed the Lord of the 1st were in the 7th and the Lord of the 7th did not aspect him, or [the Lord of the 1st] were in the 6th, it signifies the flight of the querent. If however [the Lord of the 1st] were retrograde, it signifies his flight and the breaking apart and the conquering of his side.

Then look to see if you see the Lord of the 10th in the 1st: it appears that the king is going to help the querent. If indeed the Lord of the 10th were in the 7th, it seems he will help the enemy. You may say the same if the Sun or Moon (or one of them) were joined to one of the significators (namely to the Lord of the 1st or the Lord of the 7th): because to whichever one is joined one of the luminaries, that one will be helped by the king.

Moreover, look at the significatrix (which is the Moon), [to see] if she were separated from one of the significators, and joined to the other: because it signifies the strength of him to whom she is joined, and the weakness [of him] from whom she separates; because if she is separating from the Lord of the 7th, and is joined to the Lord of the 1st, it signifies victory on the part of the querent against his enemy. And if she were separated from the Lord of the 1st, and were

---

[282] *Ibid.*

[283] I believe the two conditions are: (a) he is in the others' house but unaspected, or (b) he is in the adversary's 12th (his own 6th).

[284] Note that before, when the Lord of the 7th *was* aspected by the Lord of the 1st, the enemy was *conquered*. See next sentence.

joined to the Lord of the 7th, it signifies victory on the part of the enemy against the querent.

Then look at the place of Saturn in matters of war. Because his presence in the angles is malefic in the case of battles, since he signifies the strength and savageness of the war. Whence, if you were to see him in some angle at the hour of a question or the inception[285] of a battle, declare the strength and cruelty and great length of the war. And if he were retrograde, he will impede more and will act worse, whether he has dignity or power in the angle or not. If he were in the 1st, the war will be great and strong on the part of the querent. If he were in the 4th, it will be less than that on each side.[286] If he were in the 7th, it will be great and lasting, and especially on the part of the enemy. If however he were in the 10th, the war will be great, strong, cruel, and famous.

You may say the same if Mars were in Capricorn or Aries at the hour of the question or the hour of the inception of the combat, but the combat will not be wholly terrible. Besides, see if Mars were the significator of either side: because if he were the significator of the querent, or of the inceptor,[287] or of their helpers, and he were direct, it signifies that they will be good fighters on behalf of the querent, and in their hearts they will not imagine fleeing. And if Mars were then stationary in his second station, they will rather let themselves be killed than to flee or fall back. If however Mars were then retrograde, the fighters will be unstable, and will not persevere well in the war, unless as those who are rebelling against the other in the style of thieves and the cutters of roads. And *vice versa* if [Mars] were the significator of the enemy or his helpers: it signifies the same thing for the enemy which was said for the querent. If indeed he were not the significator of either of them, he signifies the strength or weakness of both of them according to his condition, and in his station he signifies ultimate strength in the war.

And the retrogradation of Saturn signifies the prolongation of the war, and its repetition. Indeed the retrogradation of Mars does not prolong the war like the retrogradation of Saturn. And if Mars were then in the 10th (namely at the hour of the question or the inception of the war), it will be a famous and lasting war—so long, that it will be made known in many diverse and faraway regions.

---

285 Bonatti could simply mean the time when the battle happens to start; but he probably favors the time of a battle as *elected* by an astrologer. Bonatti almost always uses the *incip-* root in the context of elections.

286 *Erit infra hoc hinc inde.* Or perhaps simply, "on that account."

287 *Incipientis,* literally, "the one beginning." I will refer to the person seeking an election as the inceptor, just as the person asking a horary question is the querent.

And if he were [located] from the 10th house up to the western angle [the 7th], the war will be lasting and will grow and be multiplied, but one of the captains of the army (or the commanders) will strive to deceive the other, and each will do whatever he does with ingenuity and cleverness.

Even consider whether Mars were in an angle (either himself or a planet who aspects him): because it signifies the strength of the war, even without the interjection of Saturn into the war, but not ultimate [strength]. If however he were in one succeeding an angle, and the one who aspected him were in an angle (or *vice versa*), it signifies the strength of the war to be greater than if both[288] of them were in an angle. And if both were succeedent to an angle, it signifies again the greater strength of the war than if they were as was said [above]. And if one were in an angle or succeedent to an angle, and the other were cadent, it signifies again the greater strength of the war. If for example both were cadent from an angle, it signifies that the war is strong, terrible, and has many conflicts, except for in the 10th:[289] because then Mars weakens the war. And if one of the malefics were in the 4th in aspect to the other, and one of these were with the Tail, it signifies the strength of the war. And Mars, if he were in Aries, or Virgo, or Scorpio, and the war were diurnal, or the question were diurnal (or if it were nocturnal, and he were in Cancer or Pisces), it signifies the middling [strength] of the war. And if he were in Taurus or Libra (and the battle or question were diurnal or nocturnal), the battle will be light [or easy], in comparison with other wars, and will not last a long time, but it will break apart in a short time.

Besides this you ought to look at the Moon, and see if she herself were joined corporally anywhere with Mars, and especially in the 8th: because then it signifies the killing of the querent, or of the inceptor of the battle, unless a benefic aspects her then. For if a benefic were to aspect her then, however much horrible dangers may oppress the querent, still it will liberate him from death, even if barely. Likewise, see if the Moon were in the 1st, and Mars were in the 7th (or *vice versa*): counsel him who wishes to go or begin the war that he should not go, nor should he begin the battle, because it signifies his being killed. And if she were in the 4th, or 6th, or 10th, he will be captured and wounded by frightful wounds, unless perhaps (as was said) she is then aspected

---

[288] *Uterque.* This word means "one of two," but Bonatti seems to be using it to mean "both" here. Robert Zoller (verbal communication) suggests that perhaps an angular Mars would make the battle end more quickly, while a succeedent or cadent Mars will make it drawn out and messy. See below.

[289] But the 10th is an angular house.

by a benefic. For if the benefics were to aspect, they will mitigate Mars's malice; and perhaps he will not be killed; still, it will always bring fear to him. If however the Moon were then separated from Mars by body, and were joined to Saturn either corporally (or by opposition without perfect reception), and the more so if it[290] were in the 2nd, it signifies the killing of the enemy, unless the benefics then aspect her (namely when she is joined to Saturn) just as was said, when she herself is joined to Mars, and this will happen more strongly if Mars or Saturn were then with the Head or Tail of the Dragon; and this will happen much more strongly, if it were in the hour of the inception of combat.

Then look at the Sun, whom likewise if you were to find him with the Head or Tail of the Dragon at the hour of the question (but more strongly in the hour of the inception of combat), it signifies the greatest killing on both sides. But it will be greater on the part of those who have their back to the south, or to the west, nor however will they be pacified on account of their conflict. Which if the Lord of the 1st were then in that conjunction (namely if the Sun were with the Head or Tail of the Dragon), it signifies that the killing will be strong and terrible and great indeed, as though all sides are killed, indeed so that it will be as though there is no one left in comparison with the amount of those who are killed. (However, it will be worse with the Tail than with the Head, and their heads will be lost.)

And you ought to know that just as Mars (and the planet to which he himself is joined, or who is joined to him) signifies the strength or weakness of the war, so the Moon signifies its greatness or smallness. Because if she were in an angle, it signifies the smallness of the war, and especially if the Lord of the house in which she is, were to aspect her, and he were likewise in an angle. If however she were succeedent, it signifies the middling size of the war, and especially if the Lord of the house in which she was, were to aspect her or were in an angle or succeedent to an angle, or were in Taurus or Cancer. If however she were cadent from an angle and were joined to the Lord of the house in which she was, and he were cadent, it signifies the great size of the combats and the battle. You could say the same if she were in Scorpio or Capricorn or in the last half of Libra.[291]

---

[290] The Latin is unclear as to who has to be in the 2nd, but clearly if it must be a conjunction or opposition, one of them must be, therefore I have translated the sentence using "it." I do not find this sentence in Sahl.

[291] I.e., the location of the fixed stars in the claws of the constellation Scorpio, and which roughly coincides with the so-called "via combusta." Perhaps it would be wise to take these fixed stars into account, instead of the location of tropical Libra?

And it always ought to be your concern lest at any time you might give an impeded Lord of the 1st, or Moon, or an impeded Mars, to him who wished to start a war, or the planet from which the Moon is separated. Which if you cannot wholly avoid it, avoid what you can: you will at least avoid the impediment of the Lord of the 1st, lest the inceptor succumb. And beware in the inception of a war or in a journey to war, lest the Lord of the 1st be joined or going to the conjunction of the Lord of the 7th: and by however much more he were willing to go off to fight, by so much more will there be worry, and it will be worse for him if the Lord of the 7th were to receive the Lord of the 1st.

Chapter 22: Which side has more allies

If indeed you wished to know who among the significators has more people or is supported by more allies, see which of them (namely the Lord of the 1st or the Lord of the 7th) is greater in its own dignity, and who aspects his own house [domicile?] better, and who is aspected by more planets, and who has more planets on his own side (namely on the side of the Ascendant or on the side of the 7th): because he who were so situated, will have more soldiers or more allies. And just as the 1st signifies the querent or inceptor, so the 2nd signifies his soldiers or allies. And just as the 7th signifies the enemy, so the 8th signifies his allies. And just as the 10th signifies the king, so the 11th signifies his soldiers or allies or ministers.

And Sahl said[292] that if benefics were in the 2nd, or were to aspect it, and the Lord of the 2nd were in a good place, it signifies the strength of the querent's helpers, and their loyalty and aid. And judge concerning the allies of the enemy through the 8th and its Lord, just as you judged by the 2nd and its Lord about the allies of the querent. And if the benefics which were in the 2nd were in a common sign, or were in Cancer or Scorpio or Pisces or Aries or Libra or Capricorn, announce that there is a multitude of soldiers or allies for the querent. And you may say the same about the enemy, for benefics that are in the 8th; and about those which were in the 11th for the king and his deputy.[293]

And Sahl said[294] that the 5th signifies the city and all who live in it.

---

[292] *Ibid.*
[293] *Vicarius.* Perhaps this could be translated (here and below) as "proxy."
[294] *Ibid.*

And he said that if an oriental planet were in its own house [domicile?], or the Lord of the 2nd were direct and oriental, the soldiers or allies of the querent pursue the truth. If indeed it were retrograde, they do not obey him.

For the king's soldiers or allies or deputies, look at the 11th, and see if some malefic planet were in it: they will not be well-behaved [or obey well]. If for example the malefic were retrograde, not only will the soldiers of the king be disobedient, indeed they will even be traitors. And this will be more strongly so if Mercury and the Tail of the Dragon were near to the Sun by 13° or less; or if one of the malefics were in the 8th house [domicile?] from the sign in which the Sun then were. If indeed the malefic were retrograde, not only will the allies of the king be malefactors or traitors, but even the king himself or his deputy will be bad and unjust. Thus you will understand if the armies will not be pacified.

If indeed you were to find that they ought to be pacified, see then the planet to whom the commanders or producers[295] of the war committed their disposition: and who has the significator who interjects himself to bring them together or bring peace between them. If you want to know what kind of person he is, see if he is in any of his own dignities. For if he were the receiver of the disposition, and the one who interjected himself to bring them together were in his own domicile, he will be of those who are in one of the armies. And if he were in his own exaltation, he will be someone powerful, who is with the whole of the land which he has to rule in that army.[296] If indeed he were in his own bound, he will be of those who have blood relatives in the army or in one of those armies who does not want anything bad to happen to them. And if he were in his own triplicity, he will be of those who have their friends or allies, who came to the army at his request. And if he were in its own face, it will be a man who must do something in the army because of his profession. And if he were not in any of his own dignities, he will be a person who comes from somewhere, for example a member of the public or a traveler. And more attentively you could know by his significator, and perhaps you can know his likeness through the same planet.

For if it were Saturn, it seems that he is an ignoble old man, and especially of he were occidental; if he were oriental, he will be less old.

---

[295] *Productores*. This should be understood in the sense of "bringing forth" or "bringing about." Bonatti may even mean those who fund the war.

[296] *Erit qui est cum communi terrae quam habet ad regendum in exercitu illo.* Zoller (*Bonatti on War*) translates this as: "who is with [these] in that army with all of the land which he rules."

And if it were Jupiter, it seems that he is of mature age, and is noble, and he could perhaps be a bishop or judge or someone similar to this.

If however it were Mars, he will be a man who tends to, or who has produced, armies; and perhaps he will be from among the leaders of the same army, and will be a lying man, and who at some time was a cutter of roads or other evildoer.

And if it were the Sun, he will be more a noble man from those who are fit for a kingdom; or perhaps it will be the king or one set over many peoples.

And if it were Venus, he will be a certain man of young age or not particularly wise or learned; but whatever he were to do, it will be done in good faith, not under any kind of *scaltimentri.*[297]

And if it were Mercury, he will be a wise and educated man, as much of natural sense as learned; or literate.

And if it were the Moon, he will be a man who interjects himself into these matters by a just motive and good will.

And if you were to see Mercury under the rays of the Sun, and the Lord of the 1st along with the Lord of the 7th were to impede him, it signifies that one side is trying to deceive and destroy the other. And then if you were to find Mars with Mercury, the treachery will be made manifest, indeed so that it will be known openly by all. And if both of the outermost planets (namely Saturn and the Moon), were to aspect the Ascendant or were in the Ascendant, or with the Lord of the Ascendant, it signifies that treachery is carried out by one side against the other. And if Mercury were not in the Ascendant, nor the Moon, but they were to aspect one another by a square aspect or the opposition, it signifies that he who interjected himself between them by means of pacifying, is neither faithful nor lawful. And if his significator were then under the rays of the Sun, it signifies that he will be discovered by those of the army against him.[298] And if the Moon were then corporally joined to Mars, or to a planet from which Mars

---

[297] Zoller (*Bonatti on War*) translates this as "treachery."
[298] Reading *invenietur* for *invenientur.*

is being separated, or who is being separated from him, he will be captured. And if in addition Mercury were oriental, he will be put into prison, but will ultimately escape. And if Mercury were then joined corporally to one of the malefics, and the malefic were northern [in latitude], he will be afflicted by him in prison, and will suffer detriment in it. And were he joined to a benefic, and the benefic were south of him, he will escape from the detriment. And if Mars were the significator of him who impedes the significator of the pacifier, he who afflicts him will be some bellicose soldier. And if it were the Sun, he will be from among the producers of the army, and specifically one greater and more excellent than he. And if Mercury were then in Gemini or Virgo or Sagittarius or Pisces, those who interject themselves to pacify things between the armies will be many. If however Jupiter were then aspecting the Ascendant or the Moon, all will come to pass with lawfulness and goodness, and no deception or treachery will then fall in that body.[299]

Chapter 23: On the knowledge of the war's victory–who will win

Look[300] even in the knowledge of the war's victory to see which of the combatants ought to be the victor. And you will see if the Sun and the Moon were located from the line[301] of the 10th house up to the line of the 4th house, on the side of the Ascendant; or from the line of the 4th house up to the line of the MC on the setting side, and they were free and clean[302] (namely fortunate and strong): because they will signify the war's victory on the side in which they are. Like if they are on the side of the Ascendant, they will signify it for the querent or inceptor. If however they are on the setting side, they will signify it for the adversary. If perchance they were unfortunate or weak, they will signify the contrary: because he on whose side they are, will succumb.

---

[299] *In corpore illo.* Perhaps by "body" he means, "the body of the army"?
[300] Reading *aspice* for *aspiciens.*
[301] I.e., the cusp.
[302] *Mundi.* Bonatti (following Sahl) makes much use of this term in Tr. 7, speaking of planets being "clean" or "cleansed" of the malefics.

Chapter 24: What was the reason why the war arose, and whether it is just or unjust

If someone at sometime were to ask (as frequently tends to happen) what was the reason the war arose, or should you otherwise wish to tell someone else, Sahl said[303] that you ought to look at Mars. Because he is naturally the significator of wars, and all wars are attributed to him (as is said elsewhere). And see from what planet he himself is being separated, or who is being separated from him, because from that one you will see him who starts the war; and from the one to whom he is joined (or who is joined to him) you will see the enemy or the adversary. If he is being separated from benefics, or benefics are being separated from him, and he is being joined to a malefic or a malefic is being joined to him, it signifies that the querent or inceptor was moved by a just cause to start the war, and that he himself uses justice and truth (and the adversary, the contrary of these). If indeed he were separated from malefics or they from him, and he were joined with benefics, it signifies that he [the querent] was moved contrary to justice, and does not use truth, and the adversary defends justice and truth. And if Mars were separated from the benefics and were joined to the benefics, it signifies that each side cherishes the just cause—which rarely happens. If perchance he were separated from the malefics and were joined to malefics, it signifies that each strives contrary to justice and contrary to truth.[304]

Then look to see if one of the malefics were in the 1st, and specifically if it were Mars,[305] because it signifies that the war arose by reason of the envy which one had against the other; or perhaps that one wanted to take some of the other's provisions away from him.

And if Mars were in the 2nd, the war arose for this reason, namely because one wanted to take away the other's goods and his substance.

And if he were in the 3rd, it seems that one injured the brother of the other, and war arose for that reason; or perhaps that he said he was not a Catholic.

---

[303] *Ibid.*

[304] The delineation assumes that the querent is the one who wants to start the war; hence the planet most recently joined to Mars will signify the querent's motives, and the one to which Mars is now (or is about to be) joined, shows the adversary's motives.

[305] Note that while the rest of the instructions assume Mars, Bonatti does suggest that we could also look for Saturn (and perhaps the Tail of the Dragon).

And if he were in the 4th, it seems that it was by reason of a city or castle that one took away from the other or wanted to take away from the other; or perhaps he wanted to take away his house or land or field or inheritance or vineyard, or he injured his father.

And if he were in the 5th, it signifies that it was by reason of the child of one, who was injured by the other; or it was because of a woman or some luxurious matter; or by reason of his paternal goods (and especially immovable ones). And if then you were to see the Moon joined to Mercury by a trine or sextile aspect, it seems that the war was because of a certain city or castle which one of them wanted to occupy for himself.

And if he were in the 6th, it was because of a male slave or female slave, or because of small animals taken away from one to the other; or it will be as if for nothing, or for a thing on account of which there should not be a battle.

And if he were in the 7th, it will be because of a kidnapped or offended or injured woman, and especially a wife or lover; or it will be because of revenge for some evildoing.

And if he were in the 8th, it will be because of some old thing because of which blood was spilled; or it will be because of the inheritance of some dead person who did not pertain much to one of them.

And if he were in the 9th, it will be by reason of religion or some religious person; or that one wanted to convert the other so that he would follow what he himself followed, and that he would revere what he himself revered.

And if he were in the 10th, it will be because of the king and his honor, and to increase his rulership. And if the Moon were then in the 10th, and were joined corporally to Mars, or were to aspect him by a square aspect or by opposition, the war will be made greater, and there will be great killing on both sides.

And if Mars were in the 11th, it will be because of friends, or it will be to defend the substance of the king or his allies.

And if he were in the 12th it will be by reason of an old enmity, and bad will which exists between the sides, or between the producers of the war. But even if the war was for this reason, still the parties will not enter into combat together in a general battle. And they will be brought together easily if there were some people who wanted to interject themselves between them in order to bring them together.

Chapter 25: On the greatness or smallness of the armies

If perhaps at some time one of the producers of one of the armies were in doubt about the army of his adversary, and wanted to know from you whether it was large or small, and you wished to look for him, in this situation look to the place of the Moon by sign and degree, and likewise Mercury, and subtract the place of the Moon from the place of Mercury, and see how many signs remain to you. Which if they were even, it will be a large army; and by how many more signs were remaining after your subtraction, by that much greater will the army be. And if they were odd,[306] it will be a small army; and by how much fewer they were, by that much smaller will the army be. If indeed the place of Mercury were not so much that you could subtract the place of the Moon from it, add twelve signs to it and after that subtract the place of the Moon from it, and do as was said.

And even see if on the setting side (which is from the angle of the earth up to the 10th on the setting side) there were a greater number of planets than the rising side (which is from the angle of the 10th up to the 4th on the rising side): again it signifies the greater number of followers[307] to be on the side of the adversary. If indeed on the rising side there were a greater number of them than on the setting side, it signifies the decreased number of followers on the part of the adversary, even if by the aforesaid reason his army were signified to be large; and *vice versa* on the part of the querent.

---

[306] *Disparia.* Cf. Ch. 15, which likewise measures the signs in between the Moon and Mercury.
[307] *Gentium.* Lit., "clans," but *gens* had also acquired a broader sense of people or followers by the Middle Ages.

Chapter 26: To know all the instruments
and other things which pertain to war

In order to know the general instruments which pertain to war, Sahl said[308] that the Ascendant signifies the one beginning the war and his reasons, and what it is which sparked the war, and whether it began with truth or lies.

The 1st signifies the one beginning the war because the first thing which comes in war is the one beginning it.

Indeed the 2nd from the Ascendant signifies whether there will be a war or not, and whether it will be for success or harm [of the one beginning it]; because the second thing which comes in war after those beginning it is the effect of those at war.

And he said that the 3rd from the 1st signifies arms and by what kinds of arms the victory or seizure will happen; and what kinds of arms will not be necessary[309] in the war; because the third thing which comes in war, are arms, because without these one could not carry out a war well.

And [he said] that the 4th from the 1st signifies the place in which the war will be, namely whether it is a level field or mountainous, and whether it is on the seashore or next to a river; and if there are fruit-bearing trees or groves. Because the location is something fit for war such that without it, it could not come to be.

And [he said] that the 5th signifies the uprightness and pace[310] and boldness and laziness of those making war; because uprightness is something without which the combatants cannot wage war well.

And he said that the 6th signifies the animals of the soldiers, which are namely horses or donkeys or mules or camels; because something which is more useful to warring soldiers are horses or other animals which bear them.

---

[308] On Quest., 7th House, "The question whether an army is big or small."
[309] I.e., what kinds will, and will not, be necessary.
[310] Incessum. Or, "attack." Sahl and Bonatti are indicating the way in which the army moves forward in the battle.

And he said that the 7th signifies the instruments with which stones are projected, and whether the war is [undertaken] with cleverness or not; because it is a very useful thing for a war after the other aforementioned instruments or arms.

And he said that the 8th signifies plagues and capture and death, fracturing [of the armies] also and the flight of the conquered: because these are themselves acts of war and into which wars have tended ultimately to devolve.

And he said that the 9th signifies the work of reconnaissance and the knowledge of the enemy's affairs, and his rumors and skillfulness; because these are things which the commander of a war very much ought to attend to, namely so that he knows the actions of the enemy, and the new things[311] which are in his power, and how apprehensive he is about the affairs of the war; and how clever or ingenious he is.

And he said that the 10th signifies the habits or acts of the senior commander and the rest of the leaders who are under his command. Because you or someone else ought to try to see whether the king or commander is troubled, and [whether he] is attending to those things which pertain to war, or not; and whether he is on his guard or shrewd in those things which pertain to it.

And he said that the 11th signifies their array of legions and their organization: in what way they are advancing against the enemy. Because this is something that serves very well so that one may know how to organize his legions and their fighters and to instruct them in how to conduct themselves in the fight. And from this alone many have yet conquered their enemies.

---

[311] *Nova*. This seems to refer to incoming intelligence about the enemy, but it also refers to innovations and developments–so it might signify new tactics that the clever general comes up with (see remainder of paragraph).

And he said that the 12ᵗʰ signifies the city and those who are besieged and assaulted in it,[312] because this is something which a combatant needs to know, and from which one would rely on for what he has to do and how he can be strengthened over his enemy.

Chapter 27: How you ought to look at what is signified by the twelve houses

Even though it was spoken above in that chapter about those things which pertain to the matters of war or contentions, still yet I will tell you certain useful things which it seems to me ought not be omitted. Nor should you believe that I wish to contradict the aforesaid opinions: because if you were to inspect well what was said, and understood it well, you will find nothing contrary to them [here]. Whence if you distinguished the times correctly, the things that ought to be in agreement, will agree.[313]

Therefore when you have inspected all the houses (as was said), and wish to know what is signified by any of them, look at all the houses for the querent or inceptor, in the order written below, starting from the 1ˢᵗ; indeed for the enemy, look from the 7ᵗʰ and make it the 1ˢᵗ of the enemy, and make the 8ᵗʰ his 2ⁿᵈ, and make the 9ᵗʰ his 3ʳᵈ, and make the 10ᵗʰ his 4ᵗʰ, and make the 11ᵗʰ his 5ᵗʰ, make the 12ᵗʰ his 6ᵗʰ, make the 1ˢᵗ his 7ᵗʰ, make the 2ⁿᵈ his 8ᵗʰ, make the 3ʳᵈ his 9ᵗʰ, make the 4ᵗʰ his 10ᵗʰ, make the 5ᵗʰ his 11ᵗʰ, make the 6ᵗʰ his 12ᵗʰ.

Then look to see if a malefic were in the 1ˢᵗ or aspected it by a square aspect or from the opposition: it signifies that the querent will not carry out well what must be carried out in matters of war, nor will he be concerned about them in the proper way; and this could be the reason why things will not go well for him in the war, unless that malefic were the Lord of the Ascendant or at least of its exaltation. And it even signifies that the querent or the one starting the war does not have justice, but more the contrary. If however a benefic were there or were to aspect by a trine aspect (instead of the aforesaid malefic), it signifies good; a malefic signifies the contrary.

---

[312] In Ch. 22, Sahl was correctly quoted as attributing the 5ᵗʰ to a city's inhabitants. The difference here is that the inhabitants' own city has become a prison.
[313] This also is repeated in Tr. 8, Part 1, Preface. The point is that apparently contradictory statements by astrological authorities are not really in conflict; rather, they apply at different times and to different situations.

If there were a malefic in the 2nd who was not the Lord of the 2nd or of its exaltation, or were to aspect it by a square or from the opposition, it signifies that there will not be a war; and if there were, it will be to the harm of the querent, and not useful to him. If however there were a benefic there, or its aspect, as was said in the [case of the] 1st, it signifies there will be a war; and if it does, it will be useful to the querent.

If indeed there were a malefic in the 3rd and it were Mars, and he were of good condition, there will be unavoidable military [clashes of] arms in the war (may you say the same if Jupiter were there); and the querent will have to use them if he wishes to win. And if Mars were of bad condition, it signifies that the use of arms, which will be on [the querent's] own side, will be of warriors, thieves, and cutters of roads, and unreliable men; nor will they be useful to him.

If however there were a malefic in the 4th, or its aforesaid aspects, it signifies that the place of war will be inconvenient and unsuitable for the querent's side if it were an open field; and if it were mountainous, they will be rough and inhabitable, and wooded. If indeed it were near water, it will be boggy and muddy, and poorly adapted to combat.

If however there were a benefic in the 5th, or its aforesaid aspects, or Mars were there and were in a good condition, it signifies that the soldiers and allies of the querent will be honest and brave and will advance easily, and be well fitted to combat. And if a malefic were there, or its aforesaid aspects, or Mars (and he were of bad condition), it signifies that they will be of low quality and sluggish and advance only with difficulty, and late, and poorly fitted to combat.

If a benefic were in the 6th (or its aforesaid aspects), or the Head of the Dragon, the animals which are used for the war will be valuable[314] horses; likewise, if Mars were there and he were of good condition, they will be equally ferocious and firm and impatient. And if there were a malefic there (and specifically Saturn), the horses will be of poor quality, as are

---

[314] Reading *pretiosi* for *preciati*.

farm-horses[315] and other very old horses, and for the most part of little value; and there will be donkeys there, and camels (if it were a region in which there are camels). And if the Tail were there, there will be mules and other animals of low quality for, and not well accustomed to, wars.

If however there were a benefic in the 7th, or its aforesaid aspects, it signifies that the instruments with which stones are thrown will be useful and will do well what they are supposed to, and it even signifies the goodness of the enemy. And if a malefic were there (or its aforesaid aspects), it signifies the usefulness of the aforesaid instruments; and that he will strive to do much combat with cleverness and deception and treachery; and it even signifies the low quality of the enemy.

If perchance a benefic were in the 8th, it signifies that few plagues will follow from the war, and few mortalities; and that the wounds will not be very dangerous, nor will there follow many captures afterwards, nor will there be great vanquishings [of the querent], nor great flights. If however a malefic were there (and especially Saturn, and he retrograde), it signifies many plagues and dangers, and great killing and captures and ruptures.[316]

If however a benefic or its aspect were in the 9th, it signifies that the enemy is well disposed and that he has hope in some rumors which he has [heard], and that these rumors are useful to him; and that he is a clever man, and that he will strive to deceive the querent if he can.

If however a benefic (or its aforesaid aspects) were in the 10th, it signifies that the querent (or he who is the major or captain of his army) is shrewd and learned in such things as pertain to war–and others to whom something of those things which pertain to war has been entrusted. If however a malefic were there, it signifies that the querent or his [military] leader or the major of his army, and the other producers of the army to whom something of the affairs of the army have has been entrusted, are all or for the most part men unfit to exercise such things.

---

[315] *Roncini*, cf. Fr. *Roncin*.

[316] It is unclear whether this means ruptures in the battle lines during combat, or between the querents' allies.

If indeed a benefic were in the 11th, it signifies that the querent or the producers of the army are discerning men, and who knew well how to organize the front points of their armies and to lead them to war; and that they know well how to go against the enemy or adversaries, and how to do all things well which pertain to that. If however a malefic or his aforesaid aspect were there, it signifies that the leader of the army is ignorant and undistinguished, nor does he know how to organize the fronts of armies, nor how to lead them to war, nor how to do those things which pertain to the maintenance of an army; even if he might otherwise be of good will.

If for example a benefic were in the 12th, it signifies that those who are in the city or another land which will be blockaded, are well disposed and fit to defend it and are unanimous, and that they are strengthened, and that they seem to fear nothing. If for example a malefic or its aforesaid aspects were there, it signifies that they are poorly disposed, and that they are not fit to defend it, and that they are not unanimous, and that they are timid people and sorely afraid.

Nor should you forget one thing which I tell you now: because even if I did not find it in the sayings of the philosophers, still I found through the test of experience that always when Mars is in the 12th, one must always fear betrayal, and the same could be said about the Tail. And just as I looked for the side of the querent from all the houses, beginning from the 1st and ending with the 12th, look for the enemy (when judging him) from all the houses, beginning from the 7th and ending with the 6th. Just as you judge for the 1st of the querent or inceptor, so judge for the 7th of the enemy. And just as for the 2nd of the querent, so the 8th of the enemy. And just as for the 3rd of the querent, so the 9th of the enemy. And just as for the 4th of the querent, so the 10th of the enemy. And just as for the 5th house of the querent, so the 11th of the enemy. And just as for the 6th of the querent, so the 12th of the enemy. And just as for the 7th of the querent, so the 1st of the enemy. And just as for the 8th of the querent, so the 2nd of the enemy. And just as for the 9th of the querent, so the 3rd of the enemy. And just as for the 10th of the querent, so the 4th of the enemy. And just as for the 11th of the querent, so the 5th of the enemy. And just as for the 12th of the querent, so the 6th of the enemy.

But you ought to know this, that if you were to find the significators of the armies (namely the Lord of the 1st and the Lord of the 7th) in all things equally strong and well disposed, or equally weak and badly disposed, then it signifies victory on the part of him who began the combat, unless the aforesaid combust hours operate against him.[317] And if one were well disposed and the other poorly, and he whose significator is well disposed was the one who began it, he will win. If however he whose significator is poorly disposed was the one who began it, he will succumb, even if they were otherwise in all things equally strong.

Chapter 28: Whether there would be a battle between armies or not

If someone were to ask you whether there would be a battle between armies or not, look then at the 1st and its Lord, and the Moon, and the 7th and its Lord, and see if they are joined corporally in any of the angles: because that signifies that there will be a battle between them. If however they were not joined corporally, see if they are joined from the opposition or a square aspect, because that signifies likewise a future battle. And if one of these [situations] did not exist, see then if some planet transfers light between them from the opposition or a square aspect: because this signifies a future battle if it were without reception. If however the heavier of them were to receive the one who transfers their light between them, it signifies that there will not be a battle; and if it were to happen, they will be pacified, either in that very engagement or shortly after the engagement. And if it were otherwise, namely that the significators of the armies (namely the Lord of the 1st and the Lord of the 7th) were not joined anywhere, nor did they hinder each other, nor were there one who transferred light between them , as was said, it signifies that there will not be a battle.

---

[317] See Tr. 4, Ch. VII; Tr. 7, 7th House, Ch. IV; Tr. 9, 12th House, Ch. VI.

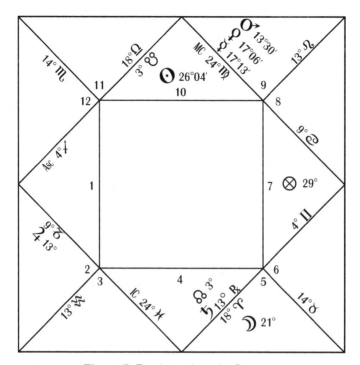

Figure 7: Battle against the Luccans

Of which topic this [figure] was an example. When Count Guido Novello was the administrator of Florence, and we were with the army above the district of the Luccans,[318] and the Luccans were maintained in the heart of their district with their army of near to one thousand men or less, he asked whether there would be a battle between the armies or not.

I looked at this question, whose Ascendant was Sagittarius, 4°; and the Midheaven Virgo 24°; Mars in it, 13° 30'; Venus 17° 6'; Mercury 17° 13', cadent from the angle;[319] and the Sun in the same, 26° 4', in the angle of the 10th house.[320] Libra was the 11th house, 18°, the Tail in it, 3°. Scorpio the 12th house, 14°. Capricorn the 2nd house, 9°; and Jupiter in it, 13°. Aquarius the 3rd house, 13°. Pisces the 4th house, 24°. Aries the 5th house, 18°. The Head in it, 3°. Saturn

---

[318] I.e., in Lucca, Italy, in northern Tuscany. This chart would have been cast at 11:51 AM LAT, on September 12, 1261 JC. I have reproduced Bonatti's own values in the chart above.
[319] Here Mercury is cadent by quadrant houses only.
[320] I note that Bonatti emphasizes the Sun being in the *angle* of the 10th house. If we read the Sun as being in the angle of the 10th *domicile*, then he would seem to be distinguishing between the Midheaven as the tenth sign, and the *angle of* the 10th as the quadrant house upon it.

in it, 13° (retrograde). The Moon in it, 21°. Taurus the 6th house, 14°. Gemini the 7th house, 4°. The Part of Fortune in it, 29°. Cancer the 8th house, 9°. Leo the 9th house, 13°. This was in the era of the Arabs, at 658 years, 9 months, 16 days (approximately). The altitude of the Sun before the meridian was well nigh 48°, the 12th day (Monday) of the month of September.

Therefore I looked at the Ascendant of this question, and its Lord (which was Jupiter), and the 7th and its Lord (which was Mercury), of which [Jupiter] was in the 2nd in Capricorn, namely in his fall–which appears to signify the low quality of the querent's side, indeed so that he would not seek battle; but because he himself was in the 2nd, it signifies some strength for him.

Then I looked at the Moon, which was void in course in Aries, which likewise signified weakness on the part of the querent, and worthlessness.

Then I looked at Mercury (for the adversary), who was in Virgo, combust and cadent from the angle, which, even though he was in his own domicile (as though they were in their own land), signified their weakness, indeed so that they would not seek battle. Whence I judged the question for him and he came back because they did not put themselves at the place of battle; and afterwards both armies parted ways, just as is said in the chapter on the occupied[321] castle below, following this.

Chapter 29: Whether a besieged or blockaded city or castle will be captured or not

The ancient astrologers did not concern themselves much with this, about which I am amazed since [such] a matter so often comes through one's hands; but it could be possibly that they did it because they considered it an easy thing, and they considered that anyone could know it; and therefore they were not concerned to speak about it. I however will append something here for you. However, Zodial[322] said something about this, whose intention I did not well understand.

Whence if a question was made to you about some besieged city or castle, or one that is blockaded,[323] [as to] whether it will be captured after the blockade or not, look at the 1st (which is the querent's), and the 4th (which signifies the besieged city or castle), even if perhaps certain moderns said that the 10th

---

[321] Reading *occupato* (with text below) for *absconso* ("hidden").
[322] Reading *Zodial* for *Zodyal*, as below. Unknown astrologer.
[323] Bonatti may be referring to cities in the Levant being blockaded during the Crusades.

signifies a city–and they were moved by this reason: that the 4th signifies the land of the querent, [and] by the same reason, the 10th signifies the land of the enemy, not making a distinction between the land or inheritance of a farm, and that of a city or castle. But to me it seems that we ought not to give the 4th to a city or castle, because the 4th signifies the inheritance of the querent, and his lands, and homes, and the 10th signifies his honors: and no honor is greater than that of conquering, and no greater disgrace than to be deposed from one's rulership. Whence if the 10th signifies the honor of the querent, which is signified more by a city or castle than through other forms of wealth, it is necessary that the 4th signify the honor of the adversary, which is opposite the honor of the querent; and so it appears that the 4th signifies the city or castle of the enemy.

Nor however should you believe this to be the contrary of what Sahl says: for he himself seems to want to say that the 12th signifies a city or besieged castle, but his intention was concerning a city against which there would be an army without a pitched-camp siege around it, but it is entered violently by enemies into its jurisdiction, and [he spoke] concerning the defenders of that city or castle.

Whence if you were to find the Lord of the 1st strong and fortunate, or you were to find him joined to the Lord of the 4th (or with the Moon) in the 1st, or in the 10th or even in the 11th, or in another place which is not unfortunate (as the 12th or 8th or 6th are), indeed so that the Lord of the 1st receives the Lord of the 4th, or even if the Moon receives him (even if she is not received by him), it signifies the taking of the city, and its capture. Likewise if the Lord of the 4th were in malignant places, not aspecting its own domicile (except if the Lord of the 7th were in the 4th, because then it signifies its protection). Likewise if the Lord of the 4th were with the malefics, impeded, it signifies its capture; or if there were malefics in the 4th without one of the benefics or its praiseworthy aspect, it signifies its capture. May you say the same if the Tail of the Dragon were there, because it signifies loss and evacuation.

If however one of these [situations] I told you about did not exist, see if the Lord of the 4th were in the 4th, strong or fortunate (indeed so that it were not retrograde, nor combust, nor besieged by the malefics), or the Lord of the 7th were there, free from the malefics and from all other impediments, or if Jupiter or Venus or the Sun or the Head of the Dragon were there, nor does the Lord of the 1st receive the Lord of the 4th, nor impedes him: it signifies that the castle or city will not be captured by that army, especially if the Lord of the 1st were impeded, not having dignity there, even if it were by one of the malefics in the 4th, so long as a benefic is there who goes first to the line of the angle of the 4th,[324] [rather] than a malefic, especially if the Lord of the 1st were weak, as I said. If indeed some benefic were there, and the Lord of the 1st were strong and fortunate, and aspected the 4th (or the Moon), it signifies capture. If perchance he did not aspect [the 4th or the Moon], or were impeded, it signifies that the side of the querent, because of its low quality and sluggishness, will desist from the activities by which besieged castles are captured. And indeed from the negligence and low quality of the assailants, the besieged castle will remain, when it could be taken.

Now, Zodial said that the Ascendant (and its Lord) is to be examined for the querent, the 7th and its Lord for the city or castle. And he said that whichever one of them were poorly disposed or retrograde, or were in its detriment–his significator will be overcome. And if the Lord of the Ascendant enters the 7th house, and the Lord of the 7th gives him virtue,[325] the city or castle will be captured. If the angles are joined to benefic and malefic planets, support will come to both (namely to the city *and* the assailants). And the Moon is always to be considered, whether she is made fortunate or unfortunate; which if she is in the 10th house up to the beginning of the 4th house (on the eastern side), support will come to the querent; if in the other half, to the center of the city.[326]

---

[324] Bonatti means that the benefic will be the first to reach the IC by primary motion, which it would be if it were closer to the cusp.

[325] *Dat ei vim*. I am not sure what technical meaning Bonatti has in mind for this phrase. He may be copying this phrase from "Zodial."

[326] *Medio urbi*. This could simply mean "the city" construed as the opponent.

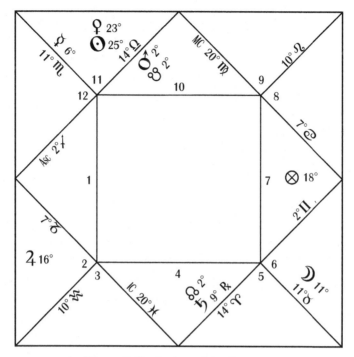

Figure 8: Besieging of the Luccans

An example of which is this. The said Count [Guido Novello], when he was besieging a certain castle of a company of Luccans, asked if he was going to occupy it.[327] The Ascendant of the question was Sagittarius, 2°; Capricorn the 2nd house, 7°; Jupiter in it, 16°; Aquarius the 3rd house, 10°; Pisces the 4th house, 20°; Aries the 5th house, 14°; the Head of the Dragon in it, 2°; Saturn retrograde, 9°; Taurus the 6th house, 11°; the Moon in it, 11°; Gemini the 7th house, 2°, the Part of Fortune in it, 18°; Cancer the 8th house, 7°; Leo the 9th house, 10°; Virgo the 10th house, 20°; Libra the 11th house, 14°; Mars in it, 2°; the Tail in it, 2°; Venus combust in it, 23°; the Sun in it, 25°; Scorpio the 12th house, 11°; Mercury in it, 6°.

And so Jupiter (who was in 16° Capricorn, aspecting the 4th)[328] signified the capture of the castle, and especially since he himself was the Lord of the 1st, and was the Lord of the 4th, and because one and the same planet was the Lord of

---

[327] These actions would have taken place about a month after the previously-described chart, at 9:51 AM LAT, on October 11, 1261 JC (cast for Lucca, Italy). See Introduction.
[328] Note that Jupiter aspects both his domicile and the degree of the 4th.

the 1st and 4th, it seemed that he ought to have it in harmony, *provided that*[329] first the things that needed to be done to capture it, came to pass. And the Moon (who was in her exaltation in Taurus) signified honor on the side of the querent. And Mercury (who was near the 12th house, not yet actually located there) signified the weakness of the querent's enemies.

But even though Jupiter seems to signify the capture of the castle, still, because he himself was in his detriment, and aspected the 4th and not the 1st; and even though the Moon was in her exaltation, still, she was in the 6th, cadent from an angle and from the Ascendant. This signified that their baseness and sluggishness and tardiness and weakness was so great that they would not apply themselves to those things by which the castle ought to and could be taken. And this was the reason it was not taken when it could have been taken. Because even though the Head was in the 4th, still Saturn was near it, so that he was placed toward the entrance of the 4th house.

Whence I responded to him under these circumstances, and I said to him that their low quality seemed to me to be so great, that the castle would more likely stand than be taken. In the end, they behaved so basely and so weakly, that in no way did they carry out any of those things which they had readied for the capture of the castle; and indeed it remained practically unharmed, and the army left the field, and so many remained in the army that they could well have assaulted the castle if they had wanted to do what had to be done in such matters. At last they resolved to ask me about the mutation of the air before they left camp, and I found that it changed greatly from the day of the question until three days [later], and it was that they were very happy when they were on the way back home, for it had been four months since it had rained.

Chapter 30: Whether someone has open or hidden enemies

The benefics are more numerous than the malefics, yet misfortunes seem to be more numerous than fortunes–not because they are greater in number, but because they are felt more [strongly]. Whence certain men are fortunate, nor is it known why it is so, unless perhaps it is by skills. Likewise certain men are unfortunate, not knowing why these things happen to them: for they serve all alike, even if perhaps one more so than another, they are devoted to no one, and still some people (and sometimes many) are inimical to them; nor do they

---

[329] Emphasis mine.

know how to assign the reason why [others] hate them, unless perhaps they are moved by envy, because they see them as good and not bad. Whence they sometimes ponder these matters and consult the astrologer, asking whether or not they have enemies, because of which contrary things happen to them.

Whence if someone were to pose to you the question whether he has enemies or not, you should know whether he is asking whether a [specific] named person is inimical to him or not, or whether he is asking absolutely, "Do I have enemies or not?"

If indeed he named someone to you, seek him from the 7th. If the Lord of the 7th were to aspect the Lord of the 1st, or the Moon, from a square aspect or from the opposition, you would know that he is inimical to him and slanders him, and he causes the querent's troubles. Likewise if he were in the 12th from the Ascendant, or were in the 12th from the [location of the] Lord of the 1st or from the Moon, or were joined with some planet who is in opposition to the Lord of the 1st or to the Moon or by their square aspect without reception. If indeed it were not so, he will not be his enemy.

If however he were to ask absolutely whether he has enemies, seek this from the 12th house and see if the Lord of the 12th were in the opposition of [the Lord of the 1st] or in the opposition of the Moon (whether with reception or without reception), or in a square aspect without reception: he has enemies who intend evil things for him, and they do them when they can (without rumors so that it is not publicly known), and they pretend to be his friends. Then look to see in whatever house the Lord of the 12th is so disposed,[330] [and] say that those people who are signified by that house, are those who are inimical to him. And even see if another one of the planets were in opposition to the Lord of the 1st or to the Moon, or in their square [aspect] without reception: because the people who are signified by the house of which that planet is Lord, will be inimical to him. Understand the same about those who are signified by the house in which this planet is, when he is opposed by the Lord of the first or by the Moon; and all of these people are moved by envy more so than by another cause. | |[331]

---

[330] I.e., so disposed as to indicate enemies–as the previous sentences explain.

[331] Here begins Section A, which begins in the middle of col. 322, as Ch. 7 of the 8th House (*Utrum faciat vindictam…*). I place it here as it refers to enemies and assigns the 7th house to the enemy. I am retitling it as Ch. 30b so as not to interrupt the flow of chapter numbering. See Introduction.

Chapter 30b: Whether or not one someone will get revenge for an injury inflicted on him

If an injury were inflicted on someone, just as often tends to happen (like if his father or uncle or brother or child were killed, or someone were struck, or an injury were inflicted upon him of such a type that he wanted to seek revenge), and he were to pose you the question whether he would get his revenge or not, you must in this case look at the 1st and its Lord, and the Moon, and even the 4th. And see if the 1st and the 4th were both movable signs (namely Aries or Cancer or Libra or Capricorn) and the Moon were in one of these four signs: it signifies that the revenge asked about will happen, unless the Lord of the 1st were in the 1st or aspected it by a trine or sextile aspect, and the Lord of the sign in which the Moon was, likewise aspected it,[332] or the first and fourth signs were fixed: because if it were so, without a doubt the revenge he seeks will come to pass—unless he was unmoved, [so] that he did not want to carry it out (but he will not have the skill to do it if he wanted to)—and shortly after the question was made. And if the Lord of the 4th house were to aspect the Lord of the 7th from any aspect, or its Lord from a square or the opposition, the querent will carry it out if he wants revenge, with his own hands, by spilling the blood of him who committed [the injury] against him and inflicted injustice upon him.

But if, in addition to what I have said, the Moon were joined to one of the benefics, it signifies that the revenge will not be able to come to pass, unless by a form of betrayal; and it will be because they will make peace, and afterwards, under the safety of the peace, the querent will kill him who injured him; and even stronger is if the benefic (to which the Moon is joined), is joined with some malefic by opposition or by square aspect: because then it signifies open betrayal. If however the aspect were a trine or sextile, it signifies that the wrongdoer[333] will be captured and kept in chains or on a stake because of it. And if the significator of the wrongdoer, or a benefic planet to which the Moon is joined (or a malefic to which is joined the benefic with which the Moon is joined) were in Aries or Cancer or Libra or Capricorn, and the Lord of the sign in which one of the aforesaid is (according to the method I told you) were quick in course and aspected the significator of the wrongdoer (namely the Lord of the 7th), he will be released from his confinement shortly. If however it were in a common sign, or the malefic to which the benefic is joined were of equal

---

[332] I.e., the first sign.
[333] I.e., the original villain.

course,[334] he will stay in captivity longer than he believes. If however it were in a fixed sign, or the aforesaid planet were slower in course or stationary, he will be held captive for a long time, and will be held in chains. If indeed the benefic to which the Moon is joined were in a movable sign, and the Lord of that sign were to aspect him by a trine or sextile aspect, he will be freed from confinement: because he who were to have power over the capture or over the confinement, will release him without impediment; and if he were to aspect him from a square aspect or from the opposition, it will come to be less. | |[335]

Chapter 31: On hunting birds and wild animals on land and water

The methods of hunting are two: one is on land and by means of land, the other in the water and by means of water. However, the hunting which is on land is twofold: for it is either directed against wild animals or birds. Insofar as it is directed towards wild animals rather than birds, it is again subdivided, for it is either in mountains or on flat land.

If a question were made to you (and the determination of the hunt) about hunting on land, and it was about wild animals, f the Ascendant were an earthy sign, then look at the Ascendant and its Lord, and even look at the Lord of the hour, because the Lord of the hour has much to do in the topic of hunting (whether by land or water). Even look to see if he were in quadrupedal signs, because it works the same as does an earthy sign when hunting in land for wild animals. Even look to see if your hunt were in the mountains: because if the Ascendant were then one of the fiery signs, it will be good. If [the hunt] were on flat land, and the Ascendant were one of the fiery signs, it will be good. If [the hunt] were on flat land, and the Ascendant were earthy or quadrupedal, it signifies likewise how much good there is in it.

When hunting for birds, however (whether they are aerial or terrestrial or in swamps), the airy signs must be adapted. Then look at the 7th (which signifies the hunt) and its Lord, and see where it is. And see if they were to aspect each other by a trine or sextile aspect: it signifies the catching of the prey without great labor, and without much searching; and it is even better if the Lord of the first were to receive the Lord of the 7th: because then it signifies catching the

---

[334] *Aequalis.* This is not usually the word Bonatti uses for a planet's "average" course or speed, but he could mean that. Since the five non-luminaries travel on their epicycles, they will never be of absolutely steady or unchanging speed (which is another meaning for *aequalis*).
[335] Here ends Section A, which ends in the middle of col. 322 (...*ab oppositione minus fiet*).

prey with ease and agreeableness. And if they were joined from the opposition or a square aspect, it signifies that whatever is caught from the hunt, will be gotten with much labor and with much exhaustion, as if after giving up hope.

If however they were not joined from any aspect, nor by body, and there were some [planet] who transferred their disposition or virtue (namely from one to the other, i.e., that of the Lord of the 7th to the Lord of the 1st), and the Lord of the 1st did not then commit its disposition to another, it still signifies the catching of the prey, even if not much of it, but only a middling amount. If indeed the Lord of the first were to commit his disposition to another, or some [planet] were to transfer his disposition to the Lord of the 7th, it signifies that he will be closing in on capturing the prey, but will not capture it; however, he will be happy with what he sees on the hunt, such as the chase, and the like. If indeed they were not joined together by conjunction or by aspect, or by the transfer of light, it signifies that nothing will be caught on the hunt.

If however, you were to find that he got the prey, and the seventh sign were Aries or Taurus, or the last part of Sagittarius, or Capricorn, and the question were in the hour of Jupiter, and the Lord of the hour were in the 1st or the 10th, he will catch fast-running, quadrupedal prey from the forests, like deer, roe, hares, and the like. If however it were Leo, his hunt will be for quadrupedal animals of the forest that cause wounds, like bears, wolves, foxes, boars, and the like. If however the 7th domicile were of the domiciles of the malefics, and it signified getting the prey, see if the benefics are in it or aspected it, because it signifies catching the prey with the safety of the hunter. If however the benefics were not in it nor aspected it, it signifies great exhaustion on the hunt, and in finding the prey, and he will not get enough, and it is feared for the hunter lest something unlucky will happen to him on account of the hunt, or to his own person from the prey itself.

And if Saturn were the Lord of the 7th, or were to have some dignity there, the question signifies the getting of the prey, [but] the beginning of the journey to the hunt will not yield much;[336] but it is feared lest someone wound him on the hunt, perhaps thinking he is striking the animal [but actually harming the hunter], and by other means. Nor however will it be a great wound, but if he were to wound himself, it could be severe for him; because the pouring out of blood pertains to Mars (whence [Saturn] impedes less), because all blood which is shed on a hunt naturally pertains to Mars; and for this reason [Saturn's] malice is mitigated in such a case, and he wounds less. But if Jupiter (who is the natural

---

[336] *Vel principium itineris ad venandum adipiscetur de venatione non multum.*

dissolver of all malicious things) were to aspect Mars then, the hunter will not be impeded, and especially if Jupiter were the Lord of the hour, or the Ascendant were Sagittarius or Pisces: the hunt will proceed with the safety of his body, and he will catch much prey, and easily, with little labor and little exhaustion, and quickly.

If however the seventh sign were earthy or airy, and a benefic were in it (even if the Lord of the 7th were a malefic and the Lord of the hour were likewise a malefic), still he will be saved and not wounded on the hunt, but he will [not] get everything he intends and believes he will get; and the wild animals and birds which he intends to hunt, will sense him and his dogs or leopards (or other animals with which one pursues from afar), and they will flee terrified from him, indeed so that he will not catch them, and he will conduct his search boldly and laboriously; nor however will anything useful follow from it; with him being safe; [so] that if Jupiter (the breaker of malice) or Mercury were with the Lord of the 7th, or with some malefic who is the Lord of the hour, the hunter will not stop until he catches it. For then Mercury takes over for Mars in matters of hunting in such a case.[337]

Chapter 32: On the greatness or smallness of the catch

If however you wished to know the quantity of the catch (whether the hunter will get many or few), look first at the hour of the question or of the hunt's departure, and see the tenth sign of the figure; so that if it were Aries or Scorpio, or you were to find Mars in it then, and Jupiter or Mercury were to aspect him, and the Ascendant were one of their two domiciles, and Mars were in the 10th. And if the Ascendant were not one of their domiciles, but the Lord of the hour were one of the two [i.e., Jupiter or Mercury], and in addition [Jupiter or Mercury] aspected Mars, it signifies catching much prey, and he [the hunter] will find great quantities, indeed so that he will get it by hardly any instruments but even by his own hands and without great labor—unless Saturn were to aspect Mars then. For if [Saturn] were to aspect [Mars] without the aspect of Jupiter, and the aspect were a square, or it were from one of the angles, or [Saturn] were in the 10th, or the 10th house were Capricorn or Aquarius, perhaps he will not get [even] a middling amount (because then it reduces the catch, and introduces labor into the hunt, and sadness and difficul-

---

[337] This paragraph derives from Sahl, *On Quest.*, "A question on the seeking of prey and what kind of catch it will be."

ties). For if Jupiter did not aspect Mars then, and [Saturn] himself were in one of
the places signifying a hunt [or prey], and especially in an angle, an impediment
to the person of the hunter or the master of the hunt is then feared; and the
prey will disappear before his eyes, and he will be oppressed by going on the
hunt; and if any prey were gotten, it will be small, and he will not rejoice over it;
and perhaps that he will lose the prey after it was caught, and especially if it were
a hunt on land (whether it were flat or mountainous).

Chapter 33: On hunting by water

And if it were your intention (or that of the ones going) to hunt for fish,
which is called a hunt by sea–and likewise understand under this heading every
place for fishing, of whatever sort of water (whether in a river or lake or swamp,
or whichever other place it is), provided that it is a place for fishing (because all
of these hunts fall under a hunt by sea).

See if the Ascendant were a watery sign, of which the most useful is Pisces,
then Cancer; and Scorpio is subordinate to Cancer [in usefulness]. Nor is Mars
useful then, because he impedes hunting by water. Whence if the Moon or the
Lord of the hour were then joined to Mars, [the fisherman] will not catch them
unless Venus is then in conjunction with the Moon: for Venus in this case
breaks the malice of Mars. For if the Moon (which has great virtue on [such a]
hunt) were joined to Mars in a hunt by water, it signifies middling usefulness in
fishing, or nearly none. And that which is [caught], will be [caught] with
difficulty and burdens; likewise with the impediment of those fishing. The next
worse is Saturn, for he himself does not impede the Moon in hunts by water,
just as Mars does not impede in hunts by land. On the contrary, if the Moon
were joined to Saturn on the hunt, it multiplies the catch, unless Mars aspects
her.

And if [Venus] were joined by any aspect [to Saturn],[338] unless she herself
were in Libra or Capricorn or Aquarius, it will be feared that the hunter or fisher
will suffer shipwreck, or be suffocated by some other means. If indeed she were
in Capricorn or Aquarius, it is feared he will fall into the water, but will not be
drowned. If however she were in Libra, it signifies his getting wet by rain or by

---

[338] This sentence is based on Sahl, *On Quest.*, "A question whether the hunters would catch
much or little." Bonatti makes it seem as though the Moon is involved in this aspect, and
omits to say with whom the aspect is. Sahl is clear he means Venus, which is further
underscored by the comment that the harm will be mitigated if she is in Libra (her own
domicile) or Capricorn or Aquarius (in which case she would be received by Saturn).

trees or by plants moistened by dew; and this happens because Mars and Saturn are enemies of Venus.

In the Treatise on elections I will tell you (out of the sayings of the ancients) other things which will have to be said in matters of hunting, whether they are by water or mountains or flat plains.[339]

Chapter 34: Whether an exile (whether expelled or banned) will return to his own land or not

Sometimes people are expelled from the homes or cities in which they live, or they withdraw from them in some other way. Perhaps they wish to know whether they are going to return to the house or land in which they were used to living, and they consult an astrologer about this. Therefore you must know in which situation he who asks about the aforesaid is, because someone can be outside his home or land in many ways and for many reasons: for he could be expelled, an exile, a foreigner,[340] a fugitive, banned, missing,[341] and deported.

If therefore you were asked about one of the above, see who it is who asks: whether he himself [is the querent], or [he is] another person [asking] on his behalf. If he is another person who is worried about [the exile's] affairs, see what business it is of his, and in what way he wants to inquire (namely whether he is the father or mother or brother or child, etc.). Give the 1st to the querent; to the quaesited person you will give the house through which the quaesited person is signified, and judge according to it. Because if the Lord of the house through which the quaesited person is signified, aspects the 1st, or were in the 1st, or were joined to some planet who did not aspect the 1st–[but] if it were joined to another planet who aspects the first, and who raises up[342] its virtue and light to the 1st–it signifies his return. You may understand the same about the Moon; so that if the question were about a brother, and the Lord of the 3rd

---

[339] See Tr. 7, Part 2, 7th House, Ch. 12.

[340] *Peregrinus*. This word can also mean a wanderer or a pilgrim.

[341] *Absens*. Literally, "not present," and translated by astrologers like Lilly as someone "absent." I use "missing" here because (a) by definition, anyone not at home is absent; and (b) questions about "absent" people in Lilly and elsewhere tend to concern people whose whereabouts are unknown. Below I will use "absent" when the context seems most neutral between the different ways of being away from home.

[342] *Relevet*. This could be read as *revelat* ("discloses"), which is an interesting metaphor; but Bonatti is drawing on Māshā'allāh (*On Reception*, Ch. 2). Of course it is possible that John of Spain's translation of Māshā'allāh was mistakenly printed as *relevet*; but, lacking other sources, we follow John of Spain's Māshā'allāh.

aspected the 1st; or the Lord of the 4th in the case of a father; if about a child, the Lord of the 5th; and understand this about those signified by all the houses.

If indeed he who asked, were asking about himself, namely that he himself was the same absent person who asked: see if he is a missing person who left of his own will, hoping and intending to return (as merchants do sometimes), or those who leave for important offices and other commands, or even if by some other means: by reason of moneymaking, or having fun, or by whatever means so long as it is voluntary (unless he himself is a foreigner), always the 8th is given to the querent for his own person; indeed the 1st is given to the land from which he has retreated (even if he suspected that something bad would happen to him, on account of which he was expelled); however he is said to be missing and not expelled, unless after leaving something happened to him so that he dare not return. Whence if the Lord of the 8th house were to aspect the 1st or the Moon from any aspect, it signifies his return; but if it aspected from the angles or by a trine aspect, his return will come quickly; if indeed from the succeedents or by a sextile aspect, his return will be delayed somewhat more. If however by the cadents or by the square aspect, he will tarry more. If however by the opposition, again he will tarry much, and his return will be postponed.

Indeed to a pilgrim[343] is given the 12th on account of the anger and sadness and tribulations which happen to him in his sojourn. And some people give him the 7th: you however can pick the one which seems more fit to signify what you intend.

If however the absent person were violently expelled from his land, or flees it or were an exile, or got himself out because of some fear, or were banned or deported or were a pilgrim[344] (because a pilgrim is compelled in a certain way to go on his sojourn, indeed so that he cannot renege on what he proposed to do on his pilgrimage without offending God), look for him in another way. For if he who asks were expelled, or banned or deported, or got himself out on account of a fear of the authorities or an enemy or of someone else, the 7th (and its Lord and the Moon) is given to him for his person, and the 1st is given to his land (from which he was expelled). Whence if the Lord of the 7th or the Moon were in the 1st, it signifies his return. If however [either of them] were not in the 1st, and [the Lord of the 7th] or the Moon aspected the 1st, or were joined to the Lord of the 1st (if [the latter] aspected the 1st), it signifies his return. If however

---

[343] *Peregrino.* Perhaps, "foreigner."

[344] *Peregrinus.* Here Bonatti makes it clear he means a pilgrim. Recall that Bonatti was writing at the close of the Crusades—for many people, their foreign journeys to the Middle East or elsewhere were part of religious pledges.

[the Lord of the 7th] did not aspect the Lord of the 1st, but aspected some other, and this other one aspected the 1st, but is joined to another which does not aspect the 1st, and this other is joined to another which does aspect the 1st, even if the conjunction came to be from one planet to all seven planets (as it seemed to Māshā'allāh),[345] one raises up the other and renders its light to the first,[346] and perfects the matter of the querent, even if with the interposition of multiple persons, and through them the matter which is signified by those houses could come to pass (the Lords of which [houses] are the planets which interpose themselves). If indeed you were to find none of the above, it signifies that he will not return.

But if an absent person were to ask about his own affairs, the 1st is given to [his] person; the 4th is given to his city or land, and even to any one of this stable things; to his other concerns are given the appropriate houses deputed to them. | |[347]

Chapter 35: On the arrival of one who is absent[348]

Very often questions tend to come to astrologers regarding people who are gone, [asking] if they will return or not, and when they will return–which is difficult, even if those who ask do not believe that it is greater work to answer than to ask.[349]

Whence, if you were asked about someone who is absent–whether he will return or not, and when–look at the Lord of the house through which the absent person is signified, just as I told you above in the preceding chapter,[350] and see if his significator is in the Ascendant (whichever type of journey it is), or if it is in the 9th (if it were a long journey), or in the 12th (if it were the longest journey), or in the 5th (if it were a moderate journey), or in the 3rd (if it were a short journey)–for a short journey is considered one day; I say a moderate one [is] from one to three days; a long journey from three to sixty days; the longest journey from sixty up to as long as one can go–or were joined with a some

---

[345] Again, a reference to Māshā'allāh's allowing multiple transfers of light, from OR.
[346] Again, a whole sign aspect to the rising sign, as in Māshā'allāh.
[347] Here begins Section H, which begins at the top of col. 323 (*De adventu alicuius absentis*)
[348] The title is in the 1550 edition, but the numbering of the chapter is mine, based on the topic and two clues in the following passages (see below).
[349] Bonatti expresses this irritation again when speaking of dream interpretation below–he must have had many clients asking questions on both topics.
[350] This is a clue to the proper placement of this section in the 7th house.

planet who is in them, to whom it commits its own disposition: it signifies that the absent person will return.

And if it were in the 7th, it signifies his return, but not quickly, but rather his return is deferred; and it signifies that he himself is in the land for which he set out, nor has he left it hitherto with a reason for turning back; still he is concerned about his return. If however it were in the 4th, it signifies a greater prolongation of his return than when it is in the 7th; still, he intends to head back when he can do it, and he will return, unless it is impeded by one of the malefics in its[351] own domicile. And if it were in the 3rd or 9th, and were joined to some planet in the Ascendant, it signifies that the absent person is ready, or prepares himself immediately for the return. And if you were to find it in the 2nd, and it were joined to some planet in the 9th house, or in the 10th house, it signifies that he prepares himself for the return; nor will there be a great delay in his arrival.

If however you were to find him cadent from the Ascendant, indeed so that he does not aspect [the Ascendant],[352] even if he were not otherwise impeded, it signifies his tardiness, and hardness and prolongation in his arrival, and that he does not care to return; and if he does care he cannot make it. If indeed he were cadent from the Ascendant, and were otherwise impeded, nor were joined to any planet who raises him up, and who aspected the Ascendant, and renders his light to the Ascendant, it takes away his hope of return; and it seems that he will not return. If indeed the significator of the absent person were retrograde, or were itself (or the Moon) joined to some retrograde planet, and aspected the Ascendant, it signifies his quick return. And if it were impeded by some planet, see which it is that impedes it. For if it were the Lord of the 4th, it seems that he is detained; if it were the Lord of the 6th, it seems that he is sick; if it were the Lord of the 8th, he is feared dead; if it were the Lord of the 12th, it seems he is shut up in a jail. These things seem to be those that impede his return. Nevertheless if the Lord of the 8th were to impede him, nor did [the significator] receive [the Lord of the 8th], then even if the Lord of the 8th received the significator of the absent person, it does not signify death. And if the significator of the absent person were not impeded as I said, then the judgment reverts to the significatrix (which is the Moon): which if she were joined to the significator of the absent person, and committed her disposition to him in the Ascendant, or above the line of the Ascendant by 3°, or below it by 12°, it

---

351 I believe Bonatti is referring to a malefic in the domicile of the significator.
352 In the 12th, 2nd, 8th, 6th.

signifies his quick return. If however she committed her disposition to him, beyond the line of the Ascendant from the third degree to the fifth [above it], or below it from 12° through the rest of the whole house, it signifies the tardiness of his return, even if not by much.

If however the significator of the absent person were impeded outside of the aforesaid houses, it does not signify a great impediment, even if perhaps there is some. If however the significator of the absent person were in the 8th, nor were he otherwise impeded, his arrival will be put off longer, and there will be delay in it. If indeed it were impeded, doubt will return to him, and it is feared he will not return, just as was said above. If indeed the Moon were separated from the Lord of the 4th or from the Lord of the 7th, or from the Lord of the 9th, or from the Lord of the 3rd, or from any planet which was below the earth (which is said to be left of the Ascendant),[353] and were joined to the Lord of the Ascendant, or to a planet who was above the earth (which is said to be to the right of the Ascendant), it signifies the return of the absent person; and even if the Moon were cadent from the Ascendant, and were joined to the Lord of the Ascendant, nevertheless however it signifies his return. And if the Moon were joined to a planet to the right of the Ascendant located in the 10th, it signifies his return, even if with delay: because the Moon will then be to the right of the Ascendant. But if she were to its left, and were joined to a planet in the 10th, it signifies impediment and duress and tardiness in his return.

Sahl however, as I told you in another chapter, gave the 1st to the absent person.

Moreover you must consider something else about the absent person: because the absence can be of many and diverse types, just as was said in the preceding chapter.[354] For someone is absent if he is an exile, a foreigner [or pilgrim], expelled, banned, deported, a fugitive–whence the absent person is like a certain general thing: however, an absent person proper is said to be he who, of his own accord and will, has absented himself, whether he went to a fixed or determinate location or not, provided that he went with the proposal or intention of returning, as is said elsewhere.

A man is called an exile who leaves his land not knowing the reason why, unless perhaps he is led by some folly, or perhaps goes off while waver-

---

[353] Here and in the rest of the paragraph Bonatti is mixing up his terminology about being "right" or "left" of the Ascendant or the heaven (Tr. 2, Part 3, Ch. 3). The reader should simply pay attention to the planets being above or below the horizon.

[354] Again, a clue to the correct placement of this chapter.

ing[355] or searching to see if he can find a land that is more suited to him than the one in which he was; and perhaps the place to which he was going was [not][356] premeditated, nor did he leave with the thought of returning or not returning, but went like one roaming.

A man is called a pilgrim who, of his own accord and of his own will absents himself, to go off to some place in the manner of a king[357] or in the service of God, or if he wished to cross the sea or go to St. Jacob's or St. Peter's, and the like.

A man is called expelled who was expelled against his will from the land he inhabited by some enemy of his, or more likely through some party [taking sides], just as sometimes it is between factions of citizens, castles or other lands, when one side expels the other.

A man is called banned, who is expelled on account of some wrongdoing or for some other reason, such as if the authority or people of the land in which he lived, expelled him from the land and banned him, nor does he dare to return, even if he wanted to.

A man is called deported, who by the people of his land was sent for some reason under custody to a predetermined location, nor can he leave without the permission of those who guard or preside over him.

A man is called a fugitive, who, from some fear that something bad will happen to him, flees the land in which he lived, and fears returning to it: nor however was he put under a ban for this; but still perhaps there are some who are eager to harm him if he were to return.

Whence all such people in whichever one of the above situations are absent people. And if a question were raised about some one of them, whether he will return to his land (whether [the question is asked] by him himself or through another), the 8th is always given to the person of him who left of his own accord and with the thought or intention of returning (as I said), and the 1st is given to

---

[355] I.e., he is not sure what he wants to do or where to go.
[356] Adding *non.*
[357] Reading *regis* for *regionis.*

his land, unless to a foreign man:[358] to the persons of all other absent people (like the expelled, banned, and fugitives, and foreigners), is given the 7th, and the 1st is given to their own land, just as to the expelled, as was said in another chapter.[359]

On the time of the absent person's arrival

To know the time of the absent person's arrival, see by how many degrees his significator is distant from the line of the cusp of the house in which it is, if it were in one of the above mentioned houses; and if it were not in one of them, see by how many degrees it is distant from a planet (in some one of them) to which it commits its own disposition, degree by degree; because if it were a short journey, it signifies that he will come within so many days; if it were a moderate one, it signifies that he will come within so many weeks; if it were a long journey, it signifies that he is going to come within so many months; if it were the longest journey, it signifies that he will come within so many years. | |[360]

---

[358] In Ch. 34, Bonatti says a foreigner can be assigned to either the 12th or the 7th, though his reasons for distinguishing foreigners is not clear to me.
[359] See Ch. 34.
[360] Here ends Section H, which ends in the middle of col. 325 (*infra tot annos sit ventus*).

ON THE EIGHTH HOUSE

Chapter 1: On one who is absent or someone else who has set out, whether he is living or dead

Sometimes certain people are accustomed to being gone from their home or land, and this for many and varied reasons; for certain people take off for reasons of pilgrimages, others because of commerce, others because of fun, perhaps others because of some [official] command, others to wield arms [in the military]–and by many other reasons they take themselves far from their children or family, indeed so that among their people there is no news of them, nor is the truth [of their condition] known. And perhaps someone worried about one of them wished to know from you whether or not the one he is worried about is alive, and he poses you a question about him, and you wished to respond to him about it.[361]

Look then to see who it is who asks you, and see about whom he asks, whether for a father or brother or child or slave or wife (or a wife for her husband), or for a religious person, or for a master or for a friend or for someone who does not like him (who pretends to be his friend sometimes), and the like. You will then give the 1st to the querent; you will give to the quaesited the house which signifies him (and likewise the Moon). And see if you were to find him in the 4th or the 8th from his own domicile, or even [in the 4th or 8th] of the question: for then it signifies his death. Likewise if he were in the 12th from his own domicile with one of the malefics, or one of the malefics were to aspect him by a square aspect or the opposition; and if the Sun were impeded, or the Moon, it likewise signifies his death.

However, Sahl said[362] that one must look at the Lord of the Ascendant and the Moon: if they were in the 4th from the Ascendant or in the house of death (which is the 8th from the Ascendant), or were combust, or in their own descension, or with the Lord of the house of death, it signifies death. And he said that if you did not find one of them disposed as was said, see the aspect of the malefics and the benefics toward them: if the Lord of the Ascendant were in the 4th retrograde, or in the house of death retrograde, or separated from the Lord of the house of death by retrogradation, look to see if it has returned to the degree of combustion–he will be dead. Likewise he said, if the Moon is

---

[361] Bonatti includes more information about absent people and their condition in the 9th House, Ch. 8. See also 7th House, Chs. 34-35.

[362] On Quest., 8th House, "Whether an absent person or some man is living or not."

joined to a planet below the earth, he will be dead; and if she is joined to a planet above the earth, he lives. Moreover, he said, if you were to find the Lord of the Ascendant in the 12th with the malefics, or the malefics aspected him, and one of the luminaries were impeded, you will judge him to be dead. And he said, if the malefics were also with the luminaries (which are the Sun and the Moon) in one sign (that is, joined corporally), without the aspect of the benefics, it signifies death. And likewise if the Moon were in the 4th with Mars, and the benefics did not aspect him. And he said, likewise if the Part of Fortune were with the malefics in the 4th or the 7th or the 8th or the 12th from the Ascendant, and the benefics did not aspect it, it signifies the same. And he said, know that what is above the earth signifies life, and what is below the earth signifies death. And he said, therefore if you were to find him combust under the rays, and no benefic were to aspect him, and the Moon were below the earth, cadent from the Ascendant (in the 3rd or the 6th), know that he who is inquired about, is dead, especially if it should happen that she is in Scorpio and in the third degree of that same sign,363 impeded by Saturn (who naturally signifies death). You will guarantee the death of him about whom the question is.

To which I (who am familiar enough [with this]) agree, except for his assigning of houses. Because he seems to want to give the 1st to the absent person, whoever he may be who inquires: to me it seemed that the house which signifies him ought to be given to him.364 However, it could be that this was an error in translation or transcription. You, however, take the method which you want, because when you are experienced once and for all,365 you will see which of these methods is more correct. Because it is not my intention to detract from any honest man, but to recommend and approve whatever they have said, and to believe that they spoke in good conscience.

If however the significator of the absent person were in the 6th from his own domicile, or in the 6th from the Ascendant or joined anywhere with the Lord of the 6th, or in his square aspect or opposition without reception or the aspect of an unimpeded benefic, it signifies that he has been taken ill. If indeed it were seeking the conjunction of [the Lord of the 6th] according to the aforesaid conditions, it signifies him to be sick. If however it were | |366 going away from

---

363 I.e., the degree of the Moon's fall.
364 This is in accordance with Bonatti's usual practice of giving the Ascendant to the absent person only if he has knowingly sent the querent to the astrologer.
365 *Semel et pluries.*
366 Here begins Section B, which begins in the middle of a sentence, two-thirds of the way down col. 322 (...*vadens a coniunctione*); but it fits seamlessly with this passage.

a conjunction with the malefics by body or by any of the aforesaid aspects, indeed so that it is separated from them, or escaping combustion, it signifies he has escaped from illness or from another impediment similar to an illness. However, you will judge the seriousness or ease of the illness, according to the completed[367] conjunction you were to see, from which the significator were to have escaped.

But you must take into consideration that you do not judge him ill unless you first see whether he were then sleeping;[368] nor judge him dead, unless you first see whether he were then drunk; nor judge him wounded, unless you first see whether he had let his blood, of which you could have such knowledge. You will consider if the significator of the absent person is in the 6th, nor were he joined to the Lord of the 6th, nor to any malefic impeding him; and [if he] were joined to one of the benefics, [the benefic being] strong and free, not impeded; or to one of the planets friendly to him while fortunate, and strong, not impeded: it signifies that he is not sick, but rather drowsy; and not wounded, but more likely having let his blood. May you understand the same if it were in the 8th under the aforesaid conditions, because it signifies he is inebriated, and not dead. | |[369] | |[370]

On the death of the querent

Sometimes some people fear the arrival of death, and they fear lest it over-take them before their time (which naturally seems to be a convenient one); and lest they cannot arrange their affairs well: they consult an astrologer so they can be assured of these things. Whence if someone were to pose a question to you about his own death, whether he were to make it absolutely or determinately, look at the hour of his question, and erect the figure for the question based on it, namely the 1st and 10th and the rest of the houses; and the places of the planets according to their degrees and minutes, and their direct motion and retrogradation, and according to their longitude and latitude.

If for example he were to ask determinately, saying: "see if I will die one, or two, or three years from now, or more or less," according to how it will seem to him it ought to be asked. Look at the Lord of the 1st and the Moon, and to each

---

[367] *Transactam.*

[368] Perhaps, as Bonatti suggests, he has endured bloodletting and is unconscious.

[369] Here ends Section B, which ended at the bottom of col. 322 (*& non mortuum.*).

[370] Here begins Section G, which began as a new heading in the middle of col 325 (*De morte interrogantis*). It ends abruptly in the middle of a sentence that matches perfectly with what follows.

of them in this matter, and see where they are: whether in the angles or in the succeedents, or if they are in the cadents, or are in their dignities, or are peregrine, or are void in course or joined to any [planets]. For if the Lord of the 1st is joined with one of the benefic planets, and committed his disposition [to it], and that planet were strong (so that [the Lord of the 1st] did not commit its disposition to another), see then if the good planet, and the benefic, is the Lord of the 8th. Because if it were not the Lord of the 8th, and were so disposed, as I said, it signifies that he will not die within the quaesited time. If indeed he to whom the Lord of the 1st is joined and commits its disposition, were the Lord of the 8th house (whether he were a benefic or malefic), it kills: and it signifies that the querent will die within the quaesited time; and all the more so if the Moon were then impeded, unless another planet is joined with the Lord of the 1st, who receives him (or at least the Moon): because then it signifies that he will not die within that time (whether the one who received the Lord of the 1st or the Moon were a benefic or malefic), except if he were the Lord of the 8th.

Even look to see if the Lord of the 1st were joined to some malefic planet who did not receive [the Lord of the 1st] by domicile or exaltation or by two lesser dignities, and the Moon were then impeded: it signifies his death. Say likewise if the Lord of the 1st were joined to the Lord of the 8th, unless the Lord of the 8th were to receive him; provided however that the Lord of the 1st did not receive the Lord of the 8th, even if [the Lord of the 8th] received [the Lord of the 1st]. Because if the Lord of the 8th were to receive the Lord of the 1st, and the Lord of the 1st [were to receive] the Lord of the 8th, one ought to fear his death, whether the Lord of the 8th were benefic or malefic. But if the Lord of the 8th were to receive the Lord of the 1st, it does not impede, whether he were a benefic or a malefic, provided that the Lord of the 1st did not receive him.

If however you were to see that he will not die within the quaesited time, see if[371] the Lord of the 1st will be joined to a planet who receives him by complete conjunction: because from that time in the year[372] he will be safe, and certainty will return to him that he will not die. If however you were to see that the same man will die, look to see when the Lord of the 1st will be joined[373] to the Lord of the 8th, or when he will be joined to the aforesaid malefic planet who does not receive him but impedes him: because when their conjunction is complete, whether by body or by aspect, then it signifies his death. If however the Lord of

---

[371] Reading "if" with Māshā'allāh, *OR*, Ch. 3.
[372] Reading *in anno* for *ib anno*.
[373] Reading *iungetur* for *iungatur*, as the next phrase shows.

the 1st were so disposed so that you do not believe yourself able to judge about the man's death, or [his] avoidance of death, look then at the Moon according to the sayings of Māshā'allāh,[374] and judge by her, just as you ought to judge using the Lord of the 1st, by means of the aforesaid conditions for death or its avoidance. If however, as I touched on for you above, the Lord of the 8th and the Lord of the 1st were joined together and each of them received the other, or at least the Lord of the 1st received the Lord of the 8th, it signifies his death in the aforesaid time period, that is when the one[375] reaches the degree in which the other was at the time of the aspect. May you understand the same, if within the quaesited time it were to experience the misfortune of combustion.

On the time of the death of someone asking absolutely about death

If however the question were absolute, because he did not make his question to you determinate, but said, "See for me when I will die," look then at the Lord of the 1st and the Moon and the Lord of the 8th, and the planet to which the Lord of the 1st or the Moon is joined, and judge death for him according to the distance in degrees existing between the Lord | |[376] of the 1st and the Lord of the 8th or a planet to whom he himself or the Moon is joined: because within so many months he will die. If the Lord of the 1st were in an angle, within so many years he will die. If it were in a succeedent, within so many months. If it were in a cadent, within so many weeks. If however it did not signify death, it signifies that he will live for so many years, or for so many months, or for so many weeks which are the degrees of that distance–that is, by how many degrees away will the Lord of the 1st be from the Lord of the 8th or from a malefic planet impeding [the Lord of the 1st]: so many will be his years or months or weeks.

And may you know this, because in this case you ought to observe the Lord of the 1st more so than the Moon, because he is stronger than the Moon in this matter. Whence one ought to fear the conjunction of the Lord of the 1st with the Lord of the 8th (or with some impeding malefic) more so than with the Moon. Because the Lord of the 1st signifies the life and body of a native, through its own nature [and] not accidentally. If however the Lord of the 1st were separated from the Lord of the 8th or it from him, or from a malefic planet

---

[374] I.e., according to Māshā'allāh's standard rules for determining whether the Lord of the Ascendant or the Moon is best suited to signify the querent. See *OR*, Ch. 2.

[375] Reading *unus* for *onus*.

[376] Here ends Section G, which ends 2/3 of the way down col. 326 in the middle of a sentence (*existentium inter dominum…*).

who impeded [the Lord of the 1st], it does not kill [the querent], nor will it kill him until so many years (if it signified years for him), or months (if it signified months) or weeks (if it signified weeks), just as was said above: how many degrees fall between the separated planet and the conjunction which they made together. And the conjunction of the Moon with the Lord of the 8th does not kill unless the Lord of the 1st were joined to him, and he were otherwise strong and free from impediments (which does not happen from the Moon). Because even if the Moon is strong and free, if the Lord of the 1st were joined to the Lord of the 8th or to a malefic according to the above conditions, the goodness of the Moon will not be enough to make the native or querent escape, even if she herself has the greatest signification with the Lord of the 1st in other matters.

Chapter 2: Whether the wife or husband will die first

And if a man or woman asked you which of them was going to die first, look at the Lord of the 1st and the Lord of the 7th, and see which of them is going to fall into the misfortune of combustion first, or will first experience one of the aforesaid impediments and conditions: it signifies that one will die first whose significator is so disposed.

Chapter 3: By what death the querent will die

And if he said to you, "see by what death I am going to die," look at the Ascendant and its Lord. Which if you were to find it in the 8th, and the 8th house were Leo, and its Lord made unfortunate or impeded, he will be torn by the teeth or claws of some beast, or it will signify he will die by beasts in some other way. But if Saturn were joined with the Lord of the 8th, and he were to impede him from Scorpio or Pisces, it will be feared that he ought to die either by the sting of a serpent or some other poisonous animal. Which if he were to escape this, drowning in water will be feared. Which if Mars were joined with the Lord of the 8th in the 8th or the 6th or the 4th or the 12th without perfect reception with the Lord of the 1st, and [Mars] were to impede [the Lord of the 8th, *etc.*], you will announce that he will perish with a sword or by fire; but more likely a sword. However in other places it will not render him secure.

ON THE NINTH HOUSE

Chapter 1: On a journey or pilgrimage, whether they will happen or not; and if they do, whether they will be useful or not

Sometimes some people propose to make a journey and they agree amongst themselves to make it; or perhaps there were only one among them who proposed to make a journey and wants to know whether the journey will happen or not, and poses you the question if the journey is going to happen or not happen; and if not, what it will be that impedes it.

Look then at the Lord of the 1st and the significatrix (which is the Moon), who both are significators of the querent; and look at the 9th and its Lord, which signifies a long journey or pilgrimage (the 3rd a short journey, the 5th a journey of moderate length, the 12th the longest).[377] | |[378]

Because if you were to find the Lord of the 1st (or the Moon) in the 9th, or one of them were joined to the Lord of the 9th (and stronger than this if it were in the 3rd or 5th or 7th or 11th), the journey or pilgrimage will take place, and the querent himself will be the reason why the journey takes place; nor will something external or extraneous happen to him which moves him to the journey, unless he is moved on his own account and voluntarily.

Then look at the Lord of the 9th and see where he is: which if he were in the 1st, it signifies that news will come to him regarding the place to which he intended to go, which will move him to go to the place, and faster than he was going to. If however, in addition to this, the Lord of the 1st (or the significatrix, namely the Moon) were in the 9th, such news will come to him that it will hardly or never happen but that he will go. If however it were the case with this [situation] (namely that the Lord of the 9th were in the 1st, such that he were joined with the Lord of the 1st), such things will overcome him that he will in no way be able to act but that he will go,

---

[377] I have set the following paragraphs apart because they are admirable examples of Bonatti applying several (in this case, the main four) forms of perfection to a single question. In order, they are: joining, location, transfer of light, collection of light. The only form left unmentioned is benefic reception.

[378] Here begins Section D, which appears from the middle of col. 325 (*quoniam si inveneris*).

unless perhaps the querent wished to make the force of nature from his own will.[379]

If indeed the Lord of the 9th were not in the 1st [and] joined to the Lord of the 1st, see if one of the planets renders the light of one of them to the other:[380] for it signifies that the journey will take place.

If however there were no planet who transferred the light of the Lord of the 1st or of the Lord of the 9th (namely of one to the other), see then if the Lord of the 1st and the Lord of the 9th were both joined to some planet who is heavier than they, and the heavier one were to aspect the 9th house: it signifies likewise that the journey will take place. If however the Lord of the 9th were not joined with the Lord of the 1st, nor were there a planet who transferred the light between them, nor were they joined to a planet heavier than they (who aspected the 9th house), judge for the querent that the journey he inquires about will not take place.

Moreover, if the Lord of the 1st were in an angle and were joined to some planet who was in the 3rd, it signifies that the journey will happen if it were free from the malefics, as certain people said, with whom Sahl seems to agree.[381] If it were joined to a planet who was in the 2nd, it signifies a journey just as if it were in the 3rd, provided that it is free from the aspects or conjunction with the malefics. If indeed the Lord of the 1st and the Moon were joined to some planet in an angle, nor were they in the aforesaid places which signify a journey, just as was said, it signifies that the journey will not take place.

This however you ought to consider: that if the Lord of the 1st were joined to the Lord of the 9th, and it appeared by this conjunction that the journey ought to take place, and you were to find some one of the malefics in the 1st which did not have dignity there, and it impeded them (or one of them), [the journey] will be annulled and will not take place; and the destroying cause will be something

---

[379] *Nisi forte interrogator vellet facere vim naturae ex arbitrio suo.* I think the point is that the querent will be compelled to go, so that he would practically have to make his own will into a force of nature to *avoid* going.

[380] I.e., if another planet transferred light between the Lords of the 1st and the 9th.

[381] Sahl, *On Quest.*, "Whether there would be a pilgrimage or not; and if cannot be perfected, what would prohibit it." Bonatti is right to say "it seems," since Sahl says something a little more expansive: "Moreover, if the Lord of the Ascendant were in an angle and were joined to a planet who is in the left side of the Ascendant (that is, between the Ascendant and the third), and he were free from the malefics, it signifies a pilgrimage."

which happens to the querent, impeding his journey so that it does not take place, even if he were to begin it.

If however the malefic were in the 2nd, something will happen to his substance that disturbs the journey, or else with a member of the household who detains him.[382]

If it were in the 3rd, it will happen by reason of his brother; and if he did not have a brother, it will happen by reason of one of those things signified by the 3rd house.

And if it were in the 4th, it will happen by reason of his father; which if he did not have a father, it will happen by reason of one of those things which are signified by the 4th house, like by reason of land.

And if it were in the 5th, it will happen by reason of his child; which if he did not have a child, it will happen by reason of one of those things which are signified by the 5th house.

And if it were in the 6th, it will happen by reason of illness or by reason of a slave or of one serving his household, or by one of those reasons which are signified by the 6th house.

And if it were in the 7th, it will be by reason of rumors which come to him from that land to which he wanted to go, or by reason of something which he intended to own, or by reason of his wife, or by reason of enemies or thieves. And Sahl said[383] that if he were to aspect from the Ascendant, murder or one of those things which are signified by the 7th house is feared.

And if it were in the 8th, it will happen to him by reason of death or one of those reasons which are signified by the 8th house.

---

[382] Omitting *non* and reading *eum* for *ei*. Otherwise it would read, "who does *not* detain him." But the malefic signifies delays and the prevention of a journey.
[383] *Ibid.*

And if it were in the 9th, it will happen to him by reason of rumors which he will hear concerning the journey, or perhaps because the road is not defended, or one of those reasons which are signified by the 9th house.

And if it were in the 10th, it will happen to him from someone who rules him (such as the authorities and the like), so that he does not permit him to make his journey, or by one of those reasons which are signified by the 10th house.

And if it were in the 11th, it will happen to him by reason of a friend or one of those reasons which are signified by the 11th house.

And if it were in the 12th, it will happen to him by reason of one of those who pretends to be his friend but is not, and is secretly his enemy; or by one of those reasons which are signified by the 12th house.

If indeed the Lord of the 1st were joined to the Lord of the 9th, after he were joined to a malefic by conjunction or from the opposition or a square aspect, and he were peregrine, it signifies destruction which will occur after he has left. And Sahl said[384] that the destruction will be according to the amount of enmity of that malefic: so if it were the Lord of the 6th, it will be illness. If it were the Lord of the 4th, it will be prison or another sadness. And if it were the Lord of the 8th, it will be death. And if it were the Lord of the 7th or the 12th, it signifies destruction by thieves and enemies. And if it were to aspect from the Ascendant, murder is feared. If from the 2nd, it signifies detriment to substance. Likewise the square aspect from the Ascendant[385] signifies detriment to the body; and the other, second square aspect,[386] namely of the 7th and the 10th, signifies detriment to substance. And he said that if you were to find the Lord of the Ascendant in the 7th or 8th, it signifies labor in the foreign journey (and especially if it were a malefic).

Nevertheless, if the Lord of the Ascendant were in the 8th, nor were it a malefic, and it received the Lord of the 8th, nor were [Lord of the 1st] received

---

384 *Ibid.*

385 Reading *ab ascendente* with Sahl, for Bonatti's "*ascendentis*" ("of the Ascendant").

386 The "second" (or "following") aspect is the dexter aspect cast against the order of signs to degrees earlier in the zodiac. See Abū Ma'shar's use of the "first" (or "leading") aspects and the second or following aspects in Tr. 8, Part 1, Ch. 116.

by [Lord of the 8th], it signifies that the traveler will be occupied with good foreigners [or strangers] in the place to which he intends to go.

Then look to see if the Lord of the 1st were free from impediments (namely, retrogradation, cadence,[387] combustion, the conjunction of the malefics, or their square aspect or opposition), it signifies that the journey will be guarded and easy, neither difficult nor laborious. You will say likewise that the journey will be easy, without impediment and labor, if the Moon were received with perfect reception by domicile or exaltation, or by two lesser dignities–and especially if she were received by the Lord of the 9th house, or [the Lord] of its exaltation (even if the receiver were a malefic, nor were impeded by a terrible impediment). If indeed the Moon were not received, it signifies the difficulty of the journey, and slowness and delay, and entanglements in it; and that the journey will not be useful, nor lucrative; and that he to whom he goes (or they of the land to which he intends to go), will not view him well or receive him. And it will even be hateful to him.

And Sahl said[388] that if you were to find the Lord of the Ascendant in the Ascendant, or in his other domicile, joined to the Lord of the 9th, it signifies that he will travel, even if the sign were fixed. And he said that a fixed sign does not destroy a journey.[389] Moreover he said: and know that the Ascendant signifies the foreign journey and the Midheaven his affairs, and the 7th from the Ascendant the land to which he goes, the 4th from the Ascendant signifies the end of the matter. If however you were to find a benefic in the 1st after you saw that the journey would happen or that it will not be prohibited, it signifies that his journey will be good and useful and with the health of mind and body. If indeed there were a benefic in the 10th, it signifies that the merchandise or things he carries will be evident if he carries his wares away with him.[390] If however there were a benefic in the 7th, the land to which he intends to go will be good and useful for him, and he will rejoice and be happy in those things he finds in it, for he will find in it what he desired to find. If indeed there were a benefic in the

---

[387] *Casus.* This could also mean "fall," but Bonatti usually includes cadence in his standard list of the most important impediments.

[388] *Ibid.*

[389] This is misleading. Sahl says that if the Lord of the Ascendant were in the Ascendant and *not* joined to the Lord of the ninth, the journey will *not* take place *especially* if the sign is fixed, for a fixed sign *does* destroy a journey. Bonatti is only *inferring* that an aspect to the Lord of the ninth will allow a journey even if the sign is fixed, but I am not sure this is legitimate simply on the basis of Sahl's text.

[390] *Merces seu res quas portat erunt perspicue si defert secum mercationem.* This departs somewhat from the conditions Sahl lays down. Bonatti seems to mean that his wares will be made known and readily available for sale.

4th, it signifies that his trip will come to an end so that he is pleased with himself, and what happens to him in the journey will take place pretty much according to his will.

Indeed if you were to find one of the malefics in the aforesaid places, not having a dignity in them, the journey will not go according to his wish, but rather to the contrary of it: because if it were in the 1st, something horrible will happen to him when he is on the road. If it were in the 7th, a horrible illness will befall him, that is something of the sort in the land to which he intends to go. If it were in the 10th, worsening conditions and damage will happen to the things he bears. If indeed it were in the 4th, distress will befall him, and a decrease in goods, and the labor which he endures will be most frustrating and useless. | |391

Chapter 2: For what purpose the journey is entered upon, or why the journey comes to be

Sometimes, certain people tend to conceal from the astrologer what they intend to seek, at other times the reason for doing it, and at other times the reason for concealing their intentions, because they do not want to disclose to someone what they have in mind–as oftentimes [happens] with journeys lest perhaps some people lie in ambush for them, or perhaps for some other reason, in accordance with how it seems to them. If indeed after a question was made, you were to see that there was going to be a journey, and you wished to know to whom the traveler wished to go, look at the significatrix (which is the Moon), and see to whom she is joined. Because the planet to which the Moon is joined, signifies him to whom the traveler intends to go, or for what reason the trip happens for him.

If the Moon were joined to Saturn, he goes to low-class and ignoble persons, or to monks, or other religious people wearing black vestments, or to old men, or decrepit men, or to Jews.

And if she were joined to Jupiter, it seems that his journey is to citizens,392 or to bishops or the secular religious, or judges, or to those skilled in law.

---

391 Here ends Section D, which ends at the bottom of col. 328 (...*frustratorius & inutilis*).
392 *Cives*. The medieval context suggests important or wealthy or prominent citizens.

And if she were joined to Mars, it signifies that he goes to warriors or to bellicose soldiers or pirates or to cutters of roads.

And if she were joined to the Sun, it signifies that he goes to the king or to some noble magnate, and a rich man, and an honorable man.

And if she were joined to Venus, it signifies that he goes to women or to other playful people who have womanly duties.

And if she were joined to Mercury, it signifies that he goes to philosophers or writers or other wise, literate people, or to merchants, or to masters of works.[393]

If indeed the Moon were then void in course, his journey will be for this: to find an absent person who is known to him.

If indeed in addition to this (namely if she were void in course) she were then separated from Saturn, his journey will be because he is pestered by creditors, on account of relief in hand[394] which he makes for someone else, or even because of his own debt, because he is not in a position to satisfy the creditors.

If indeed she were separated from Jupiter, it signifies that the trip will be for the reason that he is separated from (or wants to separate himself from), some bishop or other prelate, or a judge, or from some noble citizen.

And if she were separated from Mars, it signifies that journey will be for the reason that he intends to separate from someone who is wont to produce armies (who is then the leader of a certain army); or from some bellicose soldier, insofar as you see Mars in his dignity: because if Mars were then in his own exaltation, he flees or intends to flee from the king; if in domicile, from a duke. If in one of his lesser dignities, from a belli-

---

[393] *Ad magistros operum.* I am unsure what Bonatti is referring to.
[394] *Manu levationem.* This seems to indicate debts he incurs on behalf of someone else to whom he gives money, so that the creditors go after him.

cose soldier. If he were peregrine, he flees or wants to flee from thieves or cutters of roads.

If indeed she were separated from the Sun, it signifies that he is separated from some king or a very noble magnate, or intends to separate himself from him, perhaps fearing him.

And if she were separated from Venus, it signifies that his journey is for the reason that he is separated from some woman, or intends to separate himself from her; or perhaps that he is deceiving her, and has betrayed [or hurt] her.

If however she were separated from Mercury, it signifies that the journey or flight is for the reason that he is fleeing (or intends to flee or separate himself from) some writer, or other literate man, or from some merchant.

Moreover, see to which of the planets the Moon is first joined (if she is void in course): which if it were in its own domicile, he to whom the traveler goes will be from that region; and if it were in its own exaltation, he will be from outside the region, but has some lay dignity there, or authority, and the like. If it were in its own triplicity, it signifies that the man is from outside the region, but spends time in it just as if he were a citizen of the region or its land. And if it were in its own bound, it will be a man who spends time in the region, and whose parents live there. And if it were in its own face, he will be foreign-born, but now spends time in that land or region, and is considered a citizen.

And if the Lord of the house (in which is the planet to whom the Moon is joined), were to aspect [the planet], he to whom the traveler intends to go will be famous in the region in which he spends time. If indeed he did not aspect it, [the man] is not publicly known in that region or land in which he now spends time. And if [the Lord] aspected it, see by what aspect he aspects it, whether by a good or bad one. Because if he were to aspect him by a trine aspect, he will be a man whom all his neighbors love and honor, and is very mild-tempered. If he were to aspect him by a sextile aspect, he will be loved and honored in that land, but will be someone lower [than in the previous case]. If the aspect were a square, he is not loved much, nor is he hated much; and certain people say good things about him; but there are more who say bad things than who commend him. If by chance it were an aspect of opposition, he will be a man about whom men as a whole and unanimously say bad things, and as though those who have to communicate with him, hate him, and he is considered contentious and a whisperer. If indeed it were a corporal conjunction, it signifies that he is a verbose man, who interjects himself into many of his own–and others'–dealings, and from this interference he tries to get money from people; nor does he get involved in something, unless from it he can gain by all means (lawful and unlawful); he busies himself so he may extort money from others.

Moreover, look to see if you saw that the querent made a proposal, and see if the Lord of the Ascendant (or the Moon) were impeded by one of the malefics, [and see] who the malefic that impedes is, and see in what sign it is. Because an impediment will come according to the nature of the sign in which the impeding malefic is, and according to what is signified by the house in which it is. You ought to know well what is signified by the houses, [so] it is not necessary to repeat them here.

And if it were in Gemini or Libra or Aquarius, or the first half of Sagittarius, the impediment will come from men, whence you ought to warn him that he should beware of thieves, and *scarrani* and robbers, or cutters of roads.

If however it were in Cancer or Scorpio or Pisces, tell him to beware (if the malefic were Saturn) of shipwreck or submersion, or drowning in water. If it were Mars, tell him to beware of pirates sailing by sea, or thieves by sea or land.

If however it were in Aries or Taurus, or the last half of Sagittarius, or Capricorn, to beware in situations with beasts or their kicks or beatings.

If it were in Leo, tell him to beware of lions or wolves or bears, or even dogs, and scorpions, and spines and spiders, and the like.

And if it were in Pisces, tell him that he should beware of water snakes, and other poisonous animals that come out of the water.

And if it were in Virgo, tell him to beware lest some tree (or some limb) fall on him, or impede him in some other way; and he should even beware of shorelines, or falling from a place high up, and he should even beware of poison.

And Sahl said[395] that Mars is of greater impediment on land, and Saturn impedes more in the water.

Chapter 3: How it will go for the traveler in the city into which he enters

If, at some time, some traveler or pilgrim wanted to know what would happen to him in a city or foreign land when he entered it, or if you yourself wished to know it for yourself. Look at the 1st house when the traveler enters into that land, or when the querent asks, and see if the Lord of the 2nd house (which signifies the substance of the city) were direct: [then] he will return in no great time, and quickly enough he will perfect what he intends. If indeed it were stationary in its second station, there will be a delay in his return, but still he will perfect the matter for which he went; however many impediments contrary to his business will happen to him, so that he will not believe he [can] perfect it. If indeed it were stationary in its first station, he will believe himself able to perfect what he intends, but in the end he will not perfect it, and will return angry after some delay, because it will not be profitable–rather, he will spend more than he makes. If however it were retrograde, he will return quickly from that land, and he will not perfect the matter for which he went, nor will he make any money there, nor will any good come to him in it.

If indeed the Lord of the 2nd were in the 1st or 10th or 11th, his journey or entrance into that land will be useful and good and profitable; he will rejoice and be happy for that reason.

If however the Lord (namely of the 2nd) were in the 7th, many contrary and horrible things will happen to him; and he will have to litigate because of it, because perhaps those with whom he had dealings will not tell him the truth, and especially if their significators (namely those which are the Lords of the 7th)[396] were malefic; and contentions and hindrances will happen to him, and

---

[395] *On Quest.*, 9th House, "Whether a pilgrimage would be or not; and if it could not be perfected, what would prevent it."
[396] I believe Bonatti means to include the Lords of the 7th by exaltation, triplicity, etc., in addition to the domicile Lord.

many other things which will disturb him, and will bring grief and sadness to him.

If indeed the Lord of the 2nd were in the 3rd or the 9th from the Ascendant, it signifies the instability of the querent, and his movement within the land which he had entered or into another to which he had gone; and he will not delay in it unless moderately or almost not at all, and if he delayed there, it will not be by his own desire, but contrary to his will, and more likely if he were coerced to remain there.

If indeed [the Lord of the 2nd] were in the 4th, and one of the malefics were to aspect him from a square aspect or from the opposition (unless it were to receive him by a good reception), he will not journey beyond [that] easily. And if it were joined corporally to him, it does not seem that he will ultimately return to his own house; and it seems that he is going to die there. If indeed Mars were the malefic who impeded the Lord of the 2nd, and the Moon were joined to him (namely, to the Lord of the 2nd), or were joined to Mercury from a square aspect or the opposition or by body, and then Mars were to aspect the Moon, horrible things will happen to him, and he will fall into contention with some bad people, and those who enjoy things which pertain to Mars and are signified by his appearance, indeed so that they will injure him, and will wound him with frightful wounds, indeed so that if the Moon were then in the 4th and Mars were to aspect her from any aspect, the querent or traveler will die from it. If however she were in the other angles, he will not die from it. But if he were wounded, scars will appear in the locations of the wounds. And if he were tortured, vestiges of the torture will remain in narrowed places[397] by the iron [instrument] of the torture. If indeed the Moon were in the aspect of Mars, and Jupiter or the Sun or Venus or Mercury did not aspect him, [then] if he himself were then in a good condition, a horrible thing signified by the sign or house [domicile?] in which Mars is, will happen to the querent or traveler. If indeed one of the aforesaid benefics then aspected the Moon, perhaps then the horrible things I said will not happen; still, if they happen, the querent or traveler will be freed from them, and will escape, and relief will be found by all of these, and escape from them. If indeed one of the aforesaid benefics did not aspect the Moon, it is feared then that the horrible things are vicious and adhere to the traveler or querent in such a way, that he will die from them.

---

397 *In locis coartatis.*

Chapter 4: How it will go for the traveler on his journey or with his reason for going, whether he is a king or some other person

Sometimes men are wont to ask, when they go on some trip or foreign journey, or some such thing, how it ought to turn out or go for them in the journey or in their goal. Or perhaps you wished to know for yourself how it ought to turn out for him.

Look[398] at the Ascendant in the hour of the question if he were to ask, or at his departure[399] if he did not ask, and verify all the houses from the 1st up to the 12th, and see the disposition of the significators of all the houses, and their nature [or condition]. And whichever one of them you were to find well disposed, judge good about it; and whichever of them you were to find poorly disposed, judge bad about it.

Moreover, you will judge for him concerning his nature [or condition] according to another, less particular mode, namely that you ought to look at the planets which are between the 1st and the 4th, and specifically those which are in the 2nd. And if a malefic planet were there, which had[400] domicile or exaltation or bound or triplicity or face, it signifies at least that harm will come to him in those things which he leaves behind him. If he were the king or another great noble, the harm or detriment will be in his kingdom or duchy or his retinue, and in those things which pertain to him in his relationships. If however it did not have one of the aforesaid dignities, nor did it have a face[401] or *haym*, it signifies harm in the affairs of both great and low persons; and specifically if it were a low-class person who did not have an empire or city or castles, it signifies harm to what he possesses, and as much in the movable possessions in his house as in others, and to whatever things the detriment signifies in those close to him and in the blood relations who love him. Which if Mars were the malefic which were in the 2nd, the detriment will happen to him because of a battle or another contention, or through burning by fire, or the shedding of blood, or through cutters of roads, or in the desruction of small animals or of male slaves or female slaves, insofar as Mars were then disposed to signify one of the aforesaid. If however it were Saturn, there will be a horrible thing or detriment

---

[398] The following paragraphs are elaborations on Sahl, *On Quest.*, "A question about the nature of a journey of princes or kings, and the condition of those who follow or remain."
[399] *Motus.* I have translated it this way because I believe Bonatti wants (as he often does) the same technique to apply to elections.
[400] Omitting *non*.
[401] This probably refers to the essential dignity, but it is possible that this is Bonatti's Latinized form of "facing" (*al-muwājahah*).

because of shipwreck or submersion or ruins or thieves or the death of large animals, or illnesses. If indeed the Tail were there, it will be on the occasion of each of the things signified by some house, because harm will come from that thing which is signified by that house whose Lord were impeded. If however it were a malefic having dignity in the 2nd, and it were direct or were received, its malice is removed; nor will it impede by a very perceptible impediment. If indeed it were retrograde, its malice will not be wholly removed, however it will kill very little, because it is received. But if it were retrograde and were neither received nor in its dignity, its malice will be increased, and will kill more. You will say the same if it were in fall or in its descension.

If however it was the benefics instead of the malefics (namely, in the 2nd), say that the journey will not be fearful for him on account of his goods which remain behind him; nor will they diminish for that reason, but rather they will be improved and grow.

And Sahl said[402] that if the Lord of the Ascendant or the Moon were impeded, it signifies difficulty and sadness on the road. Whence if you were to see that some trip or foreign journey threatened harm to him, you ought to see which planet is he who impedes, who inserts the fear, and who is the cause of the detriment which seems ought to happen to the traveler, and where [the planet] himself is. And if he were between the 1st and the 10th, as Sahl says, the detriment or harm will come on his return. If it were between the 7th and the 10th, on his departure;[403] and if it were between the 1st and the 4th below the earth, in those things which he acquires on his departure.[404] If indeed it were between the 4th and the 7th, on his return.

To me however, it seems that he who translated [Sahl's book] did not understand the Arabic language well.[405] Whence he could have erred in translating, because it would have seemed more appropriate that the impediment ought to come if the impeding malefic were between the 1st and the 4th, in his departure[406] from the land in which he was, by going to the other one up to the middle of his journey. If it were between the 4th and the 7th, [the impediments] ought to happen from the middle of the journey up to the land to which the traveler intended to go. And if it were between the 7th and the 10th, it will

---

402 *Ibid.*
403 Reading *discessione* with Sahl for Bonatti's *descensione* ("going down").
404 See above note.
405 This may be true, insofar as Bonatti's source read *descensione*; but Bonatti's point is in regards to something else, as he explains.
406 Again, reading *discessione* for *descensione*.

happen to him on his return up to the middle of the path of return (and especially in those things which he acquired). And if it were between the 10th and the 1st, it will happen after the middle of the return to his own house or land.[407]

Here ought to be put down the accidents according to whichever house, and according to whichever one of the planets [indicates the events signified]: and so that you will know it in particular, look at the helping benefics and the impeding malefics, and see in which houses they are. Because in those proportional parts of the journey the things they signify will happen, insofar as they are benefic or malefic. For if they were in the 1st, they will happen in the beginning of the journey a little outside the gate of the land from which he leaves, or perhaps they will happen in the gate. If they are in the 2nd, they will happen within a fifth part of the journey. If they were in the 3rd, they will happen within a third part of the journey. If they were in the 4th, they will happen in the middle of the journey. If they were in the 5th, they will happen in the third part of the journey that is left over after the middle. If they were in the 6th, they will happen after two parts of the journey left over after the first middle. If they were in the 7th, they will happen in the place to which the traveler heads. If they were in the 8th, they happen in the separation from that place or near the fifth part of the journey's return from that place from which he returns. If they were in the 9th, they happen in the third part of the return journey. If they are in the 10th, they happen in the middle of the return journey. If they are in the 11th, they will happen after the second part of the return journey. If they are in the 12th, they happen near the land to which the traveler returns.

Then look to see in which of the aforesaid houses a benefic may be found, because there the traveler will rejoice and good things will happen to him: like if it were Jupiter, it will signify the money that is sought; if it were Venus, he will be happy with women and gourmands and the like. If however the malefics were found there, contrary things will happen to him: like if it were Saturn, harm will come to him because of a thief, fire, secret and obscured affairs, or because of shipwreck. If however it were Mars, they will happen because of fire or cutters of roads or because of the shedding of blood and the like.

---

[407] In other words, Sahl sees the whole eastern half of the figure as representing the return, and the western half as the departure. Bonatti thinks the quadrant from the 1st to the 4th should represent the departure, from the 1st to the 10th the return, and the other quadrants points in the middle of the round-trip journey.

Chapter 5: In what direction it would be better to go

And if the traveler (or someone else) were to ask you, saying, "In what direction is it better for me to go?" Look at the figure which you have erected, and see in which quarter are the benefics, and which are more fit, and in a better condition, and say to him it would be better to go according to that. If in the east, toward the east; if in the south, toward the south, if in the west, toward the west; if in the north, toward the north. And in whichever quarter there were more benefics (and better disposed), it is better to go in that direction.

And say the same about the malefics, because in whichever quarter there are more malefics, it is worse to in that direction. And it even seems that something ought to happen to the traveler, because if the Lord of the 1st were joined with one of the significators of the question, he will meet them on the road. If it were the Lord of the 3rd, he will meet his brother. If it were the Lord of the 4th, he will meet his father. If it were in the 5th, he will meet his child–if he were to have a brother or father, *etc.* And understand the same about all things signified by the houses. And if the significator of the brother were in the 1st, his brother will come to him. And if the Lord of the first were in the 3rd, the traveler will go to his brother. And say the same about all the significators of the houses, if the querent or the traveler were to have a brother or father, *etc.* And let it always be your concern to look at the 2nd and the 8th in journeys: according to Ptolemy,[408] beware of malefics in the 8th and their aspects when going out on a journey and in the 2nd upon returning, because an evil or malefic [planet] in the 8th signifies detriment in the land to which the traveler intends to go, and in the 2nd in the land to which the traveler intends to return. Whence you ought to put a benefic in the 8th in any journey,[409] or make it so one of them aspects [the 8th]; and if you could put the Head with it, it will be better. And beware then the Tail, and if it should happen that you cannot avoid having a malefic there, put the Tail with it, and beware then the Head. May you understand the same about the 2nd when someone returns, just as I told you about the 8th when he leaves, [that is], that there not be a malefic there nor aspecting it; and if you cannot avoid having it aspect, let its aspect be a trine or at least a sextile. And always put a benefic there, or make it so that it aspects it.

---

408 *Cent.*, Aph. 41.
409 Here and in the rest of the paragraph, Bonatti is making recommendations about elections.

Chapter 6: Of two lands or houses or whatever things, or of two or more business deals or journeys (and the like): which will be better for the querent

Sometimes some men have more than one business deal on their hands, and they do not know which of them would be more useful, and they consult an astrologer to choose for them which of the business deals would be better for them.

Whence if someone were to come to you who had some business deals on his hands (or journeys or purchases or sales or offices or marriages or changes [of place] from land to land, or from one house to another, or something similar to these), and he wished to satisfy himself about it: it seems that there is diversity among our ancient sages. But if one were to consider it correctly, there does not seem to be diversity to me. Rather, one said more than another, just as it seemed to him, not by way of contradicting the saying of the other, nor by way of violating [the opinion of], among others, Māshā'allāh and Abū Ma'shar (who seem to me to have spoken more subtlely, even if more obscurely). However, those who are in my own time period (as is Hugo Abalugant,[410] Benduardinus Davidbam,[411] Joannes Papiensis,[412] Dominicus Hispanus,[413] Michael Scot,[414] Stephanus Francigena,[415] Gerard of Cremona,[416] and many others) worked in all of the above matters with the 1st and the 7th; however their indications enlarged those two means [or ways].[417] Bellonus Pisanus[418] used the four angles for all of the above; Grandeus,[419] the son of the said David, used a certain secret method of his own which he revealed to no one, and things went well for him in his judgments. However, I, not by contradicting any of them (neither the ancients nor the moderns), have worked just as I tell you, and (praised be our Lord, Son of the Blessed Virgin) good and authentic judgments were made, because I used to use[420] this method, and I advise you to use it–

---

[410] Unknown.
[411] Unknown.
[412] Unknown.
[413] Unknown.
[414] See Introduction.
[415] Unknown.
[416] *Girardus de Sabloneto Cremonensis.* See Introduction.
[417] *Extendebant sua indicia istos duos modos.* It is possible the last part of the sentence should read *istas duas domos,* "those two houses," since he is implying that these other astrologers forced these two houses to signify too much.
[418] Unknown.
[419] Unknown.
[420] Reading *utebar* for *utebatur.*

namely that if one of the aforesaid questions came to me, which contained more than one of the same matter, I fearlessly took three things under one Ascendant, and I judged about them just as [I would] about one: and I used the Lords of the triplicity signifying the quaesited matter, and judged concerning them.

For example, someone wanted to take a wife, and had many women at hand, and he posed a question and framed it thus: "I have verbal acceptance to take Mary as a wife, and Berta and Invelda: see which of them is better or more useful to me; and if the marriage will be concluded between me and one of them, and with which one the marriage will be concluded." And let it be put that the Ascendant was Aries, which signifies the querent. And Libra was given to the [potential] woman,[421] whence I looked at the Lord of the triplicity of Libra, namely Saturn (who is the first), Mercury (who is the second), and Jupiter (who is the third).[422] And the one of them I found in conjunction with Mars (who is the significator of the querent), I said the marriage would be perfected with her. And if Mars were joined with two of them, or with all, I said that the marriage would be perfected with her whose significator was more closely conjoined with Mars. And if all of them were equally joined to him (whether by body or aspect), I said that it would perfect with either. But if one were joined to Mars by aspect and another by body, the marriage would be perfected with the one that was joined [by conjunction?] and was more dignified.[423] May you understand the same about all of the other things signifying what is better and more useful; you will judge by the planet which is better, and best disposed, and more fortunate.

If however the question were about exactly one [thing], you will judge by the Lord of the 7th house or by whichever house it is signified.

And if he were to ask about more than three things, then you will change your judgment: if there were four things, you will give the Lord of the house signifying the matter to the first thing; the first Lord of the triplicity to the second thing; the second Lord of the triplicity to the third thing; the third Lord of the triplicity to the fourth thing. And again, if he were to ask about five things, in the same way you will change your judgment again, and you will give the Lord of the house to the first thing; the Lord of the exaltation to the second thing; the first Lord of the triplicity to the third thing; the second Lord of the triplicity to the fourth thing; the third Lord of the triplicity to the fifth thing.

---

[421] I.e., the 7th house was in Libra.
[422] Bonatti seems to be assuming a diurnal chart.
[423] But which significator signifies which prospective bride?

And if it were not the exaltation of any planet, you will give (as was said) the Lord of the house to the first thing; the first Lord of the triplicity to the second thing; the second Lord of the triplicity to the third thing; and the third Lord to the fourth thing; indeed you will give to the fifth thing the Lord whose bound was the degree of the house signifying the quaesited matter.

Look in each matter and in every question according to this method which I have given you: like if you were asked about someone who is in some land and it is not going well for him there, or if for some other reason he wants to change [locations] from there to another one (or from one house to another, or from one official duty to another, or from one art to another, or from something similar). And if he were to say to you: "See which of these is better for me, whether this or that," see in what sort of condition the Lords of the 1st and 7th are. If the Lord of the 1st were of a better condition than the Lord of the 7th, it is better to stay in the land or the house in which he is, or to hold on to the art which he practices, or to exercise the official duty which he exercises. If indeed the condition of the Lord of the 7th were better than the condition of the Lord of the 1st, it is better and more useful for him to go to the land which he wants to, or to move into another house, or to take up another art.

Moreover, look to see if in addition the Moon were separated from some benefic (whether he received her when she was conjoined to him or not), or from some malefic who is not impeded, who received her when she was joined to him; [or] she were joined to some malefic without perfect reception, indeed so that her condition was made better from the reception: say that the land in which he is (or the house in which he lives, or the art which he practices) is better for him. If indeed she were separated from some malefic and were joined to one of the malefics, tell him that he should beware of moving from there. Say likewise about the Part of Fortune if the benefics are being separated from it, and malefics are being joined to it: say it is bad. If the malefics are being separated from it and the benefics are being joined to it, say it is good, which-ever of them is good for him, or he wants to do what he intended or not. But it will be better for him whose significator were of a better condition. If indeed both were malefic, the condition of both is bad for him, but [the one] whose significator is of a less bad condition will be less bad for him. Say likewise about the Moon and the Part of Fortune. If however the condition of the Lord of the 1st were good, and the Moon were separated from the benefics, and the benefics were to aspect the Part of Fortune, say that the thing which he does (or the home or the land in which he lives) is most useful to him, indeed so that he cannot improve it. If indeed one of them is missing, it will be below this, in accordance with how one of these aforesaid good things is missing. If however the condition of the Lord of the 7th were bad and the Moon were joined to malefics, and the malefics aspected the Part of Fortune, it signifies that the matter which he wants to undertake (or the house or the land to which he wants to go, or the lands [he wishes] to alter) is not right for him, so that it could not be worse. If indeed one of these [conditions] were missing, the evil will be less than this, according to the quantity of the defect of one of the malefics.

Chapter 7: Whether that land is better for him

And Sahl said[424] if someone were to ask you if "the land in which I am is better for me, or the one to which I want to go," look at the Moon. If she were separated from a malefic, leaving will be better for him. If indeed she were separated from the benefics, it will be better to stay. But he said, and if he were to ask you, saying "Is it good for me if I leave for this business deal, or [even] to make it," look at the Lord of the Ascendant and the Moon. If they were separated from the malefics or joined to the benefics, instruct him to do as he wishes. If indeed they were separated from the benefics and joined to the malefics, he should not go near that undertaking. If indeed the condition of the Lord of the Ascendant were good, it will be better for him to stay. If however the condition of the Lord of the 7th were better, it will be more useful for him to go. And if the Moon were separated from a malefic [that is] oriental, direct, and strong, receiving her from a trine or sextile aspect, and she were joined to impeded benefics not receiving her, it signifies that it is worse to do the thing about which he asks, than to let it go, even if it is to do good. And if she were separated from a benefic that is impeded and poorly disposed, not receiving her, by a square aspect or from the opposition, and she were joined to a malefic [who is] direct, oriental, and strong, and well disposed, receiving her from a trine or sextile aspect, it signifies that it is worse to let it go than [not][425] to do it, even if it is not to do good. I say the same if she were separated from them, as was said, and she were void in course, nor should she be separated so as to be

---

[424] On Quest., 9th House, "A question whether the land in which someone is, is better, or that to which he is going to go."
[425] Adding non.

joined to a benefic.[426] To me, however, it seems that I have satisfied you on all of these things.

However, if the significators of the quaesited matters were equal in strength or debility, so that you could not discern the truth through some one of them, nor likewise through the Moon, then subtract the place of one of the significators from the place of the other significator, and add the degrees of the ascending sign to the result, and project from the Ascendant, and see where the number were to fall: because you could judge about the matter according to that place, and according to the Lord of that sign, and according to [its] condition. So if it were disposed well, you could say good; however, if poorly you will judge the contrary; while if their places were equal, [then] what is signified will remain in the ascending degree.[427]

Chapter 8: On someone put in jail or fetters: what will happen to him concerning his incarceration, namely whether he will be freed from the prison or not, and how long until then

When some prisoner asks you (or someone else on his behalf and with his words) whether he will be freed from his prison or not, and how long until then, not fixing another length of time concerning the time of his liberation,[428] look at the Lord of the Ascendant and the Moon. And see if they were both in angles: it signifies the holding of the captive, and the prolongation of his imprisonment. Likewise if the Lord of the 1st, and the Lord of the 10th, also the Lord of the 7th and the Lord of the 4th, were in angles: it signifies his being held for the whole year.

And if all four of the Lords of the said houses were not in the angles themselves, and there were three of them, or only two, it signifies likewise his being held for the whole year. Moreover, if even the Lord of the 1st were in an angle, then even if the Moon were not in an angle, it signifies his being held, and the prolongation of his incarceration. Likewise if the Lord of the 1st or the Moon were in a fixed sign, it signifies the prolongation of the incarceration. If indeed

---

[426] *Nec sit separata iungi fortunae.* This does not seem grammatical, and I have translated it as though it had read *nec sit separata ut iungatur fortunae.*

[427] I.e., if the two significators were conjoined by body, then there would be no (or very little) distance to project from the degree of the Ascendant. Presumably then, we would have to examine that degree.

[428] This seems to mean "without asking whether he will be freed within a specific length of time"–i.e., an absolute question.

[the Lord of the 1st] were in the 1st, it will be so (namely, the prolongation of his imprisonment). If it were in the 10th, his stay in the prison will be longer, because what it signified in days in the 1st, in the 10th it will signify a week; what signifies a week in the 1st, will signify a month in the 10th; what will signify a month in the 1st, in the 10th it will signify a year. And if it were in the 7th, what will signify a day in the 1st, will signify a week in the 7th; what will signify a week in the 1st, in the 7th it will signify a month; what will signify a month in the 1st, in the 7th it will signify a year. If it were the 4th, what signifies an hour in the 1st, in the 4th will signify a day; what signifies a day in the 1st, in the 4th it signifies a week; what will signify a week in the 1st, will signify a month in the 4th; what will signify a month in the 1st, in the 4th will signify a year.

And see if then the Lord of the 12th were to aspect the Lord of the 1st, namely while [the Lord of the 1st] or the Moon was in the 4th: difficulty and evil will happen to him in prison, indeed so that the death of the one incarcerated is feared from the incarceration and the difficulties.

And Sahl said[429] that if the Lord of the Ascendant were cadent from the Ascendant, and were joined to a planet in an angle, it signifies that his imprisonment will be prolonged after he hoped to escape. If indeed the Lord of the 1st were in an angle, and were joined to a planet who was cadent from an angle, it signifies that the prisoner will lose hope in prison—however, he will escape later. Then look to see if the Lord of the 1st were joined to some malefic planet located in the 4th, or [if] the Lord of the 8th were in the 1st: the prisoner will die in that prison. And may you understand the same about the significatrix (which is the Moon), as was said about the Lord of the first.

If indeed the Lord of the 1st and the Moon (or even one of them) were joined to the Lord of the 3rd or the Lord of the 9th, it signifies that the prisoner will be freed. But if the Lord of the 3rd or the Lord of the 9th house were the Lord of some angle (namely the 10th, 7th or the 4th), his exit from the prison will be delayed; however he will escape it later, nor will there be someone to take him out of prison, but he himself will break the bolts of his door or his shackles and will flee; or he will work in another way so that he goes out of the prison. If however the Lord of the 3rd or the Lord of the 9th were lighter than the Lord of the 1st, indeed that one of them were joined to him, it signifies that someone is working on his behalf without the prisoner seeking it, and would make it so that he would be liberated. If however the Lord of the 1st were joined to the Lord of

---

[429] On Quest., 9th House, "A question about someone conquered: what will be so regarding him."

the 12th, or the Lord of the 12th were joined to him, or [if] the Lord of the 3rd or the Lord of the 9th were joined corporally with the Lord of the 12th, it signifies that the prisoner will flee from the prison, and will be freed.

But if the Lord of the 1st and the Lord of the 3rd (or the Lord of the 9th), when they are joined together, were then joined to some planet heavier than they, who received their disposition,[430] and the heavier one were in an angle, it signifies that the prisoner will not leave his captivity until the heavier planet who receives the disposition of the aforesaid significators leaves the sign in which he is–or until he transits as many degrees of the sign in which he is, as there are which made the house up to five degrees near the line [of the house] succeeding the angle.

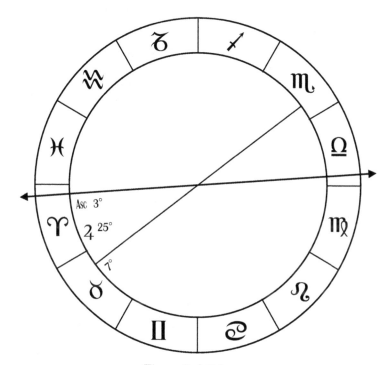

Figure 9: A Prisoner

For example, the line of the angle was the fourth degree of Aries; and the line of the one succeeding the angle was the seventh degree of Taurus. And the

---

[430] This is similar to collection of light, except that Bonatti does not generally require the two lighter planets to be joined to each other as well.

heavy planet who received the disposition was in the twenty-fifth degree of Aries: by this method [or in this way] the prisoner will not leave until the receiver of the disposition transits all of Aries. And there are five degrees left to transit [in Aries], and two degrees of Taurus: because the other five are from the succeedent, as you know, up to its twenty-seventh degree.[431]

And even look to see if the planet who is the Lord of the house in which the Moon is, were joined to the Lord of the 1st or not; which if it were joined with him, it signifies the prolongation of the incarceration, and a delay in the prisoner's departure from the prison.

And Sahl said,[432] after you have finished looking at the Lord of the Ascendant and the conjunction of the stars with him, look at the place of the significatrix[433] (which is the Moon); which if she were in a movable sign, it signifies the speed of his liberation—except for Cancer, which is slow because it is her domicile. And Aries and Libra are faster in liberation than is Capricorn. And he said, and he will not delay in the prison, and he will find many helpers there. And he said, indeed Capricorn signifies delay and worry and sorrow, and enemies will labor so that he will be kept in fetters. And he said that if she were in a fixed sign, it signifies the delay of his departure, and slower than all [the others] is Aquarius. And he said that if the Moon were in a common sign, and he were not liberated before she herself leaves the same sign, his imprisonment will be prolonged; and all the more strongly if it were the domicile of Jupiter, and he did not aspect her. And he said, if indeed she were in the domiciles of Mercury, he will find good and joy in the prison. And he said, then look at her conjunction if she were in an angle, and were joined to a planet to the left of the Ascendant, and the Lord of the Ascendant were to give testimony: it likewise signifies liberation. And he said if the Moon were cadent and were joined to some planet in an angle, it signifies the prolongation of the incarceration, unless the planet were the Lord of the 3rd or the 9th: then he will be liberated when that planet has changed [signs]. And if the Moon were cadent from an angle, and she were joined to some planet who was the Lord of some angle, the prisoner will have hope and firmly believe he will exit the prison: nor does he believe that

---

431 This passage is a little confusing. First, the text combines both written words and Arabic numerals for its ordinal numbers. Second, Bonatti (or the typesetters) seem to be conflating ordinal and cardinal numbers. But the point is this: the heavy planet must traverse 7° before it comes within 5° of the succeedent cusp: 25° Aries plus 7° equals 2° Taurus, which is within 5° of the succeedent cusp at 7° Taurus.

432 Ibid.

433 Reading *significatricis* for *significatoris*.

anything could prevent him but that he will leave; and this hope will endure with him, and it will be in him[434] until that planet to which the Moon is joined goes from the place in which he is, to the sign which was the angle when the question was made (or when the man was put into prison), and it transits again all those degrees which then made the angle to which he was closer;[435] and then he will despair and afterwards will not believe himself to be able to leave the prison. But even if he loses hope, if the Lord of the angle to which the Moon is joined is [itself] joined to another planet who is in the 3rd or the 9th, nevertheless he will leave the prison after his loss of hope, and better than was believed. And may you always have this in mind: because when the Moon is joined to the Lord of any angle (unless another helps her, as was said), it indicates delay in his departure from prison.

Afterwards, consider (if you were to see that the prisoner is going to leave the prison) if there were a malefic planet in the 4th, who did not have [the dignity of] domicile, or exaltation, or two of its minor dignities there, and in addition were direct [in motion]: it signifies misfortune that will happen to him after his departure from the prison. If it were Mars, he will be killed. If it were Saturn, he will be submerged [in water], and perhaps he will be suffocated from the submersion, or he will be beaten with sticks, or he will be thrown down [from a height], indeed that he could die from the fall, or break a part of his body, and this will happen to him according to what is signified by the sign in which the malefic was.

Which if the Lord of the 1st were then entering into combustion, so that he is already touched by the rays of the Sun, it signifies that the prisoner about whom the question is, is dead (or he is sick with a fatal disease). I say that if a malefic were in the 4th, who did not have dignity in it, [it will be] as was said.[436] If indeed the Lord of the 1st had transited combustion by one minute up to one degree,[437] it signifies that he is sick or will be sick with a dangerous disease (however there is hope of his being freed from the illness). If indeed it transits it, that is, that it is separated from the body of the Sun more than one degree up to five full degrees, it signifies that he is ill or will be ill with a very strong disease, but he will be liberated. If indeed it were separated from the degree of the Sun up until

---

[434] Reading *eo* for *ea*.

[435] I.e., until he transits the sign forming the angle closest to him in the order of signs.

[436] Bonatti's sentence ends abruptly. I do not know whether he is saying that a combust malefic will mean the same thing as a combust Lord of the 1st, or that a malefic in the 4th *in addition* to the combust Lord of the 1st will indicate it more strongly, or what.

[437] I.e., it is just entering combustion. The next sentences detail further stages of combustion.

it is elongated from him by twelve full degrees, it signifies that he is sick or can be made sick by a not-very-strong or dangerous illness. If indeed it were separated from him by more than 12° up until its appearance from under the rays of the Sun, it signifies that he was sick, but has already escaped from the illness, and is free. And may you understand the same about any absent person whose condition is unknown: because if you were to find his significator thus, you will be able to judge about him.[438]

And Sahl said[439] that by how much more you were to see the malefic (who is in an angle) is far from the degree of the Sun, by that much more will his disease be easier and he will be freed from it more quickly. If however the Lord of the 1st were then so disposed (namely joined to the Lord of the 8th or with the Lord of the 4th), the prisoner or absent person will die from the illness. If however you did not find him to be sick, but only incarcerated, and he were joined corporally to Saturn, or he were to aspect [Saturn] from the opposition or a square aspect without perfect reception, it signifies impediment to the body of the prisoner, and the diminution and detriment of his substance. If indeed Saturn were then impeded, then even if he received the significator of the prisoner, still he will impede him (but not as gravely as [he would] if he did not receive him). If however it were Mars instead of Saturn, it signifies that he will be afflicted by a powerful affliction; and that his prison will oppress [him], and it[440] will be more strengthened than usual.

And look at the significatrix (which is the Moon). Which if you were to find her impeded, contrary things and impediments will happen to him in the prison, which come from unknown causes and for reasons not discovered; and some by nature, and some by accident, even without the deeds of the guards or those who hold him in jail–unless the Lord of the house in which the Moon was, aspects her. Because if the Lord of her house were to aspect her, it takes away the malice and alleviates it.

Even look to see if Mars were in the 12th: for it signifies the death of the prisoner before he leaves the prison, and the master of the prison is the reason for his dying. The same must be said about the Tail. Likewise if Mars were the Lord of the 12th, and were joined with the significator of the prisoner, and even more strongly if their conjunction were in the 8th. If however it were Saturn instead of Mars, it signifies his death for reasons of illness.

---

438 See further material on the condition of absent people in the 8th House, Ch. I.
439 Ibid.
440 This probably refers to the illness.

On those people who are against him in prison

If however you wished to know if there are people who are working against the prisoner himself so that he will be kept in prison and not released from it (whether the reason he is incarcerated is just or not), look to see whether the Lord of the 1st and the Lord of the 7th aspect each other with an aspect of friendship (namely, by a trine or sextile aspect): because if there were someone who works against him so that he will not be freed from prison, he is moved by a just cause, and makes him to be held in fetters, lest, if he were to leave, harm would come to him from it. Whence, fearing this, he attempts this [goal] so that he does not leave, unless he is first reconciled with him; nor is it found in a bad way against him.[441] If indeed they were to aspect each other from the opposition or a square aspect, it does not seem that he who works against him (so that he is not freed from prison) acts with justice, and he goes after him with inconveniences and injustice, and seeks with the greatest perseverance so that he may be given to him in his fortune, believing himself to be extorted by him for something, announcing himself to be in the right, so that he would have to be handed over to him. And look at the Lord of the prison (which is the 4th): if the prison is not very harsh, it is tolerable. And if it were intolerable and unusual, that is, very harsh, it is signified by the 12th. If you were to find the Tail of the Dragon there, it signifies the emptying of the prison, and that he who was inquired about has left the prison–unless the Lord of the 1st or the Moon were found in it: because the Tail always signifies evacuation and decrease.

Chapter 9: Whether those things which appear in dreams signify something or not, and when they do signify something, and when they do not signify something

Sometimes things tend to appear in dreams which terrify men, and certain things which sometimes make them happy; and sometimes horrible things appear to them which are unnatural, sometimes certain ones which seem to be natural; and sometimes certain ones appear which happen afterwards just as they seemed in dreams (or almost as they seemed); sometimes nothing comes from all the things which appear, and sometimes they have some effect, and sometimes none; and sometimes men remember what they see when dreaming,

---

[441] *Nec invenitur malo modo contra ipsum.* This seems to mean that things will not be so bad for him.

and sometimes they forget them, and do not remember any of it. Whence men, not knowing the difficulty of judging about dreams, and who are unable to know what is signified by them in terms of whether they will come about afterwards, often ask of the astrologer that he may tell them the truth [about] what their dream signifies. Whence, even if we cannot respond to them in accordance with what they want, it is necessary that you tell them what can be said about the dreams.

If therefore someone were to come and pose a question to you about something he dreamt, or he were to relate the dream to you, and he wished to know whether it signified something or not (and if it were to signify something, what it signifies), [then] look at the Ascendant at the hour of the question or of the relating [of the dream], and all the other houses,[442] and verify their twelve cusps, just as best you can.

Then, since this chapter is under the heading of the 9th house, and because it signifies religion in some way, it is necessary that it be begun from the 9th house and that what can be discovered from it, be discovered. Therefore, you will look at the 9th house and give it to the dream. If perchance you were to find one of the seven planets in it, then it will signify concerning the dream.

Which if it were Saturn, it signifies that the dreamer or querent dreamt that he saw something which he greatly feared and which brought fear to him, and it was some extraordinary thing which is not truly natural, [though] it seemed to him that it was. If however it were the Tail instead of Saturn, or it were in the same place with him, again he saw something more horrible and more fearful, and[443] he saw some people who were chasing him, and he himself feared they would kill him (or something of a sort similar to this), and it hardly seemed to him that he could escape, and so on.

Then look to see in which house Capricorn were to fall, and in which Aquarius were to fall, because fear or something horrible came to him from the thing signified by that house. That is, if Capricorn or Aquarius were the 1st house, the dreamer himself, or the querent, was the reason why the fear or horrible thing came to him. And if it were the 2nd house, his substance was the reason why the horrible thing came to him. If it were the 3rd house, the horrible thing came to him because of brothers; and if he did not have brothers, the cause of the fear was one of the other things which are signified by the 3rd house. And if it were

---

442 Reading *domos* for *modos*.
443 Omitting *si*, which could be a typographical error for *sic* (but without changing the meaning of the sentence).

the 4th house, the fear came to him because of the father or uncle; which if he did not have a father or uncle, it was one of the other things which are signified by the 4th house. And if it were the 5th house, the fear happened to him because of children; which if he did not have children, it happened to him because of one of the other things which are signified by the 5th house. And if it were the 6th house, the cause of the fear was his slave or slave-girl or a client; and if he did not have a slave, it was one of the other causes which are signified by the 6th house. And if it were the 7th house, the cause of the fear was an enemy or his wife or partner, or one of the matters which are signified by the 7th house. And if it were the 8th house, it was death which terrified him, or capture, or a dead person, or something of those which are dignified by the 8th house. And if it were the 9th house, some journey was the reason for the fear, or flight, or something else of those things which are signified by the 9th house. And if it were the 10th house, it signifies that it was an authority or king or [death by] hanging, or one of the things which are signified by the 10th house. And if it were the 11th house, it signifies that it was a friend or the substance of the king or some one of those things which are signified by the 11th house. And if it were the 12th house, it signifies that it was an enemy or incarceration, or something else of those things which are signified by the 12th house.

If indeed you did not find any planet in the 9th, consider the 10th and see if one of the planets is in it, and judge according to it just as you judged with the 9th house: because whichever planet were in the 10th, will be the significator of what the dreamer dreamt, whether he dreamt something good or evil. If however there were no planet in the 10th, then look at the 1st, and if one of the planets is in it, it will be the significator. If indeed you did not find any planet in the 1st, then consider the 7th: if one of the planets were there, it will be the significator of the dream. If indeed you did not find one of the planets in it, then consider the 4th: if one of the planets [is there], it will be the significator of the dream. If indeed you did not find any of the planets there, then consider the 3rd: which if you did not find one of the planets there, you must then [see if] there is one in the 2nd, or the 5th, or the 6th, or the 8th, or the 11th, or the 12th, which all six houses signify the falsity of the dream, and that the dreams which then took place will have no effect. And it could be that the dreamer has forgotten the dream, and thus his dream disappeared and came to nothing.

If however Jupiter[444] were in the 9th at the hour of the question or the hour of the relating of the dream, then the dreamer saw something delightful, namely of those things which are of the nature of Jupiter, as are the dignities of magnates; or he saw those magnates or noble kings themselves, or those who are fit for a kingdom, or those who are placed in dignities and preferments, and things in which men rejoice and are elevated. Whence one must then see where Jupiter is, and in which house Sagittarius or Pisces fell: which if one of them (and in particular Sagittarius) were the 1st house, it seems that the dreamer himself will be the reason for the delightful thing which came to him. If the 2nd house, his substance will be the reason for the delightful thing which came to him. If the 3rd house, his brother or one of his blood-relatives will be the reason for it, or one of those things which are signified by the 3rd house. And understand the same about all the other houses, just as was said above in the things signified by Saturn: in whichever of the aforesaid six houses [Jupiter] were to be found (namely the 9th, or 10th, or 1st, or 7th, or 3rd), he will be the significator of the dream. If however he were not found in any of them, he will not have any signification concerning the dream; but he who was found in one of them (namely the first of them) will have signification concerning the dream. Because if there were one planet in the 9th and another in the 10th, he who is in the 9th is put first, and is the significator of the dream; and understand [the same] about the others.

And if Mars were the significator of the vision, so that the dreamer saw something horrible in his dream (namely of those things which are of the nature of Mars), like the shedding of blood, or he saw men mutilated; which if he did not see this, he saw burning or a battle or a conflict of arms or the mangling of beasts of prey, or perhaps the hunt itself or the consumption of raw or putrid meat; or perhaps he saw the instrument of destruction of the things of the enemy with which stones are projected to kill,[445] or something else of those things which are signified by Mars.

And if the Sun were the significator, it signifies that he has seen a king. And if the Head were with him, he dreamt he saw God or heavenly things; or he saw luminaries, namely multiple Suns or multiple Moons or

---

[444] Remember that Bonatti has already discussed Saturn above.
[445] *Cum quo proiiciuntur lapides nocumenta inferentes.*

things up for auction, or gold; or he saw himself flying or a stranger flying, or something which is of the nature of the Sun, and the like.

And if Venus were then the significatrix, it signifies that he dreamt he had sex with women (and if Saturn were to aspect then, he dreamt he misused them or misused boys in the abominable way, namely the sodomitical one), or he was with housemaids or other women, and delighted himself with them; or he saw games, singing, and drinking bouts, and odiferous things, and necklaces and beautiful clothing, especially those in which he delights; precious stones, and other things which are of the nature of Venus.

And if Mercury were then the significator, it signifies that he saw paintings or writings, and coins, and the selling of wares, or houses of prayers and people praying in them; or something else which is of the things signified by Mercury.

And if the Moon were then the significator, it signifies that he saw sailors or those sailing the sea, or that he himself boarded a ship, or saw overflowing waters in which he swam; or he saw his mother or other women, and more likely little old women than young ones.

And if the Head were in one of the aforesaid places (whether alone or with some planet), then it signifies that he saw gold and odiferous things, and delightful pleasure-gardens, and in which he delights, and the like.

And if the Tail were the significatrix, it signifies that he saw obscure smoky things, or perhaps that he saw someone consumed by fire, or he saw mist or sick people or illnesses or weeping, and a murmuring [or rushing] sound, and dead people, or the burying of the dead, or tombs, and he was very scared for this reason; or he saw verbal fights between some people, or a beheading, and the like.

And Sahl said,[446] and if the significator of the dream were in a masculine sign, it signifies that he saw a sunken place, or as though he seemed to ascend from the sunken place to a high place, and he could not complete his ascent; or

---

[446] On *Quest.*, 9th House, "The question of a vision or dream."

he dreamt he crossed over through some place breaking away beneath his feet (nor can he cross without great labor and much entanglement), and he seemed to go through a narrow place. And if the sign in which the signifying planet was, were feminine, it signifies fear; that the dreamer saw some great, elevated shore from which he seemed to fall, or another place [like] a tall rock, namely something similar from which he feared he would fall; and he saw himself sink into some fearful place, or perhaps he saw storms on the sea, or the greatest wind terrifying him. And if the significator of the dream were in Aries, Leo, or the first half of Sagittarius, it signifies that he saw an obscure mistiness, black, or someone hanged or decapitated, or burned, or skinned. And if the significator of the dream or the planet inducing fear were in Taurus, or in Virgo or Capricorn, or the last half of Sagittarius, it signifies that the dreamer or querent saw himself pierced or stoned,[447] or he saw himself besieged, and therefore he feared lest he be overpowered, or he seemed to him he fell from a bank [over water], or from some other elevated place; or he fell into a place in which he was concealed and compressed, nor did it seem he would be able to get out of it; or he went along a road or tight and narrow place. And if Saturn were the significator, or the Tail were there, it signifies that he saw the Devil or a dead person bringing fear to him. And if it were in Gemini or Libra or Aquarius, it signifies that he saw birds or winds or the climbing of trees;[448] and he saw himself or a stranger flying, or he was chased by someone and he fled, indeed so that he could be caught. And if it were in Cancer or Scorpio or Pisces, it signifies that he saw himself board a ship, and it seemed to sink under water, or he saw the shipwreck [of another ship], or the testing out of a ship, or it sinking, an excessive overflowing of waters, and that sometimes in places where there is not usually water, or perhaps he saw the sea or a flood.

And look then to see if the Moon were in a fixed sign: because then the dream will have an effect (whether it appeared for good or bad). If she were in a common sign, something will appear from it. If she were in a movable sign, it will totally disappear and it will not have any signification for him.

Then look at the significator of the vision, and the Lord of the Ascendant and the Moon; and see if they are all (or two of them) joined together; if they are all (or two) joined, or only one of them is joined with a good planet, it signifies that from one of them follows usefulness and good; and especially

---

[447] One would think that the first half of Sagittarius would indicate piercing (the human archer half), and that the last half would indicate the same as the bestial signs of Aries and Leo.

[448] *Ascensiones arborum.*

from the thing which is signified by the house whose Lord was the planet which was the significator of the dream (just as was said). If it were the Lord of the 1st, usefulness will ensue from his own person. If it were [the Lord] of the 2nd, there will be improvement in his substance. If it were [the Lord] of the 3rd, it will be in his brothers and because of brothers or from one of the reasons that are signified by the 3rd house. If it were the Lord of the 4th, it will be in his father or because of his father or uncle or one of the reasons that are signified by the 4th house. If it were the Lord of the 5th, it will be in children or one of those reasons which are signified by the 5th house. And if it were the Lord of the 6th, it will be in slaves or because of slaves or small animals or one of those reasons which are signified by the 6th house. If it were the Lord of the 7th, it will be in wives or because of them, or one of those reasons which are signified by the 7th house. If it were the Lord of the 8th, it will be because of death or some prison, or one of those reasons which are signified by the 8th house. If it were the Lord of the 9th, it will be because of a journey or religion or a religious figure, or one of those things which are signified by the 9th house. If it were the Lord of the 10th, it will be because of the king or the kingdom, [or] his own office, or one of those reasons which are signified by the 10th house. If it were the Lord of the 11th, it will be because of friends, or a reason which come to him from an unexpected thing, or one of those reasons which are signified by the 11th house. If it were the Lord of the 12th, it will be because of horses or cows, or those people who do not like him and pretend to be his friends, or one of those reasons which are signified by the 12th house.

If however the planet to which the Lord of the 1st were joined, were the significator of the vision, or either of them (whether with the conjunction of the Moon or without her conjunction) [were] malefic, say that something evil will come to him according to what is signified by the house whose Lord that malefic was, just as I said about assistance; and judge according to this method alike for the succession of the twelve houses or cusps.

Chapter 10: Concerning a bishopric or abbacy or cardinalship, or any other clerical dignity (whether in an Order or religious), the intention of the querent being whether he will get it or not

Even if it should seem disgraceful to desire religious dignities (when it should be expected to be a divine gift from above), still there are many today who indifferently desire clerical dignities like the Papacy, a cardinalship, archbishop-

ric, abbacy, a priorship, and other dignities and clerical orders (both Brothers
and others who are called secular clerics).

Whence if someone longing to get one of the aforesaid [dignities] came to
you in order to pose the question whether he will be promoted to the dignity or
office which he desires, you will first consider what sign is on the eastern line[449]
and see if its Lord or the Moon (namely both or the stronger one of them) were
joined to the Lord of the 9th (which signifies the quaesited matter). And if the
Lord of the 9th were in the 9th or aspected it, it signifies the attaining of the
quaesited matter, but with his own labor and seeking or exertion. If indeed
neither of them were joined to the Lord of the 9th, nor he with them, look then
to see if one of them (namely the Lord of the 1st or the Moon) were in the 9th;
because it signifies the attainment of what the querent intended, provided that
the one (of them) who is in the 9th is not impeded, [i.e.,] that he is not
retrograde or combust, nor do one of the malefics aspect him by a square aspect
or from the opposition without perfect reception (because that signifies the
dissolving of the matter, even after it seemed that it ought to be perfected). If
however the Lord of the 9th were in the 1st, whether the Lord of the 1st (or the
Moon) aspected him or not, whichever sort of disposition of the Lord of the 1st
or of the Moon was, or if the Lord of the 9th were joined to the Lord of the 1st–
this is if [the Lord of the 9th] is lighter than [the Lord of the 1st]–and were joined
to him, it signifies without a doubt the attainment of the quaesited matter,
without the striving of the querent. If however the Lord of the 9th were not in
the 1st, nor were he joined to the Lord of the 1st, but were joined to Jupiter, or
even the Sun by a trine aspect or a sextile, and Jupiter or the Sun were then in
the 1st, it signifies the attainment of the matter with little labor. If indeed the
conjunction were with reception and the aforesaid aspects, the quaesited thing
will happen to him from unexpected sources, namely freely, while he sits in his
own home. If however it were a square, it will not come to him easily, even if
with reception; and it will come because reception intervened, even if the
receiver which was in the 1st did not have any authority there, and even what is
more, if the Lord of the 9th were to receive the Lord of the 1st or the Moon[450]
from whatever place the reception was (even if it were from a cadent house), it
signifies the perfection of the quaesited matter. If indeed one of these [situa-
tions] which I told you did not exist, look to see if one of the planets transfers
light between the Lord of the 1st and the Lord of the 9th, because it signifies the

---

[449] I.e, the horizon, marking the degree of the Ascendant.
[450] Reading *Lunam* for *Luna*.

attainment of the quaesited matter through the hands of intermediating legates, unless he who is heavier (to whom the transferor gives the light which he accepts from the light one) commits his disposition to the other: because that signifies detriment, even after it is believed that the matter will be perfected.

If however the Lord of the 1st were not joined to the Lord of the 9th, but seeks his conjunction and is joined to him before another cuts off their light, it signifies the perfection of the matter, but with obstacles and inconvenience.

And if it were not one of these [situations] which I have told you, but there was a transfer of light by many planets from one to the other, it is possible that the matter will be perfected, but not without great complications and entanglements, and disputes, and contentions, and many words and people involved, and threats from every side,[451] and with [loud] clashing and much discord. If indeed the Lord of the 1st were joined with some malefic who did not receive him, nor were the malefic the Lord of the 9th, nor did he [the malefic] commit his own disposition to some planet who received the Lord of the 1st or the Moon, the quaesited matter will not be perfected. But if the malefic were to commit his own disposition to some benefic who was in a strong place from the Ascendant, the matter is perfected: for a conjunction of the malefics does not perfect the matter unless they receive; but if they receive, it perfects, even if not easily.

And may you know this, that whenever some planet signifies the effecting of some matter, and it itself were in an angle, it hastens the matter. If it were in a succeedent, it slows it. If however it were in a cadent, it postpones it, even if it may perfect it later (with the exception of certain things of which nothing [will be said] for the present).[452] But you should understand concerning these and similar things which are spoken of here.

Even see if some malefic were to aspect the Lord of the 1st or the Moon from a square aspect or from the opposition without reception, (unless it would then commit its disposition): it will impede [the Lord of the 1st] or the Moon, and the querent will be angered and disturbed with him who interjects himself in order to handle the matter, and he will be inimical to him, and will tell him he has not acted faithfully. If however the aspect were a trine or a sextile, he will not be angry with him, even if it does not perfect the matter.

If indeed the Lord of the 1st and the Lord of the 9th both committed their disposition to some planet (who was not impeded) from any aspect, nor did [the

---

451 *Minis hincinde.*
452 See, e.g., Ch. 11.

third planet] go retrograde before leaving the sign in which he is, it signifies the effecting of the matter. Likewise if the Moon were received from the place in which she was, and she were free from the malefics and from all other impediment, it signifies the attaining of the quaesited matter, and that the querent will have many helpers to perfect what he intends. If however the Lord of the 1st and the Lord of the 9th were[453] joined at the same time somewhere, nor were one of them impeded, and the Moon were to commit her own disposition to one of them, it signifies that the matter would be wholly perfected. If indeed [one] were impeded, it will not be perfected. And it does not only happen in this, but even in any matter when the Lord of the 1st is joined with the Lord of the quaesited matter, and the Moon commits her disposition to one of them, that the matter is wholly perfected. If however the Moon did not commit her disposition to any of them, but were received by one of the planets, and they were joined together, as was said, it still signifies the perfection of the matter (even if more slowly).

You will say the same if the Lord of the 9th is joined to the Lord of the 4th, and the Lord of the 4th is joined to the Lord of the 1st: it signifies that the quaesited matter will be perfected for the querent, and without great labor. If for example the Lord of the 1st were joined to the Lord of the 4th, and the Lord of the 4th were joined to the Lord of the 9th, it even signifies the perfection of the quaesited matter, but with the greatest labor and duress and delay and complications, indeed so that the querent will lose hope that the quaesited [matter] will be perfected for him, even if however it is perfected afterwards. After which, [if] you were to know he was going to attain the quaesited [matter], and you wished to know something else about his accidents, you will judge for him through the 9th house according to what you find. Below [you will judge] for a king through the 10th house, namely if in [the matter] he is going to attain it or not, and what ought to happen to him from it. And in all things you will follow these steps: because all these things are stated more copiously there.

Chapter 11: Regarding a letter or rumor: when it will come, and whether there will be good in the letter or not

Sometimes certain business deals arise in some locations, and about which the truth is not known by certain people, and thence they desire to know something. Perhaps they ask the astrologer, saying, "When will we have news of

---

[453] Reading *fuerint* for *fuerit*.

the business deal?" Or perhaps they are expecting that some letter will come to them from some direction: they say, "When will the letter arrive?"

Look then at the 1st and the 2nd, and see if Mercury were in the 1st or the 2nd, indeed near the end of the 2nd, so that it seeks to go to the 1st, namely that it is one or two degrees below the 2nd, going to the 1st;[454] or if the Moon were joined to the Lord of the 1st, or the Lord of the 1st were joined to the Lord of the domicile of the Moon, or [the Lord of the domicile] to [the Lord of the 1st]; or if Mercury were the Lord of the 1st, just as it seemed to Sarcinator: it signifies the arrival of the letter or of the rumor about the quaesited matter.

And [Sarcinator] said if Mercury were not in the 1st, that the letter or rumor will come in the hour in which Mercury will have entered the Ascendant.[455] And if the Moon was joined to Mercury, it will come in that hour in which they will be joined as one,[456] or in that hour in which the Moon will have come to the Ascendant.[457] And if it were not so, see if the significatrix (which is the Moon) were to receive light or nature from Mercury in the ascending degree, or from its Lord: the time of the arrival of the letter or rumor will be when the Moon has reached the Lord of the Ascendant or to the Ascendant, just as that same wise man said.

When the letter was made

And if you should wish to know how long it was since the letter was made, or the herald who was supposed to bear the rumor began his journey, look to see from what planet the Moon is separating, and see by how many degrees she is elongated from him, and see if she herself is in an angle, and likewise the planet from which she is already separated, if he is in an angle: it signifies that there are so many months. If indeed they were in succeedents, it signifies weeks. If they were in cadents, it signifies so many days. And if you wished to know when it will arrive, see to whom the Moon is joined, and how many degrees are between her and him to whom she is joined, or to whom she will first join. According to that number, put months or weeks or days by the aforesaid conditions.

---

[454] I.e., by the primary motions of the heaven.
[455] I think Bonatti means, "when Mercury will have entered the rising sign by secondary motion [i.e., through the zodiac]."
[456] I take this to mean that if they were joined by *aspect*, it will come when they are joined by *corporal conjunction*.
[457] Again, this must mean "when the Moon enters the rising sign."

Chapter 12: If at some time it is unknown to whom a letter is sent, and you want to know of whose nature it is

If at some time it is unknown to whom a letter or rumor is sent, and [there is someone] fearing to open the note or letter.[458] Look at the Ascendant in the hour of the question, and see to whom the Moon is joined: because through her conjunction with the planets, you will be able to know the nature of him to whom the letter is sent.

For if the Moon is joined to Saturn, it is sent to an old man or a Jew or a religious person dressed in black or blackish clothing, or to people of a low-class nature, like a farmer, and so on. If however she is joined to Jupiter, it is sent to a noble or a great religious figure, or to a bishop, and the like; or to a judge or a great and wealthy and famous merchant. And if she is joined to Mars, it is sent to someone leading an army, or to some bellicose soldier. And if she were joined to the Sun, it is sent to some king, or some magnate of those who are fit for a kingdom, or to another famous man. And if she were joined to Venus, it is sent to some famous or beautiful or sexually attractive woman. And if she were joined to Mercury, it is sent to someone proven in Scripture and writings, or to a judge who is not very famous, or to a merchant, or to a young man.

You can even know the [social] level of the people by the place of the Moon: because by how much she were in a greater and stronger place, by that much it signifies the greater status of the people: like if she were in exaltation and in an angle, it signifies the greater status of the people spoken of above. If in exaltation and not in an angle, it will be something lower than this. If in domicile and in an angle, it will again be less than this, even if only a little [lower]. If she were in domicile and not in an angle, it will again be something less than this. And triplicity is much lower than domicile, and bound something below triplicity, and face below bound. And if she were not in any of her dignities, it will be a low-class person.

---

[458] Bonatti uses two synonyms for letter, *epistola* and *litera* (Medieval spelling); but it is unclear what he is trying to distinguish. It is also unclear to me why someone who possesses a letter would not know to whom it is addressed.

Chapter 13: What is contained in the letter, whether good or bad

Sometimes some magnates and noble men tend to want to inflict punishments on people. But in order to avoid occasional infamy, they send another to them who might inflict the punishment, and they give these same people their own letters or messages, saying to them that they are to go to such places and to such people in order that they make preparations for people taken into servitude,[459] sometimes for another reason. And sometimes it is contained in their letters, so those carrying the letters are rewarded for those taken into servitude.[460] Sometimes they are punished by the evildoers that are brought in, so they are hanged or decapitated or mutilated, and the like.

Whence sometimes one of them, fearing that something unlucky is contained in the letter, seeks to be assured by the astrologer about what is contained in the letter, and on account of this if someone were to ask you what is contained in such a letter, look first at the hour of the question, and see where Mercury (who is the universal significator of all writings) is, and see from whom he is separating: because the letter's signification is his alone; nor does the Moon participate with him in this because only very rarely does it happen to her.[461] But because she signifies rumors and especially unwritten ones, writings are given to Mercury. Which if he is separating from a benefic, good is contained in the letter; and that he who does it will be rewarded for his service. If indeed he were separating from a malefic, evil is contained in the letter.

Then see if Mercury (or the malefic from which he is separating) were in the Ascendant: it signifies the harming of the person of the querent. If it were in the 2nd, it signifies detriment in his substance. If it were in the 3rd house, it signifies the harming of the brother, or of those things signified by the 3rd house, and so on with the rest. And if it were in the 4th, it signifies the harming of an older kinsman, etc. And if it were in the 5th, it signifies the harming of the child, etc. If it were in the 6th it signifies the harming of a slave, etc. And if it were in the 7th, it signifies the harming of the wife, etc. And if in the 8th, it does not have a certain signification (except that sometimes it can signify the substance of the dead), nor in the 9th or even in the 10th. But if it were in the 11th it signifies the

---

[459] *Ut provideant eis aliquando pro servitiis collatis.* I am unclear about this sentence; from the context, perhaps it means that the enforcers would bring those punished back for indentured servitude of some sort.

[460] *Ut portantes epistolas illas remunerentur de servitiis collatis.*

[461] *Quod rarissime accidit ei.* Perhaps Bonatti means that she rarely signifies letters–see below, where she participates in *responses* to letters.

harming of the friend, *etc.* And if it were in the 12th, it signifies the taking away of horses and cows.

And if the Moon were then impeded, and she were in Aries, it signifies his decapitation or dismemberment. And if she were in Taurus, it signifies his beheading, and especially she were joined to Mars. And if she were in Gemini, it signifies the cutting off of his hands. And if she were in Cancer or Leo or Virgo or Libra, it signifies his being beaten. If she were in Scorpio, it signifies detriment to his genitals. And if she were in Sagittarius or Capricorn or Aquarius, it signifies his incarceration. And if she were in Pisces, it signifies the cutting off of his feet. If indeed the Moon were free and safe from impediments, it will be deliverance from all the things signified by the house[462] in which she was.

What the response to a letter is

And if the letter were for something other than the aforesaid things, so that it is expected there will be a response to it, and you wished to know whether his response would come to be pleasing to the sender, then you would see if Mercury or the Moon (because here the Moon has a place) were both joined to benefics: the response to the letter will be pleasing to the sender. If indeed one of them were joined to benefics and the other not, the response will be partly [so], but will not be to his liking. If however both were void in course, it will not be responded to. Indeed it seemed to Sahl that you ought to judge the response to the letter through the second conjunction more so than the first.[463]

Whether the letter is sealed or not

And if you did not know the truth of some letter which is desired, and thence you wished to know something, [i.e.,] whether it has been written or not,[464] look at the Moon: which if she were in the conjunction of Mercury, so that she is distant from him by 1° or less, it signifies that the letter has already

---

[462] This could mean either the topical house or the type of sign, since Bonatti has now discussed both.

[463] Sahl says: "And if a letter were written, and you wished to know what his response would be, look at this from the second conjunction, because the first conjunction is the significator of that which preceeded concerning the letter; and the second conjunction is the significator of the response to the same letter" (*On Quest.*, Concluding Questions, "A question: if you long to know what would be in the response to a letter"). The idea seems to be that we ought to look to the aspect being made by the Moon just after the next one.

[464] *Impetrata. Impetro* can mean "obtain" or "complete." From the context I take it Bonatti is referring to whether or not written orders have actually been given, hence my translation of "written" throughout this paragraph.

been written, but is not sealed; however, it will be sealed. If however the Moon were then separated from Mercury by 59' or less, it signifies that the letter is already sealed. (If indeed you should find Mercury joined to the Sun, or separated from him up to the limit of 3° or less, it signifies it has been written, and that it will be sealed.) But if she has transited him by 3°, it neither will be sealed nor has been written.[465]

From whom a letter may come or to whom it may be sent

And if you wished to know from whom a letter comes (or [to whom] it is sent), look at Mercury. Which if you were to find him having transited the Sun or the Lord of the 10th, or the 10th itself, by 15' or less, it signifies that the letter will come from the king or from a great noble, namely from those who are fit for a kingdom. If however Mercury were joined[466] to some one of the aforesaid, it signifies the letter is sent to the aforesaid king or great noble.

Chapter 14: On rumors–whether they are true or not, and when they are wholly true, and when they are wholly false, and when they are partly true and partly false

It seemed to certain people that a chapter on rumors ought to be put within the chapter on the 12th house, and they had this reasoning [for it]: namely, that rumors, as often found, are other than they show themselves to be; and when it is believed there is truth in them, lies are more likely discovered, even if they are sometimes true. But to me it seems that a chapter on rumors ought to be put under the 9th house, because they often come from distant regions, and it is not known immediately when they are heard whether it is as they show themselves to be, or not. And this signifies that the arrival of either [kind of] news was expected, which was conveyed from a place that is likened in a certain way to a

---

[465] This paragraph is a version of Sahl (*On Quest.*, "A question whether a letter is sealed or not"), with interpolations by Bonatti. Sahl says: "And if you were asked about a letter, whether it is sealed or not, look at the Moon. If she were joined to Mercury, say it will be signed; and if she were separated from him, and were to transit him by a quantity of approximately two degrees, and she did not transit him through a bound, say that it is already sealed. And if you were to find Mercury with the Sun, and they both were to aspect the Ascendant, say it will be signed–lacking this, not." Bonatti's addition at the end that if the Moon has transited Mercury by 3° it is neither signed nor will be delivered, must be his way of emphasizing that the Moon is too far away to show the perfecting of the matter.
[466] I.e., by application.

journey and something far removed.[467] You however may take which[ever] of these you wish.

Whence, when you are asked concerning some rumor whether it is true or false, or you hear the rumor itself and by yourself you wish to inquire into its truth, look at the [Lord of the] Ascendant at the hour of the question (or of the announcing of the rumor), or the Moon. And see which of them is stronger, and work with that. For the stronger is the one who is in an angle, free from the malefics. If however neither of them were in the angles, see if the Ascendant (and the other angles) were a fixed sign: because if it were so, it signifies the truth of the rumor, unless the Lord of the 1st or the Moon or both of them were joined with Saturn or Mars without reception, or were with the Tail.

Then consider what kind of Ascendant it is. If Jupiter or the Sun or Venus or the Head of the Dragon were there, it signifies the truth of the rumors. If however none of them were in the 1st, consider the 3rd. And if you did not find any in the 3rd, consider the 5th. And if you did not find any in the 5th, consider the 9th. And if you were to find one of the aforesaid planets (which are truth-bearing) in one of these places, it signifies the truth of the rumors, even if it is solitary,[468] provided that it is not impeded. However, the Sun, because of his clarity, does not have so much signification over rumors, as do the other benefics. For he shows certitude, which is not easily discovered in rumors. If indeed you did not find one of the stated planets in one of the aforesaid places, it is not certain whether the rumors are true or not.

See if you were to find Saturn or Mars in one of the aforesaid places, or the Tail: it signifies the falseness of the rumors, even if they are solitary.[469] Moreover, consider just as I said, if the Lord of the 1st were in an angle, free from the malefics, and were not joined with a planet who is cadent from an angle, it signifies the truth of the rumors. And if it were not [the case] with regard to the Lord of the 1st as I told you, you will consider the Moon by means of the conditions laid out: which if you were find her in an angle, free, nor were she joined to a planet cadent from an angle, it signifies the truth of the rumors; and stronger than this [is] if she were received. Likewise if the Lord of the 1st were in a succeedent to an angle, or even in a cadent house and joined to some planet which is in an angle; and if it were a benefic, the rumors will be true. If indeed the planet (to whom the Lord of the 1st is joined) were a malefic, nor were it

---

[467] *Et istud significat quod iterum alter eventus novus expectaretur qui de loco apporteretur quod assimulatur quodammodo itineri & longae remotioni.* My translation is something of a paraphrase.

[468] This must mean being either void in course or feral.

[469] See previous note.

retrograde or combust, and it received him, the rumors will be true. If he did not receive [the Lord of the 1st], the rumors will be partly true, but not wholly.

You may say the same about the significatrix [the Moon] as about the Lord of the 1st: which if she were cadent from an angle, and were joined to a planet in [that] aforesaid angle, the rumors themselves will be true. If however the malefic did not receive the Lord of the 1st or the Moon, the rumors themselves will be lies. If indeed the benefic planet who was in an angle (to whom the Lord of the 1st is joined, or who is joined to him) were to receive him, nor were he then impeded, you should then know all the rumors to be wholly true; nor must you ask nor consider anything else except for this alone, and this especially and in particular: if the planet to whom the Lord of the 1st is joined, were in the 10th: because then they will be truthful in all of their parts, without any diminution, but rather perhaps it could be there will be more to the rumors than may then be said. You may understand the same about the Moon which I told you about the Lord of the 1st.

You will even see if the Lord of the 1st or the Moon were joined to any planet which is in an angle and were to commit its own disposition to it:[470] it signifies the truth of the rumors. And see if the planet (to whom the Lord of the 1st or the Moon commits its own disposition) were in the 1st: the rumors had already been heard, and something was said about them in the land before you had heard them, or [before] the question was made to you concerning whether they were true or not. And if it were in the 4th, one had heard nothing about the rumors in the land; on the contrary they were hidden up until now. And if it were in the 7th, the rumors were already made known as though publicly. And if it were in the 10th, even if perhaps you had not heard the rumors, they already will have been divulged publicly; and the truth is known about them among men of that area.

When the rumors are not true

If indeed the Lord of the 1st or the Moon were in an angle, and were joined to a planet who is cadent from an angle, the rumors will be false, unless the cadent one is a benefic and receives [the Lord of the 1st] or the Moon; but something was said about them, so that it seems to be so. If indeed it were a benefic, and it received [the Lord of the 1st] or the Moon, it signifies the truth or the rumors, even if they are not wholly true, just as was said. And if the cadent

---

470 I.e., that either the Lord of the 1st or the Moon commits disposition to the other angular planet, and not the other way around.

planet did not receive the Lord of the 1st or the Moon, or he were a malefic
(whether he received the Lord of the 1st or the Moon, or not), the rumors will
be false, even if something has been said about them, and nothing concerning
them reached [the level of] action. If however the Lord of the 1st or the Moon
were joined to a malefic planet [who] himself is impeded, it signifies that the
rumors are false, and that the rumors will be suppressed quickly. But if the
malefic were not impeded, and it received the Lord of the first or the Moon, it
signifies some truth to the rumors, even if they are not wholly true.

Nevertheless, Sahl said[471] that you ought to look at the Lord of the Ascendant and the Moon, and see which of them is stronger, and you ought to judge
about the matter of the rumors through it. Whence his intention was not to give
force except to one of them. But to me it seems that if we can use both of them
(namely the Lord of the 1st and the Moon), then let us do so. However, it does
not seem to me that we should reject his steps.

You ought even to see whether the angles are movable signs, because by how
much they are,[472] the rumors are signified to be false. For just as when the
angles are fixed signs they signify the truth of the rumors; and more accurately
than this the rumors will be lies if the Lord of the 1st or the Moon were joined
with one of the malefics by conjunction or aspect, unless perhaps it[473] is
received by perfect reception (namely, by domicile or exaltation); but when this
[is so], there will be little truth in the rumors. But if the malefic were retrograde,
the rumors will be false, whether it or the Lord of the 1st or the Moon were in
an angle or outside an angle, which[ever] one of them were joined with it,
whether the angles were fixed signs or not, whether he were received or not;
however the rumors will be false.

And Sahl said[474] that if the Moon were impeded in an angle, and were joined
to some malefic planet who did not receive her, the rumors will be false. And
see if the Lord of the 1st or the Moon (or one of them) were joined to some
impeded planet (namely, retrograde or combust) which did not receive him [or
her]: it signifies the falsity of the rumors, even if it is said by everyone as a whole
that the rumors are true, and that it is believed to be so by everyone.

---

[471] On Quest., Concluding Questions, "A question about rumors: whether they are true or false."
[472] I.e., because quadrant house cusps may involve intercepted signs or multiple cusps on one sign.
[473] In this section it is a bit difficult to know whether these rules apply to the malefic, the Lord of the 1st, and the Moon indifferently, or whether they are meant to apply especially to the malefic. I suspect it is the malefic.
[474] Ibid.

Nevertheless, you must see or consider of whose nature are the rumors which you hear, or by whom the question is posed to you. For if they are about things which are signified and come to be through iron and fire, and bloodshed, and the cutting of roads, and the like, and Mars were there, it is said that he signifies it. And if it were about the tearing down of houses or castles or cities, and the like, and the Tail were there, it signifies the rumors to be such.[475] And if it were about submersion or about a fall from a height, and Saturn [were there] or even the Tail, it signifies the same. And you may understand the same about the things signified by any planet; and all the more so if signs agreeing with their natures are in the houses.

---

[475] *Aliquid.*

ON THE TENTH HOUSE

Chapter 1: Concerning a kingdom, or empire, or leadership position,[476] or escortship,[477] or any other lay dignity, whence the querent has hope or money to attain it: whether he will attain what he intends, or not

Men sometimes tend to desire dignities (namely kingdoms, or generalships, or escortships, or other lay dignities or offices or estate-stewardship[478]). Whence they ask of an astrologer whether they are going to get what they intend, or not. And if some question were made to you about any of the aforesaid, whether it is an empire or kingdom or generalship or authority, or judgeship, or senatorship, or whatever other office or any dignity, whether it is great or small, even if it is the custody of some castle or some city gate or castle gate–provided that it comes through some official channel–or estate-stewardship, the 1st is given to the querent, [and] the 10th is given to the kingdom or office or dignity or estate-stewardship.

Look then at the Lord of the 1st and the Moon to see if both (or only one of them) were joined either to the Sun or to the Lord of the 10th (who signifies the dignity or office), and he (namely the Lord of the 10th) were to aspect the 10th or was in it: it signifies that the querent will have what he intends, but not freely. Rather, he will have to labor and exert himself and seek by all means he can in this, in order to attain the quaesited matter. If however neither of them were joined to the Lord of the 10th, look to see if the Lord of the 1st or the Moon were in the 10th: he will attain what he intends, so long as neither the Lord of the 1st or the Moon are impeded (namely that they are not combust, nor is he retrograde, nor do the malefic planets aspect him [or her] from the opposition or a square aspect without reception). Because then it signifies the dissolution of the thing, even if it had seemed in order and that it ought to be perfected. If however the Lord of the 10th were in the 1st, whether the Lord of the 1st or the Moon aspected him or not (of whichever sort the Lord of the 1st were), or the Lord of the 10th house were joined to the Lord of the 1st (indeed so that he goes

---

[476] *Ducatus* can refer to generalships; also to princes, hence the English "duchy."

[477] *Comitatu*, again a position of attendance (particularly of the military sort) upon a lord.

[478] *Baylia*. A *baylia* (*bail, bayle*; cf. Eng. "bailiff," "bailey") was originally a managerial or administration over a manorial estate on behalf of its lord. This is related to the Fr. *Baillistre*, a man who acts as an administrative steward of an underage vassal's affairs. They were sometimes paid by revenues from the estates they managed, but later in the medieval period they became salaried officials.

to his conjunction, that is, if the Lord of the 10th is lighter), without a doubt it signifies the attaining of the empire or kingdom or magistracy or lay dignity or office or estate-stewardship, without any of his own striving or labor or any inconvenience. And if the Lord of the 10th were not in the 1st, nor were he joined to the Lord of the 1st, but he were joined to Jupiter or Venus or the Sun by an aspect, except for the opposition of the Sun (because with the others he is not impeded by the opposition as he is with the Sun), and the one to whom he (namely the Lord of the 10th) is joined were in the 1st, he will attain the quaesited thing with ease. If indeed he were joined to Mars or Saturn, and they were in the 1st, and the Ascendant were one of the their domiciles or exaltations, and they were oriental and direct, nor were one of them opposed to the other, it signifies the attainment of the quaesited matter, even if with complications and striving or inconvenience; but with little inconvenience or nearly none.

However, it seemed to Māshā'allāh[479] that whether or not the malefic received, that the matter would be perfected, and that if the aspect were a trine or sextile, and he who were in the 1st house were a benefic, the quaesited will come to him while he is in his own house, without any striving. If it were a square or opposition, or it were a malefic and it were a trine or sextile, it will even come to him with ease. If it were an opposition, and it were a malefic, it will come to him, even if with duress and delay; and all of this, whether the planet which was in the 1st (joined to the Lord of the 10th) had testimony in the 1st or not. And Māshā'allāh said again,[480] that if the Lord of the 10th were receiving the Lord of the 1st or the Moon, from whatever place the reception was, that the matter would perfect with goodness and stability and usefulness and wealth.

And if it were not one of these [situations] which I told you, see if there is some planet who transfers light between the Lord of the 1st and the Lord of the 10th: because if it were so, it signifies the attaining of the quaesited thing, but not through himself; but it is necessary that someone else interpose himself so as to manage the matter so that it will be perfected; and he will perfect it unless he who receives the disposition of the other were joined then to another to whom he himself committed disposition: because that signifies the dissolution of the thing after it is thought to be arranged; but if he did not commit his disposition to another, nor were he retrograde or combust, it signifies the attainment of the quaesited thing. Likewise if the Lord of the 10th does not seek the conjunction of the Lord of the 1st, but the Lord of the 1st seeks the conjunction of the Lord

---

[479] *OR*, Ch. 8.
[480] *OR*, Ch. 8.

of the 10th, and is joined to him before another planet may cut off their conjunction: the matter will come to pass, but not without the querent's striving, and obstacles and inconvenience. Likewise if the Lord of the 10th is not joined to the Lord of the 1st nor he to him; nor were one of them joined to some benefic, but joined to some malefic; and that malefic is joined to another malefic, and the other malefic is joined to some benefic, and the benefic is joined to the Lord of the 10th (if the conjunction of the first malefic were with the Lord of the 1st), or the last planet is joined to the Lord of the 1st (if the first conjunction were with the Lord of the 10th): it signifies the attainment of the quaesited thing, even with many and diverse interpositions of diverse people. You could know the significations of the persons through the houses whose Lords were those planets though whom the conjunction comes to be, from conjunction to conjunction, until the conjunction arrives at the significator of the quaesited matter, or to the Lord of the 1st or the 10th, as was said, [even] if the conjunction came to be from that planet all the way through the seven planets. And Māshā'allāh said that it would be the same with conjunction by body.[481]

And he said[482] that if there were no conjunction between the Lord of the Midheaven and the Lord of the Ascendant or the Moon, nor were there a planet transferring the light between them, that you ought to see who is stronger–the Lord of the Ascendant or the Moon–and work with the stronger of them. And if [the stronger] is not joined to the Lord of the Midheaven, but is joined to another (provided that the stronger is in an angle or in a strong place), that the quaesited matter will be perfected, whether or not it receives the Lord of the Ascendant or the Moon. And he said, that if he to whom the Lord of the Ascendant (or the Moon) is joined were a malefic, and received him [or her], the matter would be perfected. If however he were a malefic, and he were not the Lord of the Midheaven, nor did he receive the Lord of the Ascendant, nor did the malefic commit his own disposition to another planet, then the matter would not be perfected: because the malefic destroys the matter. But if the malefic did commit his own disposition to another malefic, and the other malefic received the Lord of the Ascendant or the Moon, the quaesited thing will be perfected. But if the malefic committed his disposition to a benefic which was in a strong place, the matter will be perfected.

---

481 *Ibid.*
482 *Ibid.*

Moreover, see if one of the aforesaid planets were in the 1st, or were in the 10th (if it were a benefic): it signifies the perfection of the matter, whether it receives or not, and that the querent will gain wealth and acquire substance because of it. If however it were a malefic and received the Lord of the 1st or the Moon, the matter will be perfected; if indeed it did not receive, it will not be perfected. If however the 10th house were the domicile or exaltation of that malefic planet, and the malefic itself were in it, it will even perfect the matter, whether or not the malefic receives the Lord of the 1st or the Moon, just as if a benefic were in the 10th, and the Lord of the 1st or the Moon were to aspect it: because then the matter is perfected, whether or not the benefic receives the Lord of the 1st or the Moon, [whether] it did or did not have dignity in the 10th. And you ought to know this: because whenever a planetary significator of any matter is in an angle, it hastens the effecting of the thing; in a succeedent it slows, in a cadent it postpones (even if the matter is ultimately perfected).

And see if a malefic were to aspect the Lord of the Ascendant or the Moon from the opposition or from a square aspect without reception: because unless he then committed his own disposition to the other, it impedes him and the querent is disturbed by him who interposed himself to manage the matter, and does not believe him to have acted faithfully; and it is possible that they are made enemies by it. And if it were to aspect from a trine or sextile aspect, he will not be angry with him, nor make charges against him, even if he did not perfect the matter. And if the Lord of the 1st and the Lord of the 10th committed their own dispositions[483] to some planet from any aspect (whether with reception or without reception; whether it was a benefic or a malefic), and it were not retrograde nor combust nor cadent, nor left the sign in which he is before the conjunction of the two Lords (namely the Lord of the 1st and the Lord of the 10th) with him is perfected, and the Moon were joined to the Lord of the 1st or the Lord of the 10th, the querent will attain the quaesited thing.[484] But if there were a collection of light or of the disposition of the Lord of the 1st and the Lord of the 10th, as I said, nor did the Moon aspect either of those two, but she aspected another who received her by domicile or exaltation, or by two other [lesser] dignities, nor were she otherwise impeded (that is, that she were free from fall and combustion, nor were besieged by the malefics, nor in their opposition or square aspect without reception), it signifies the attainment of the

---

[483] Reading the plural *commisierunt...dispositiones suas* for the singular *commisierit...dispositionem suam*.
[484] In other words, Bonatti is speaking of a collection of the light along with an aspect from the Moon.

quaesited thing, and that many people will assist the querent, so that the matter he seeks will be perfected.

However, pretty much all of those wise in the judgments of the stars seem to be in agreement that when the Lord of the 1st and the Lord of the quaesited thing are joined together, and the Moon were to commit disposition to one of them, that the quaesited matter is be wholly perfected. If however she did not commit disposition to any of them, but the Moon were joined to a planet not receiving her, and that planet were to aspect the house of the quaesited matter, or were to aspect the 1st house [domicile?], it signifies that the querent will attain part of those things he sought, even if not wholly (if the thing can be divided into parts).

And Sahl said,[485] if the Lord of the Ascendant were to receive the disposition of the Moon, it will be easier to seek a kingdom–that is, it will be had more easily. If however he to whom the Moon (or the Lord of the 1st) commits her disposition were impeded (namely that he is retrograde or combust or cadent or besieged by the two malefics, or in their opposition or square aspect without reception), it signifies that the matter will not be perfected. Then look to see if the Lord of the 1st house is joined to the Lord of the 4th house, and the Lord of the 4th house is joined to the Lord of the 1st house: the quaesited matter will be perfected for him who asks, and without great labor. If however the Lord of the 1st were joined to the Lord of the 4th house, and again the Lord of the 4th house were joined to the Lord of the 10th house, the quaesited matter will be perfected for the querent–but not without so much labor and so much duress, and complication and delay, that the querent will despair that he will not be able to perfect what he intends; ultimately however, it will be perfected for him.

Where his magistracy will be

After you were to see that the querent is going to attain the dignity or office or magistracy which he intends, look at the Lord of the 1st, and see if he were in his own domicile: and if it is so, then you will know that he will attain the magistracy or the dignity in the land in which he lives. And if he were in his own exaltation, he will attain a magistracy to which other magistracies and other offices are subordinated, and the dignity will contain within it or below it some other dignities, whether he is going to attain it in his own land, or in a foreign one; and it does not seem it ought to be a great distance from his own land. If

---

[485] Referring perhaps to *On Quest.*, 10th House, "Concerning a kingdom in which someone has trust, if he will get it or not."

however it were in its own triplicity, it seems that he is going to attain a great office or a magistracy outside of the land in which he lives, and far from it, perhaps more than two years.[486] And if it were in its own bound, he will not achieve a great office, but rather it will be less than the aforesaid; and perhaps that it will come to him because of a blood relationship which exists between him and the one to whom it is committed to give the office (or perhaps that some blood relation of his nominated him to the one to whom it is committed to give the office), and because of this he will be chosen and placed over the kingdom or office; or perhaps that some blood relation will be chosen to some office, and will commit it to him. And if it were in its own face, it will come to him because of his profession or his wisdom; and the office will be lower than what was written above. If however it did not have dignity in the place in which it is, dignity will be given to him in a land in which few or almost nobody knew him, and the office or dignity or estate-stewardship will be far below what was written.

And if the Lord of the 1st and the Lord of the 10th were the same planet (which can happen with Jupiter and Mercury), and it were received by some planet somewhere, and the Moon were joined to him from any of the angles, it signifies the attainment of the quaesited matter. If however the Moon were not joined to the Lord of the 1st, but were joined to another who receives her, and the Lord of the 1st himself were likewise received, and neither of them were cadent from the angle, nor from the Ascendant, the querent will attain part of the things which he seeks (if it were capable of being divided), but not wholly.

When he will not attain the quaesited

If indeed the Moon were impeded, and the Lord of the 1st were not received, nor were either of them in the house of the quaesited matter, the querent will not attain what he sought; and it seems that the reason why he would not attain it is because he seeks something that is not appropriate for him. If however the Lord of the 1st or the Moon did not aspect the Lord of the 10th, nor did the Lord of the 10th aspect one of them, and the angles were fixed signs, nor were it one of the aforesaid aspects signifying the effecting of the matter, look then to see where the Sun is and where Venus is, and see if both aspect the 10th, and if both are received; because if it were so, it signifies the effecting of the matter, and that the querent will acquire the kingdom or magistracy in which he has

---

[486] Bonatti seems to mean that the office will be both far away, *and* last perhaps more than two years.

confidence;[487] and it will be useful and lucrative for him, and he will acquire much money from it. If however they were not both received, but only one of them, see if the Moon then aspected the one which was not received: the quaesited matter will be perfected, because the Moon commits her own disposition and strength to him to whom she is joined. Look even at the Moon: which if she were to aspect the degree of the 10th house, or even if the Lord of the 1st himself were to aspect the degree of the 10th house, or one of them were in it, or the Lord of the 10th house were in the degree of the Ascendant itself, it signifies that his selection is already accomplished, and the rumor of his selection will reach him quickly.

And Māshā'allāh[488] and Sahl[489] said that if the Moon were joined to the light of the Lord of the Midheaven, or transited above him, namely so that she were north of him [in latitude] while she transits through his rays, or were joined to his body, and she aspected the Midheaven, he will attain [it]; and if the Lord of the domicile in which the Moon is, were to receive her, and both aspected the 10th, he will attain the quaesited. And if the Moon were in any sign in which the light of any planet was, but will not be joined to its body before she exits the sign in which she is,[490] the matter will not be perfected unless the Lord of the 1st and the Lord of the 10th (or either [Lord of the] quaesited matter) were each in places in which they have dignity, and were to aspect the 10th or the place of the quaesited thing.

And Sahl said[491] that a defective condition[492] of the Moon and of the Lord of the Midheaven signifies the diminution of the matter in its work; and worse than that is if the receiver of the Moon's disposition were impeded: because then it signifies the detriment of its work. And he said if the Moon were joined to the Lord of the Ascendant or to the Lord of the Midheaven, he will be aided in its effect. And if the receiver (and the Lord of the Midheaven) were to

---

[487] *Fiduciam.* Part of the confidence may lie in having bid money for the office: *fiducia* can also mean a deposit.
[488] Bonatti may be referring to *On Reception*, Chap. 8, where Māshā'allāh refers to either the Lord of the Ascendant or the Moon projecting its rays "upon" or "above" (*super*) another planet. But neither Māshā'allāh nor Sahl (see following footnote) refers specifically to her being in northern latitude; and the projection of rays above or upon a planet is not used by Māshā'allāh to suggest this (so far as I have seen).
[489] *On Quest.*, 10th House, "A question concerning any matter, if it he will attain it or not."
[490] In other words, if she is void in course.
[491] *Ibid.*
[492] *Vitium.*

push[493] their own strength and disposition to the planet who [a] received them and who [b] had strength in its own place and [that] of the matter, and who [c] did not aspect the Midheaven,[494] the matter will not be perfected in the same way in which it is sought. And he said that when the significator is inimical to its own house, it signifies duress and complications in striving for the matter. And enmity of his house in this is by cadence,[495] like if in the 12th [domicile] from his domicile, or in the 2nd or in the 6th or in the 8th. And if he (namely the Lord of the quaesited thing) were to aspect him from the 7th, it signifies that he will not attain the quaesited, but it will not prohibit it totally so that it does not come to be, but rather it is possible that the quaesited is perfected (but if it were perfected it will be with a lawsuit and controversy and contention).

Chapter 2: Whether he will be praised or condemned on the occasion of his rule or office or magistracy

After you have ascertained that the querent is going to have a kingdom, or something else which he intends to attain, and you wished to know what is going to befall him in his rule or office or magistracy, look at the Lord of the 1st and his place, and see how he is disposed: because he signifies what happens to the querent from his rule or magistracy.

If however you were to find the Lord of the 1st in the 10th, not far from the degree of the 10th house, by more than 3° ahead of it, or up to more than 12° behind it, or if an unimpeded benefic were there, or were to aspect the place (namely the 10th) by 3° ahead and 5° behind, or up to more than 7°.[496] May you understand the same if it were an unimpeded benefic,[497] or it aspected (as was said concerning the 10th; and may you understand about the 11th), it signifies that he will acquire honor and praise from the office or rule (provided that it is not impeded in a bad way by the aforesaid impediments), and especially if the Head of the Dragon were there; but if the Tail were there, it will destroy one-third of the honor. If however it were in the 11th, it will be less than that; still he will finish his rule well, and good will be said about him. If however it were in

---

[493] *Pulsaverit.* Sahl is referring to a version of what Abū Ma'shar later calls "pushing virtue" or "pushing management" (also known as "pushing disposition"), for which Bonatti uses the term *percussio* in Tr. 5 (4th Consideration).

[494] I have inserted brackets for ease of comprehension.

[495] *Casu.*

[496] I believe that by "ahead of," Bonatti means "in an earlier degree than the cusp's"; by "behind," he means "in a later degree than the cusp's." See my Introduction.

[497] Does he mean "malefic"?

the first, he will be praised and good will be said about him; however, certain people will try to say bad things, but they will not make their malice public. If indeed it were in other places, well-disposed, he will leave his rule or office, not so much with great honor, nor with condemnation, but just as regents step down together from their regencies,[498] provided that badly disposed malefics are not in the aforesaid places. If however there were a badly disposed malefic in the 1st or in the 10th who did not have dignity there, or [who] aspected (as was said concerning the 10th and the 1st), and especially if it were retrograde or in its own fall (and stronger than this, if the Head of the Dragon were there), it signifies that the querent will be condemned because of it. And if the Lord of the 4th were to aspect him (and [the Lord of the 4th] were a malefic) from a square aspect or the opposition, it signifies that he will be captured and detained because of it, [but] without being put into prison. And if the Lord of the 12th were to aspect him by the aforesaid conditions, he will be imprisoned. And even if the Lord of the 8th were to aspect him through the method stated above, he will be confined in prison, and will fear he will die because of it. And if the Tail of the Dragon were there, it subtracts one-third of the condemnation.

And if a benefic were in the 2nd, free, it signifies that he will acquire substance because of it, and from it will follow success and good; or [if] the benefics were to aspect (as was said concerning the other houses), and better than that if the Part of Fortune were there (and if it were elsewhere it likewise signifies good and wealth, and it increases it); if indeed it were badly disposed, it signifies evil and impediment. And if a malefic were there, or aspected from a square aspect or the opposition, it signifies the dispersion of substance and its diminution.

(And may you always have this in your mind, because whenever the Head is in any house which signifies good, he will always increase it by one-third. And whenever the Tail is in any house which signifies good, it will always take away one-third of the good. And whenever it is in some house which signifies evil, it always diminishes one-third of the evil, just as if the Head were in some house which signifies evil, it will increase it by one-third.)

---

[498] Unsure about the exact meaning, because of the generality of the terms *rector, regimen*, and *communiter* can mean "generally" or "together."

And if a benefic were in the 3rd (or were to aspect it), free, it signifies good for the brothers of the querent, and to him from his brothers (if he were to have brothers). If a malefic were there, or were to aspect by a square or opposition, it signifies evil and detriment.

And a benefic were in the 4th, free, or aspected it, it signifies that the end of his administration will be good and praiseworthy. And if a malefic were there or were to aspect it, it signifies that the end will be evil and shameful.

And if a benefic were in the 5th or aspected as was said, it signifies good and fortune from children or because of children, and that things will go well for them (if he has children). And if a malefic were there, or were to aspect, it signifies the contrary, as was said about the others.

And if a benefic were in the 6th or aspected it, it signifies that it will go well for him from slaves and attendants, and for them and the attendants. If however a malefic were there or were to aspect it, it signifies the contrary.

If however a benefic were in the 7th, or aspected it, it signifies that it will go well for those who are under him in his rule, and that it will go well for his scribes; and that his enemies will be of good opinion concerning him. And if a malefic were there or were to aspect it, it signifies the contrary of what I said.

And if a benefic were in the 8th, or aspected it, it signifies that the goods of those whom he has to rule will be increased, and will grow and be amplified. And if a malefic were there or were to aspect it, it signifies that they will suffer detriment and diminution.

And if a benefic were in the 9th or aspected it, it signifies that the regent who came before him was to be honored and revered, and that things turned out well for him in his own regency. And if a malefic were there, or were to aspect it, it signifies the contrary of what I said.

And if a benefic were in the 10th, or a malefic were there, it will be as was said above concerning the 10th house.

And if a malefic were in the 11th or aspected it, it signifies that it will go well for him in his regency or magistracy, and that it will go well for him in his rule or office, and that he will be honored and revered, and things will go well for him in it. And if a malefic were there or aspected it, it signifies the contrary of what I said.

And if a benefic were in the 12th, or aspected it, it signifies that it will go well for him with horses, mules, cows, donkeys, and camels; and that no one will scheme to his detriment. And if a malefic were there, it signifies that it will go contrary for him in the things I said; and especially if Mars were there (because then it signifies treachery).

And may you always understand when I say that if a malefic were in such a place, it signifies evil, unless he has dignity there (namely domicile or exaltation or two of the other dignities).

Chapter 3: Again on the same subject, and its end

Again consider if you were to find the Lord of the 1st in a good place (namely if it were in the 10th or 11th or 1st or 5th), well disposed, not impeded (whether it were received or not, whether it were with the Part of Fortune or not), because it likewise signifies a good end. If however it were in the 2nd or 3rd or 9th or 7th or even in the 4th (but it remains more weakly in the 4th than in one of the aforesaid places), and well disposed, and in no other way impeded, his end will be less than this, but it will not be abhorrent nor capable of being condemned. If however it were impeded in one of the aforesaid five places, it signifies impediment and evil. If however it were in the 6th or in the 8th or in the 12th, it signifies that he will be deposed shamefully from his rule or magistracy, and with opprobrium and disgrace. But in the 6th and the 12th it signifies more severe disgrace than in the 8th, unless it is received: because then it signifies that a junior regent[499] will impede him, and rise up against him in his condemnation, and all the more strongly if the Head were there. And if the Tail were there, it

---

[499] *Secundus rector.*

will be weaker; if however [the Lord of the 1st] were received he will not be impeded; and if he were impeded, he will be freed from the impediment without great obstacles or complications. And if it were not received, and it were in the aforesaid three places, and were otherwise impeded, something will happen to him after he is deposed, which will be more harmful to him and a greater condemnation than being deposed from his magistracy.

And if the Lord of the 12th house were joined to the Lord of the 1st, and [the Lord of the 12th] did not receive [the Lord of the 1st],[500] it signifies that he who was deposed will be confined in chains and disgraced, and his disgrace and condemnation will be signified more strongly if the conjunction were in one of the four angles, and more condemnatory than all of them is the 10th house. For just as [the 10th] itself signifies honor greater than the rest of the houses, so if it is turned to the contrary it signifies greater condemnation, because it signifies that he will be held publicly in chains before all wishing to see him, and all who wish to will be able to deride him. If however the conjunction were in the 1st, it signifies that he will be put in chains, and there will be a rumor from it, but it will not be as great as when it is in the 10th. If however the conjunction were in the 7th, it will be his own subjects (of whom he is the leader or regent) who put him into jail or chains. If however the conjunction were in the 4th, he will be put in chains or prison, but there will not be great defamation from it. If however in addition to this the Lord of the 1st were in the cadents from the angles, and he were above the earth, even if he is joined to the Lord of the 12th he will not be captured in the land in which he is regent or leader or estate steward[501] or an official, but rather he will be led to another place and held captive there. If however it were below the earth, he will be fettered on the road when he is being led to the place of his detention. If however the Lord of the 1st, when he was separated from the Lord of the 12th, [made his] first conjunction with the Lord of the 8th, it signifies that he will die in the prison.[502] If however the Lord of the 1st were joined to the Lord of the 10th after he was separated from the Lord of the 12th before he is joined to another, it signifies that after he is captured he will be freed from prison, and another regency or office will be given to him.

---

[500] I believe this is the proper meaning, rather than the Lord of the 1st receiving the Lord of the 12th (which according to the usual method would be very bad for the Lord of the 1st).

[501] *Baylitor.*

[502] I.e., if the Lord of the 1st transfers the light from the Lord of the 12th to that of the 8th: prison leads to death.

And you may understand the same if the Lord of the 1st were joined to Mars, because it signifies that the same signified things will happen to him as happen to him when [the Lord of the 1st] is joined to the Lord of the 12th, and even more strongly so because Mars signifies beatings and the clash of weapons, and bloodshed and sometimes death, which the Lord of the 12th does not. And if Mars were not joined corporally with the Lord of the 1st, but by opposition or a square aspect, and he were the Lord of the 2nd or the 8th, it signifies the same thing which was said above.

And even look to see if the Lord of the 1st is impeded by one of the malefics, because the affliction which he will suffer will be according to the nature and things signified by the malefic who impedes the Lord of the 1st. If for example it were Mars as I said, the impediment will be from fetters that wound and constrict the arms and legs, or both of them with skinning; and he will suffer from iron instruments and confined by iron bands, and perhaps that he will be pierced by swords and iron rods. If however it were Saturn, he will be imprisoned in a dark or underground prison, and beaten by sticks, and perhaps that he will be stoned or hit by stones.

Chapter 4: When he has entered his rule[503] or office and begun to rule or be in charge; what will happen to him in his office

And if you wished to know what would happen to him in [his] rule or office, see when he himself enters the office or kingdom or empire. And it is at the hour of his entrance, when he is placed on his throne, or begins to rule or be in charge or dispose the affairs of the kingdom or office by means of carrying out his duties.[504]

If the beginning [of his rule] were by day, look at the Lord of the 1st and the Sun. If the Lord of the 1st were badly disposed, and the Sun were anywhere joined with Saturn, or the malefics aspected him by a square aspect or from the opposition, without perfect reception, it signifies his deposing, and the deposing will be from rule or the office. If however you were to find the Lord of the 1st and the Sun in the aspect [of] or conjunction with the benefics, and they were in the 1st or 10th or 11th or 5th, and in addition they were in a fixed sign, it signifies

---

[503] Bonatti is sometimes unclear whether he means the act of ruling or the kingdom itself when he uses *regnum*; moreover, he often switched back and forth between it and *regimen*. I will tend to translate both as "rule" unless "kingdom" seems to make more sense.

[504] *Per modum generandi officium.*

that his rule or office will last and be prolonged, and he will delight in it, and things he wishes for and is happy with, will happen to him in it, and he will rejoice in them.

If however the Lord of the 1st and the Sun were in corporal conjunction, or even in the aspect of Mars without perfect reception, as I said, and he[505] were north of the Sun, or Mars were in the 10th, and the Sun were in the 1st, and the Ascendant was a movable sign, it signifies that a certain man from among those whom he must rule will rise up against him, and will try to resist him in his rule or office, and the king or official[506] will fear lest he could succeed against him, and lest he can depose him from his office or rule; and he fears he will be killed or will die in some other way before he completes his office. If however one of the aforesaid [conditions] were missing, that is, that Mars is not in the 10th, or the Sun is not in the 1st, or the Ascendant is not a movable sign, it signifies that he will not rise up against him; and if he were to rise up, he will not be able to succeed against him, and [the rebel] will succumb.

If indeed the Lord of the 1st and the Sun, or at least the Sun, were joined corporally to Jupiter, or in his aspect by trine or sextile, whether with reception or without reception, or in square or opposition with reception, or if Jupiter were in the 10th and were free from the aforesaid impediments (namely that he is not retrograde or combust or cadent), and the Sun were in the 1st or 11th or 5th, and the Sun were in addition in a fixed sign, it signifies that his rule or office will be very praiseworthy, and he will be of great honor, and will always be increased in the good; and he will last a long time in praise and fame, and that it will be useful and lucrative for him, and for a long time it will be said of such a man, "he ruled us well, and his rule was very useful to us."

You would even look to see if you saw the Sun in the 6th or the 8th, and if the Lord of the 1st were in the 1st or in the 10th, and the Lord of the 1st were Jupiter or the Sun or Venus: his office or rule will be well-disposed, and of a good end, except that it seems he ought to be saddened, because it signifies the death of him who promoted him to the office or rule.

And if the entrance to his rule or office were at night (namely when he began to exercise the office or rule), look at the Moon just as you looked at the Sun in a diurnal entrance, and see if she were free from the aforesaid impediments, and that she were not combust nor cadent nor in conjunction with the malefics: it signifies that he will complete his rule with the health and the integrity of his

---

[505] I believe Bonatti is referring to the Lord of the 1st.
[506] I.e., the querent.

body; and that he will remain well and not [be] sick in his rule. And if the Moon were joined corporally with one of the aforesaid malefics, or were in their square aspect, or in their opposition, or even in a trine or sextile aspect without reception, it signifies his being deposed from his rule, and he will be deposed shortly. And if she or the Lord of the house in which she was, were in bad places, he will find evil in that land and in his rule, and that there will be many who complain about him because his rule is not carried out or handled well.

And if the malefic who impeded the Moon were the Lord of the 10th, he will be accused of ruling them badly. And if it were the Lord of the 11th he will be accused of having stolen by evil means, or having squandered the goods of the people or the king. And if it were the Lord of the 2nd he will be accused of having made off with or having squandered the money of the citizens whom he was supposed to rule. And if it were the Lord of the 5th he will be accused of a shameful vice, that he has abused a boy. And if it were the Lord of the 7th, he will be accused that he has made use of their wives. And if it were the Lord of the 8th he will be accused of having judged some people unjustly. And if it were the Lord of other houses, it does not signify a certain or specific accusation, except for the rumors of the populace and foolish people.

And if the Moon were then near the Head of the Dragon or its Tail by 4° or less, it signifies that the office or rule will not be useful for him, nor will he acquire fame or wealth in it. If for instance she were distant from the Head or Tail by more than 4°, up to a full 12°, and the significator of the ruler were impeded or detained,[507] and the Moon were then in a movable sign, it signifies that his detention and impediment will last by so many days as there are degrees between the Moon up to the end of her separation from the Head or Tail, until she is elongated from it by the said full 12°. And if she were in a common sign, it will last so many months. And if it were in a fixed sign, it will last so many years. And if there were a fraction of a degree there, and the detention signified days, one hour will be signified for every two-and-a-half minutes. And if it signified months, a week will be signified by every 15'. And if it signified years, a month will be signified by every 5'. And if it were not detained, nor otherwise impeded, but he feared something bad would happen to him, he will have fear until the Moon is elongated from the Head and the Tail by 12°,[508] just as was said.

---

[507] *Detentus.*

[508] I.e., not when she is actually separated (which would be within two days due to her speed), but in the time signified by the timing mechanism above.

And see likewise if, when he begins his rule or when he takes his oath, the Ascendant is a degree which is of the bound of Mars of Saturn, and one of them were to aspect the degree: it signifies that he will not take good ruling actions in his office or rule, and will comport himself shamefully in it; and men will speak disgracefully about him. Even if the ruler is otherwise good there, it will take away from his goodness and he will act in a weakened way in it. You could almost say the same if the Moon were impeded in the 4th at the hour of his introduction to the rulership. If indeed [the degree] were some degree of the bound of one of the three planets Jupiter or Venus or Mercury (that planet being fortunate), and one of them were to aspect [the degree], he will complete his rule with honor and good praise, and all good will be said about him, and the sound of his name will be magnified because of it, and all wealth which he made during his rule will be called good by all those whom he had to rule. Just as he will be praised for good works when a benefic is in the 1st at the hour of his entrance into rule or the office, indeed he will be condemned if it were of the malefics, just as was said; and by so much worse because perhaps he will die because of it.

Chapter 5: How the beginning of his rule will be, good or bad, and even how its end will be

And even see, at the beginning of his rule, if there were a benefic in the 1st: his beginning will be good and very praiseworthy (if the benefic were not impeded). If however it were impeded, or there were some malefic there, oriental and direct, in its own domicile or exaltation, nor otherwise impeded, it signifies that the beginning of his rule will be praiseworthy, but not very.

And if there were in addition a malefic in the 4th, it signifies that however the beginning was, the end will be bad. And if there were a malefic in the 1st, who did not have testimony there, just as I said, it signifies that the beginning of his rule will be bad. If however there were a benefic in the 4th, well-disposed, the end will be praiseworthy and whoever said bad things about him will later praise him, and will honor him and say good about him. And if there were an impeded benefic there, or a malefic [who is] oriental, direct, in its own domicile or exaltation, nor otherwise impeded, it signifies that the end will be praiseworthy, but not very.

And if there were [a benefic] in the 1st and the 4th, the beginning and the end will be likewise [both] of high praise. If however in both there were a malefic, both will be condemned.

Likewise, see if the Tail of the Dragon were in the 1st, and the Lord of the 1st were in the 2nd or 4th or 6th or 7th or 8th or 9th (unless he were the Sun), or in the 12th—and all the more so if it [the Lord of the 1st?] were in the conjunction or aspect of any malefic planet, without reception, and any malefic were in the 1st or 10th, or the 7th or 4th, and [if] in addition the Moon were impeded by one of the malefic planets: it signifies that his household members[509] will be unfaithful; and his ministers will be low-class people, and his deputies and officials will be evildoers and will make him sad and trembling, and their actions will be such that they make him condemned in his reign or rule; and the evil deeds will be those which bring about the cause of the destruction of his rule or reign, and will sadden him; and he will always fear that evil will be done to him in his rule or office as long as he remains in it.

And may you always have this in mind: because whenever any misfortune threatens his being deposed from rule or an office, and you were to find Jupiter in the 10th or the 1st, and he were oriental, he will either wholly cancel the deposing, or make it better and delay it. And if his deposing is not signified, and you were to find [Jupiter] in the 10th, he will acquire praise in his rule or office; indeed so that because of it he will reach the greatest forms of rule and offices. If however a malefic were in it, it will be drawn out, and he will be conquered and fall under the ire of the king or another magnate who rules over him, and it will take away from him all that had reached his hands in terms of wealth and what he had sought.

If however you were to find a benefic in the 1st, and in the 10th a malefic and in the 4th a benefic, the beginning and end will be good, but the middle bad. If you were to find a benefic in all of them, the beginning and middle and end will be good. If indeed you were to find in the 1st a malefic, in the 10th a benefic, in the 4th a malefic, the beginning and end will be bad, but the middle good. If indeed you were to find in each of them a malefic, the beginning, middle, and end will be bad.

If indeed there were benefics and malefics [together] in the aforesaid places, the things signified will be according to the nature of that one which is in more degrees in the sign; but, however, the other will diminish something of the

---

[509] *Familiaris*, lit. "one of the same household" or "servant" or "intimate." In the context of ruling, this probably means lower-level workers, office staff, and servants.

signification of the other: like if a benefic were to obtain the signification (namely that it were in more degrees than the malefic),[510] it will take away from the good which the benefic signified. If a malefic were to obtain it, the signification of the benefic will take away from the malefic what the malefic signified.

And if Mercury were joined to Jupiter in the 10th at the hour of his introduction into the rule or office, it signifies that he will complete his rule wisely and with discretion and reason, and the jurisdiction of those whom he rules will accrue to him, and he will be increased[511] with regard to them. The same thing will happen to him if the Moon were joined to Jupiter in the 10th and Venus were in the same place or in the 11th or in the 1st or the 5th.

And may you know this: because whenever you were to find Mars in the 7th at the hour of his entrance into his rule or reign, it always threatens death (unless a benefic is in the 1st). If however a benefic were there[512] and he were deposed from his rule, the cause of the deposing will be fine and honorable, and he will rejoice because of it, nor will he be saddened from it; nor will any harm or shame follow from it, nor will he consider it an insult to himself.

And if the Lord of the 9th were joined to the Lord of the 1st, he himself will ask to be removed from his office. And always when[513] the Lord of the 4th is well disposed, it signifies the good end of his rule, whether it were at the entrance of the king[514] or in a question.

And may you hold this likewise as something firm, because whenever you find Jupiter in any of the places, or were he to aspect any of the places of the circle, and he himself were well disposed (that he is not retrograde or combust or cadent from an angle, nor is he in Gemini or Virgo or Capricorn), that no evil will be able to work any malice in that place which he would not break. Even if two malefics were in that place, and he himself were present, and were disposed as I said, [then] even if he could not work the good which one would want, still he will take away all the malice of the malefics.

---

[510] Reading *malo* for *malus*.
[511] Reading *ingeminabitur* for *ingemabitur*.
[512] In the 7th.
[513] Reading *cum* for *eum*.
[514] I.e., in an electional chart.

Chapter 6: If he will remain in power or that office, or will be removed from it

And if at some point someone in some office or rule were to ask of you, saying, "See if I will remain in this power or rule or not." Consider the Lord of the 1st and the Lord of the 10th, and see if they were joined together in a corporal conjunction or from any aspect; and see if the heavier of them (who is called the "receiver of disposition") were in an angle (except the fourth): tell him that he will not be removed from the office or rule before the required time. If indeed the receiver of disposition were below the earth, which is called "left of the Ascendant,"[515] it signifies that he will leave his rule or office, but will return to it again—and all the more surely if the receiver were received in the place in which it was, because then it signifies that the return will be quick and honorable.

You could also say the same if the Lord of the 1st were joined to the Lord of the 3rd or 9th, or to a planet in them, and after the separation from them were joined to a planet in an angle (except the fourth), and by that much more will his exit from rule be good and free from care, and useful. If indeed they were separated from each other, so that there comes to be a complete conjunction of them, and one were to transit the other, it signifies the departure from his rule. And if one of them (or the significatrix, which is the Moon) committed its own disposition to a planet in one of the angles (except the fourth), and it were slow in course, he will not be removed from his reign or rule until the receiver becomes retrograde or enters under the rays of the Sun or leaves the sign in which it is, because then it will be the term of his removal from his rule.

If indeed the Lord of the 1st were joined to some planet which is in the sign opposite to its own exaltation—namely, belonging to the Lord of him to whom the Lord of the 1st is joined[516]—the ruler will behave in a bad way during his rule, so that death will be feared for him for this reason. If however the Lord of the domicile opposite to the exaltation of the Lord of the first were joined to him, men of that kingdom will bring false testimony against hem, and the falsity will

---

[515] Again, Bonatti is mixing up his terminology. He means "left of the heaven." See Tr. 2, Part 3, Ch. 3.

[516] The first part of the sentence makes sense, but contrasts with the material in parentheses. Luckily this whole passage derives from Sahl, who says: "And if the Lord of the Ascendant were joined to the Lord of his own descension, he will conduct an act in which he will perish." See On Quest., 10th House, "A question about the stability of the king or about his departure."

be believed by those ignorant of the truth (and that belief will remain in their hearts for a long time).

If however the Lord of the 10th were joined to the Lord of the domicile opposite his own exaltation, his reign or the land which he must rule will suffer great detriment and depression.

Moreover, if the Moon were joined to the Lord of the 10th, and he himself were in the 10th, the king or ruler will not be deposed from his rule. And if the Lord of the 1st or the Moon (or one of them) were joined to the Lord of the 10th, and he were heavier than they, and he were in a good place from the Ascendant (namely in the 10th or 11th or 5th, free from impediments), even if he himself did not aspect the 10th, however nevertheless if [the querent] were in some position of rulership, he will be placed above another reign or rule; but if he were to aspect the 10th, he will remain firmly in his reign or rule.

If however the Lord of the 1st and the Moon were in the angles, and the angles were movable signs, and the Moon were not joined to the Lord of the domicile or exaltation of the sign in which she was, it signifies that he will leave his rule. Likewise if the Moon were joined to a planet who was not in any one of its own dignities, even if it were received (unless perhaps it were received by a benefic from a trine or sextile aspect, and it itself were in the 3rd or the 9th): he will leave the reign or rule. It will happen to him likewise if the Moon or the Lord of the 1st were in the 4th, and the 4th were Aries or Cancer or Libra or Capricorn (and all the more strongly if the Moon were then joined to the Lord of the 4th, and he himself were peregrine). And again it will happen all the more strongly if the Moon were joined to a planet who was in the opposition of the sign of its own exaltation or domicile, or she herself were in Capricorn. It will happen to him likewise if the Moon were void in course.

Chapter 7: What the king or ruler will do with the substance which he gains during his rule

Sometimes it happens to those for whom substance and wealth comes to their hands (on the occasion of their reign or rule or offices), that they have to spend it, sometimes willingly, sometimes unwillingly. Whence if you wished to know on what he had to spend it, he (or another person whose business it is) having posed the question to you, you must look in a different way than in other questions. Because in this case one must look at the Lord of the 2nd house,

which you will [examine to] see whether there were a benefic or a malefic
[there].

If however it were a benefic, and it were Jupiter, he will spend it on a
good work, and one pleasing to God and men, by building churches,
making treaties, hospitals, monasteries, by helping the needy with alms,
and the like.

If however it were the Sun, he will spend it on the things of kings, magnates, and nobles, and on those things which pertain to the temporal
honor of laypeople, or by building homes, castles, or towers, and in these
sorts of things which pertain to secular ostentation, and even by giving to
others in a vainglorious manner, and the like.

If indeed it were Venus, he will spend it for venereal uses, by giving to
women, actors, [spending on] clothing, on banquets, gourmands, and
drinking bouts, by squandering and the exercise of luxury. And if Venus
were elevated above Saturn (that is, if she is north of him),[517] it signifies
that he himself spends part of his money in a way that is to be condemned, by the use of the shameful and horrid sodomitical vice.

And if it were Mercury, he may spend it on matters from which he ex-
pects wealth, like market transactions,[518] and on these sorts of buying and
selling which are quickly repeated; and his whole intention will be in
gaining wealth, and he will carry most of his expenses in a commercial
way.

And if it were the Moon and she were in her own light, or void in course,
he will spend the substance not for his own usefulness, and he will spread
it around, not knowing how or on what, all the while he will consume it
through squandering. And if she were not void in course, he will spend it
according to what he would spend if the significator were he with whom
the Moon is joined.

---

[517] But this could also refer to the Hellenistic "overcoming," so that she is in the tenth sign
from Saturn. See Introduction and footnote to Tr. 3, Part 2, Ch. 20.
[518] *Mercibus venalibus.* This might also mean "bribed transactions." It is usually unclear whether
Bonatti means corrupt practices or normal business transactions when he uses *venalis.*

If however it were Saturn, he will not spend it justly, and he will always fear that the method of spending is harmful to him, and he will be distressed about it, and will try to spend it on the harming of others, as through he were revering them, and it will go badly for those with whom he had dealings, and with whom he gets involved.

And if it were Mars, he will spend it on all things criminal, and unjust and evil acts, as in wars, whisperings, and in perpetrating fires, bloodshed, and fornications, and in the service of friends by arming [them] for war, and the like.

Chapter 8: On someone who has been thrown out of his rule or office, or concerning an absent king: whether he will return to his reign or office, or not

If someone were thrown out of his reign or from his rule or a lay office, just as sometimes tends to happen, or if some king or leader absented himself from his reign or leadership position, just as men of that sort tend to set out for a long time,[519] and the question was put to you whether the absent king would return to his reign, or the leader to his position, or one taken from power to his rule, or an official to his office or not.

Look in this chapter just as I tell you: because if someone asks on behalf of a king whether he would return to his reign; or on behalf of a leader, whether he would return to his position (namely, when the king or leader is not there); or someone thrown out of office or rule asks for himself, the 1st is always given to him, namely to the king or leader or the one thrown out.

Whence you ought to consider if the Lord of the 1st were anywhere joined with the Lord of the 10th, and see if the heavier of them (who receives the disposition of the lighter), were to aspect the 10th: the king will return and will reign in his kingdom, and the leader will return to his position, and the one thrown out will return to the rule or office that is asked about. If however the receiver of the disposition did not aspect the 10th, look then to the significatrix (which is the Moon), and see if she herself is joined to some planet who is in the 10th or the 1st: it signifies his return.

And see likewise if the Moon were in Aries or Cancer or Libra or Capricorn: he will return quickly. If indeed it were the Lord of the 10th [in these signs], it

---

signifies the return of the absent king to his kingdom, and the one thrown out of office or rule to his rule or office.

And if the Lord of the 10th were lighter than the Lord of the 4th, and were separated from him, it signifies the return of the king to the kingdom, and of the one thrown out to his office; likewise with the Lord of the 1st. And if the Lord of the 4th were lighter than the Lord of the 10th and were joined to him, he will return and will endure in it; likewise if the Moon were joined to the Lord of the 10th, and she herself aspected the 10th: he will even return, unless she herself commits her disposition to a planet located below the earth [and] who is peregrine. Likewise if the Lord of the 1st were received by an unimpeded planet; if however it were not received, he will not return. Likewise if the Moon were joined to a planet who is in the 9th, it signifies that the king about whom it is asked, will leave his reign, unless it is a benefic. If however the planet to whom the Moon is joined were a benefic, and were in Aries or Taurus or Cancer or Leo or Libra or Scorpio or Capricorn or Aquarius, it signifies the return of the king or of the one thrown out. And if it were in Gemini or Virgo or Sagittarius or Pisces, it signifies that the king will get another kingdom, or the leader another leadership position, or the one thrown out, another office. And Sahl said[520] that the king will rule his kingdom for three years, because the receiver of the Moon's disposition would not fall until it would come to the twelfth place from the Ascendant.[521] And in the second year he will be in a better condition, and will be held more in reverence, and he will satisfy his own desires more than in the first [year].[522] And if the Moon were then joined with benefics, it will be better, unless one of the malefics came and entered the 10th before the receiver or the Moon's disposition reached the 12th from the Ascendant at the hour of the question: because if one of the malefics reached the 10th house of the question, which signifies the reign, before the receiver came to the said house, it will impede the reign which the king was going to attain, and will not permit him to attain it; and all the more strongly, if the malefic were retrograde in the sign which had then been the 10th house. And if he had achieved it and the Moon were joined to the malefics, he will acquire condemnation because of it.

---

[520] *On Quest.*, 10th House, "A question about him who departed from his reign, or about an absent king: whether he would return."

[521] Sahl (*ibid.*) seems to mean that if each sign symbolizes one year, then by profection the planet in the ninth will not be cadent again until it is profected to the twelfth.

[522] See above footnote. Sahl/Bonatti seems to consider the 10th house by profection to be the second year.

If however she were joined to a planet in the 10th, he will acquire praise from it, and will endure in it for two years. It will happen likewise if she were joined to a planet in the 5th, because he will reign in his kingdom or rule for two years.

And if she were joined to a planet in the 11th (and all the more strongly, if he received her), he will stay in power or rule for one year, provided that one of the malefics[523] did not enter into the 10th and [go] retrograde in it. Likewise if the Moon were joined to a planet in the 1st, he will stay in his rule for one year. And if the Moon were joined with the Lord of the 10th, or if they were not joined and each was well disposed in its own place, and they were in Gemini or Virgo or Sagittarius, or Pisces, he will return to his office or reign. If however he were [already] present [in office], he will persevere in it; and he will remain more strongly in it than he was thus far used to, and another reign or office will be added onto it. If you were to find the Lord of the 10th and the Moon impeded in any of the angles by the corporal conjunction of some malefic, it signifies that the absent king will not return to his reign (nor the one thrown out to his office), forever; and if he were in it, he will be removed and will remain removed forever.

Chapter 9: Whether the reign or rule is going to last or not, and how long

It was said in the preceding, whether someone was going to attain a kingdom or not, and whether an absent king was going to return to his reign or not, and the same thing about other leaders or officials thrown out of office (whether they would return to it or not).[524]

Now however we must say if the reign or another similar thing is going to last, and how long. Since you saw the hour of his entrance into his reign, or when he received it, or when he was confirmed in it, or the hour of his question, you could know the time of his duration in his reign or office, and what ought to happen to him in it, and how his subjects will revere him; and how he will be honored by them, and how the memory will be of him (concerning the things he took on by remaining in power), and how it would go for him or his reign

---

[523] *Malivolorum* (lit. "of the foes, evildoers, etc."), an uncharacteristic variant on *malus* or *infortuna* by Bonatti.

[524] In this chapter Bonatti seems to be talking about *horary* questions asked *after* the hour of the ascension to the throne, *when* that hour is known. In this case, the chart of the hour of the ascension to the throne is assumed to act as a proper root for the horary question, "How long will my reign last?"

against his enemies; and what kind of victory he will have over them, and how he will serve the goods of his kingdom, and [what he] will acquire from the goods of his enemies, and the like.

Whence we must look at the Lord of the 1st and the Lord of the 10th, and see if they both suffered the misfortune of combustion in the ascending sign (or in the 10th or the 7th or in the 4th) which existed at the hour of the entrance or confirmation, or of his question about these things, before the line of any of the aforesaid houses by 3° or after by 5°:[525] it signifies then that he will be deposed from his reign or rule.

You may understand the same about a planet who was in the 1st at the aforesaid hour, if he were one having some signification in a kingdom or office, just as was said in the other chapter before this one. If however it were not so (concerning the Lord of the 1st or a planet appearing in it, nor what was said about the Lord of the 10th), nor were it joined at the hour of his confirmation or introduction into power with a planet in the 1st who signified something about a kingdom, then see if there were some planet in the 10th who had some signification over a kingdom, namely who had some dignity in the 10th–[in which case] you could judge the same.

Likewise when Mars or Saturn reached that degree, or that minute in which the aforesaid planet then was (and all the more strongly if among them Mars or Saturn retrograded in the same degree), because then it signifies the removal without a doubt.

You could say the same if the planet who was the Lord of the 4th house of the entrance into power or his confirmation, were retrograde or combust or were in the 10th house of the entrance into power–if the 10th house was the exaltation of some planet. If however the 10th house was not the exaltation of some planet, but it was the descension of one, you will judge the same according to the planet who was the Lord, *if* the planet who was the significator of the king when the reign began, were to aspect the one whose descension was the 10th house of the entrance into power.

If you did not find a planet in one of the aforesaid places (namely the 10th or 7th or 4th), or one of the planets disposed as I said,[526] and the entrance into power or the office was diurnal, see if the Sun is joined to some planet (namely Saturn or Mars), and look at the degree in which they are joined at the entrance

---

[525] I believe that by "before," Bonatti means "in an earlier degree than the cusp's"; by "after," he means "in a later degree than the cusp's." See my Introduction.

[526] Again, this seems to be in the *horary* figure cast after someone has risen to power.

into power: because when the Sun reaches that minute in which the conjunction of them is complete, minute for minute, and that minute were found in the angle of the 10th or the 1st (and certain people wanted to say the same for the 7th and the 4th, but I have not been experienced in the 7th or the 4th as with the 1st and the 10th), directly on the line of the angle (or 1° ahead, or 2° after),[527] it signifies that the king or ruler will then be deposed. You could say the same about his conjunction with Mars, just as you said about his conjunction with Saturn. If indeed the Sun were joined to Jupiter, it signifies his deposing when Saturn reaches the degree and minute in which the Sun was at the hour of the introduction [into power]. And if were not then, it will be when he reaches the square aspect of that degree and minute in which the Sun was. And if it were not then, it will be when he has reached the square[528] or his opposition. And if were not then, it will be when he reaches corporally to the degree and minute in which the Sun was, unless the aspect or opposition precedes his arrival to that place. If indeed his arrival to that place were to precede the aspect or the opposition, the deposing will be then. If however the Sun were not joined to Jupiter, but Venus were joined to him, and she were then (namely at the introduction into power) in the 9th or 11th and had dignity there, then when Saturn or Mars were to reach to that minute in which Venus was then, or to her opposition, or square aspect, or her own opposition (just as was said in the consideration of the Sun), the deposing of the king will be [then].

If however the entrance into power were nocturnal, look at the Moon (who is the luminary of the night), and see if she is joined to Mars or Saturn: because that signifies that when one of them to whom she is joined reaches the degree and minute of one of the angles, or to the degree and minute in which the Moon was then, or to her opposition or square aspect, the one promoted will be deposed from his rule. Even see if the Moon were joined to the Sun: because the Sun signifies what the Moon ought to signify. If indeed she were not joined to him, but were separated from him, see if she is joined to Mars or Saturn (or the Sun): likewise what is signified will remain, which the Moon ought to have signified. If indeed the Moon were not joined to the Sun, nor were separated from him, or she were joined to Mars or Saturn (or Mercury, with him not located fortunately), it signifies that the king or official will not complete his

---

527 I believe that by "ahead of," Bonatti means "in an earlier degree than the cusp's"; by "after," he means "in a later degree than the cusp's." See my Introduction.
528 This may either refer to the other square aspect to the Sun, or may be a redundancy by the typesetter.

reign, whether his rule were long, whether an office or not;[529] and however it was, he will not last in it for a whole year. If indeed the Lord of the 1st and the Lord of the 10th suffered the misfortune of combustion in the 1st or 10th or 7th, or Mars were impeded, it signifies that the receiver[530] is already in the haste of removal[531] from his honor or magistracy; nor could he deceive without his being removed in short order or at least before the year of his reign or office is completed.

And if you wished to know when the deposing will be before the year is completed, see when the Lord of the 1st and the Lord of the 10th suffer combustion, [and] in what place will be the combustion of whichever of them; and when Mars or Saturn reaches to that place; and when one of the aforesaid malefics reaches that degree: then will be the deposing of the promoted man from his office or rule. And if Mars or Saturn did not reach the degree in that year, the deposing will be when one of them comes to [the degree's] opposition or square aspect (namely, of the place in which the aforesaid combustion was).

Afterwards, look to see if the Moon were joined to Mercury, and their conjunction is in Taurus or Leo or Scorpio or Aquarius or Gemini or Virgo or Sagittarius, and the rule were for a year: he will be deposed within five months. If however it exceeded a year, he will be deposed within eight months after one year. If indeed their conjunction were in Aries or Cancer or Libra or Capricorn, and his office or rule were for a year, he will be deposed within five months. If however it exceeded a year, he will be deposed within ten months.[532] If indeed the Moon were joined to another planet which is impeded (however he were [impeded] by the malefics, or if he were combust), see how many degrees there are between him and the malefic who impedes him, or between him and the degree in which his combustion will be completed (namely in which degree he will be united with the Sun), because within so many months he will be deposed, if the rule were for one year. If however it were a reign which is believed to be perpetual, or for a long time, he will be deposed within so many years. If however the Moon were received in the place in which she is, it even signifies that he will stay in power through one year. And if she were not received, and were in the exaltation of some planet, and he whose exaltation it was were received in the place in which he was, it signifies likewise his stay in

[529] I.e., no matter how long one is standardly expected to remain in that position.
[530] I.e., the person who has received the honor of the office–and is now about to be removed.
[531] *In praecinctu remotionis.* I have tried to translate this phrase exactly–it means his removal is already beginning to take place quickly.
[532] I do not understand the rationale for these months.

rule or reign for one year; which if the Moon were not received, nor the Lord of the exaltation of the place in which she was, it signifies his removal or being deposed from reign or office.

If he will reign for a second year

And when you find that he is going to remain in power through one year, see when the year will be completed: and it will be the full time when the Sun returns to the same point in which he was when the king or ruler ascended: that is, when he entered his rule, and assumed his lordship or magistracy; for then one year will be completed, when the Sun travels around a full 360°; and then will begin the second year, when he begins to enter the same minute which he entered when his reign or rule began.

For example, in the beginning the Sun was in the first minute of the fifth degree of Taurus; and he had already crossed 4" of that minute when the Sun traveled around the whole zodiac, and reached the fourth second of the first minute in 5° Taurus, then the year will be complete, and when he touched the fifth second of the fifth degree of Taurus, then the next year will begin, and it will be the second year after the first. Therefore reckon the planets to that hour and to that minute of the hour, and verify the twelve cusps, namely the 1st and the 10th and the rest of the houses; and then you will know whether he is going to remain in power in the second year or not, and what ought to happen to him in the second year, and do in the rest of the years if you see that he is going to remain in power for more.[533]

On the third year

And likewise see where the Lord of the hour is (namely of the Ascendant of the revolution of the year),[534] because through it is known if the said promoted man will remain in his rule again for another year or not. For if it were well disposed and free from the impediments of the malefics, it signifies that he will stay again for another year. And you may understand this in any revolution: because always when the Lord of the Ascendant is free from the impediments of the malefics, it signifies that he will remain again for another year in his rule.

---

[533] Bonatti is now (and below) saying that one can treat the leader's reign just as one does with a solar revolution for a native or an annual mundane ingress for a nation.
[534] Bonatti seems to mean the solar revolution based on the entrance into power, *not* the mundane revolution of the entrance into Aries.

If however the Moon were joined to a planet who received her, see if the receiver were free from the malefics. Because if it were free, it signifies that he is going to stay in his rule more than was thought at the beginning when he was elected[535] to his rule. Which if he were not free, see by how many degrees he is distant from the degrees of the malefics impeding him, or from their aspect, degree by degree, and take that number and use it, and take the number of the lesser years of the Lord of the Ascendant of the elevation to the kingdom. See also[536] if the Ascendant of the elevation to the kingdom were one of the domiciles of Saturn: add 30[537] to the number of degrees which are between the planet who receives the Moon and the degree of the malefic impeding him (if it were in the domiciles of Jupiter, add 12; if it were in the domiciles of Mars, add 15), and make the degrees of the aforesaid distance and the lesser years of whichever of them [it was] into one number, and revolve the year to so many years beyond that in which the elevation to the kingdom was; and see if in that year the Lord of the Ascendant of that revolution were combust in the 1st or the 10th or the 7th or even the 4th, or if the aforesaid malefic were joined with the Lord of the 10th in the 10th: because it signifies the destruction of the kingdom or the land which he had to rule or lead; and the same if it were to signify months, within so many months. If it signified weeks, within so many weeks. And if the malefic in the revolution were in the 1st, it signifies the destruction of his deputies and his officials. And if the Lord of the 1st were combust in the 10th, it signifies that the promoted man will die in his reign or rule. And if the malefic in the revolution were in the 2nd, it signifies the destruction of the substance of the promoted man and of his subjects in that year during his reign or rule. And if it were in the 10th, it signifies the loss of his rulership, and his depression. And if it were in the 11th, it signifies the loss and destruction of the tribute or tax revenues of the kingdom.

Whence you must see who among the aforesaid higher[538] planets were to have authority in the elevation or introduction of his rulership: which if he were strong in the 1st, and some other [planet] committed its own disposition to him, then it will signify that the rulership is going to last for so many years (as how

---

[535] *Fuit electus*. This could simply mean "chosen," but it also suggests Bonatti seems to want to make this pertain to assumptions of power that were also intentionally chosen by an electional chart.

[536] Now Bonatti's example begins.

[537] The number of years here and immediately below are the lesser years of the planets: see Tr. 3, Part 1.

[538] *Altioribus*. Bonatti must mean the superior planets, since these were the ones identified in the formula earlier in the paragraph.

many degrees of distance are between him and the malefic, [plus] his lesser years). If indeed he were weak, that is, that no planet committed its own disposition to him, it will signify months instead of years. And if again he were very weak, that is, that he is not in the 1st or in any of his dignities, nor did some planet commit its own disposition to him, it will signify weeks instead of months. And if again he were weaker, namely that he were outside his dignities,[539] nor did any [planet] commit its own disposition to him, and in addition he were retrograde or combust, it will signify days instead of weeks.

On his infamy after his fall

Indeed after you were to see the wasting or destruction of his rulership, see if the Lord of the Ascendant of the elevation to power (or the Lord of the 10th of the same) were retrograde or combust in the revolution of the year which had threatened the detriment.[540] Because if it were next to the line of any of the angles of the Ascendant of the revolution (that is, by 3° ahead or by 12° after), the detriment will be predicted by the vulgar for a long time, and it will be in the voice of the people; and it will be openly said by the men of his region, "what will happen to us?"–but not knowing what they are saying (but they will speak almost in a prophetical manner). If indeed it were far from the line of the angle by 4° ahead or 15° behind, some evil or destruction will come quickly, and it will be predicted and known beforehand by certain men of the region, but not openly as before. And if it were far from the angle by more than 4° up to a full 5° ahead, or behind from 15° up to the full size of the angle, the evil or destruction will come suddenly, and unexpectedly, and in a hidden way, and hurried as though unforeseen.[541]

If however you were to find Jupiter in the 1st or the 10th of the elevation to power or leadership or other rulership, and he had some dignity there, or one of the planets committed its own disposition to him, in this it will signify that the reign or rulership is going to last as many years as there are degrees of distance between the planet receiving the Moon at the hour of the elevation to power or rulership and the malefic just as was said, by adding the number of the lesser

---

[539] I.e., peregrine.

[540] Here "detriment" probably has its political connotation of an overthrow. See Tr. 2, Part 2, Ch. 7.

[541] In this paragraph, I believe that by "ahead of," Bonatti means "in an earlier degree than the cusp's"; by "after" and "behind" he means "in a later degree than the cusp's." See my Introduction.

years of Jupiter (namely, 12). If indeed he were weak, it signifies months instead of years, *etc.*, as was said in the case of Saturn.

If indeed it were Mars instead of Jupiter, and he were strong and fortunate, or one of the planets committed its own strength to him, it signifies likewise years according to the number stated above. And if he were weak, it will signify months instead of years, *etc.*, as was said in the case of Saturn, and by that much more and worse. Wherefore if Mars were in the 1st or in the 10th, and the Moon in the 4th or in the 7th, or even the Moon in the 1st or in the 10th, and Mars in the 4th or the 7th (unless Jupiter or the Sun or Venus were to aspect him or the Moon), it signifies then the destruction of the kingdom or region in which he was elevated to rule, by vigorous killing and much beheading and bloodshed.

If however the Ascendant were Leo, and the Sun were strong in the 1st or the 10th, or one of the planets committed its own disposition to him, it signifies the reign is going to last 19 years. If however the Sun were weak, it signifies months instead of years. Again, [if] weaker, it signifies weeks or perhaps days instead of months.

If however the Ascendant of the elevation or introduction into power were one of the domiciles of Venus, and she were in the 1st or the 10th, strong in one of her dignities, or one of the planets committed its disposition to her, it will signify the durability of his reign or rulership for so many years as there are degrees distancing the aforesaid planet receiving the Moon from the degrees of the malefic impeding [him], with the superaddition of the number of Venus's lesser years (which are 8). And if she were weak, it signifies months instead of years. And if she were weaker again, it signifies weeks instead of months. Therefore revolve the year by so many years added to the year of the elevation to power or rulership, and see if then one of the malefics were to fall in the 1st or in the 10th of the elevation or the revolution. Because then it signifies the destruction of his reign, and it even confers the fear [of] the same, and [the fear] will be great if he were to escape.

And if it were Mercury instead of Venus (namely that the Ascendant were one of his domiciles), and he were [positioned] just as was said about Venus, it will signify that the reign will endure for as many years as there are degrees of distance of the aforesaid, and in addition for as many months as his lesser years are (which are 20). Because on account of his repeated misfortune of combustion, he cannot give years. And if he were weak, it will add to the number of years in distance, weeks or perhaps days instead of months. Revolve the year to that time, judge according to what you judged in the case of Venus. Moreover, if

Mercury were combust in one of the angles in the revolution, and the Lord of the 10th were found in the opposition or square aspect of Saturn or Mars, or were joined to him corporally, it signifies the destruction of his kingdom or at least the deposing of the king.

Moreover, see if Mars were then in the 1st or the 10th in the revolution. If the misfortune of combustion were to happen to him within as many months as there are of his lesser years (which are 15), and the combustion were complete (degree by degree) in one of the angles of the revolution of the elevation to power, it signifies then the destruction of his kingdom or rulership; and it is possible that it would signify his own destruction (namely of the one promoted).

Which if the Ascendant were then Cancer, and the Moon were free from the impediments of the malefics, and were joined to the Lord of the domicile or exaltation in which she was, it signifies the durability of his reign by 25 years added to the number of the distance. And if the Moon were weak, it signifies months instead of years, *etc.*, as was said in the case of Venus. Likewise, look to see if the Moon is joined to some planet to whom she commits her own disposition: which if [it]542 were combust in one of the angles, it signifies the destruction of his rule or rulership. And if the planet to whom the Moon committed her disposition were received by one of the seven planets, it signifies the durability of his reign continuously through so many years as there are lesser years of that planet. And if the receiver were then weak, it signifies months instead of days, *etc.*, as was said in the case of Venus. You will judge likewise when Mars or Saturn reaches the degree in which the Moon is, or to the degree of the planet to whom she committed her own disposition, or to the opposition or square aspect of that degree: because then it signifies the destruction of his kingdom, or at least his being deposed from it.

You even ought to know that if one of the aforesaid planets were to signify some time which would show the durability of some rule for a fixed number of years, and, in the year of some revolution it was going to receive an impediment in one of those signs which were the angles in the hour of the elevation or introduction to power, you ought not to lose hope concerning his deposing in that year because of it, unless you first look at the revolution of the next year. This having been done, you will see if the aforesaid planet were free from the malefics and from combustion and retrogradation: because if it were so, he will

---

542 *Qui si fuerit combusta,* using a masculine ending for *qui* and a feminine ending on *combusta.* But based on the context it must refer to the receiving planet.

still complete his rule. And if it were impeded by one of the aforesaid impediments, it will signify impediment and being deposed from his reign or rule.

Then look in the revolutions of years to the rays of the planet who was the Lord of the revolution (or of the profection),[543] by giving one sign to each year; and according to this you will be able to judge what will happen to him in that year which you have revolved. And see how far distant his rays are from the malefics, or the malefics' rays from his, and you will judge according to the lesser distance. Which if they were in angles, you will give a month to each degree of distance; if they were in the succeedents, you will give a week[544] to each [degree]; if they were in the cadents, you will give a day to each [degree]. Whence, [for] how many degrees there are between the ray of the planet who is the Lord of the revolution and the body of the malefic, or between his body and the rays of the malefic who impedes him, there will be so many months or weeks or days up to the hour of the arrival of that impediment which is going to come in that year.

And always make the Lord of the Ascendant of the revolution and the Lord of the Ascendant of the elevation or introduction into power or rule, and the Moon, participators with him;[545] so if he were well disposed, and the Lord of the Ascendant of the revolution and the Lord of the Ascendant of the elevation were well disposed (and likewise the Moon), it signifies that they will take away and remove the malice of impeding malefic, indeed so that he will not particularly kill. And were he poorly disposed (and likewise the others), the malice of the malefic will be increased, and will impede more and faster. If for instance he were well [disposed] and the others poorly, his goodness will not be particularly able to be of much use. If indeed he were poorly [disposed] and the others well, his bad disposition will hardly harm [the querent]. If however he were well or poorly [disposed] and one of the others were well and another poorly [disposed], the one who is well disposed will aid his goodness, and the poorly disposed one will increase his malice and decrease his goodness.

And even though I said "the Lord of the revolution" to you, do not think that he is the Lord of the Ascendant of the revolution: because, as it often happens, [the former] is different from [the latter]. Because he is the Lord of the

---

[543] Below Bonatti clarifies that the "Lord of the revolution" is the same as the profected Lord of the Year (or *sālkhudāy*).
[544] Bonatti suddenly drops the Greek-derived *hebdomadas* and uses the Latin *septimanam*.
[545] *Fac ei participes*.

profection for every year, according to one sign.[546] For example, the Ascendant of the elevation or introduction was 10° Pisces; Jupiter was then the Lord of the elevation to rule. In the following year Mars was the Lord of the revolution or of the profection, which is the Lord of the second sign from the Ascendant of the elevation–namely, Aries. In the third year the Lady of the profection was Venus, who is the Lady of the third sign from the Ascendant [of the elevation], namely Taurus (which is the third from Pisces). In the fourth year the Lord of the Revolution or of the profection was Mercury, who is the Lord of the fourth sign from Pisces, namely Gemini.[547] And may you understand this successively according to the Lords of all the signs, up to their end.

Even see if the benefics aspect [the Lord of the profection], because it will signify the good condition of the king in the year of that revolution, if the Lord of the Ascendant of the revolution were of good condition. If however [the Lord of the Ascendant of the revolution] were not of good condition, the condition of the king or leader will be less than what I said. And see where are the benefics aspecting [a] him or [b] the Lord of the Ascendant of the revolution or of the elevation, or [c] the Lord of the 10th of either of them, or [d] the Moon–or of what house he is the Lord:[548] because thence will come the good and the fortune. If however the malefics aspected him and impeded him, see from what houses he is impeded and of which houses they are the Lords: because thence will come the impediment to him, and from that place will come that which will be the reason for his being deposed, just as the reason for his confirmation and stability will come from the benefics and their places; and the deliverance [or salvation] of the Moon will have much efficacy in this; and her impediment harms much.

Whence it must always be put in your work, and you must always fear this: because whenever the Lord of the 10th of the revolution is impeded by retrogradation or combustion or besiegement from the two malefics, it always signifies the shameful and horrible deposing [of the ruler] in that year. If however he were free, it signifies his great strength and stability. And if he were oriental of the Sun, and were fortunate, and he were one of the superiors, it

---

[546] See above–so far Bonatti has spoken of (a) the profected Lord of the Year; (b) the Lord of the Ascendant of the revolution; and (c) the Lord of the Ascendant of the querent's elevation to power (the Lord of the elevation). These are three distinct *roles*, although the same *planet* may take on more than one role in a given situation.

[547] Bonatti is referring to the *sālkhudāy*, the profected Lord of the Year. See Tr. 9, 12th House, Chap. 7.

[548] Bonatti does not indicate who this "he" is, but it is probably the Lord of the revolution/profection–in which case Bonatti means to see what houses are ruled by this Lord.

signifies his being renewed in the rule or office. And if it were of the inferiors, and were occidental and fortunate, it will be likewise. And if it were of the superiors, and were occidental, it signifies detriment and deposing; and all the more strongly if the Sun were cadent from the angles and the Moon were in the 7th or the 12th. And if it were of the inferiors, and were oriental, it signifies the same. Likewise if the Lord of the 10th were joined with the Lord of the 4th, because it signifies deposing and evil; less good however will be if the Lord of the 4th were joined to the Lord of the 10th, because then it signifies stability.[549] And see if the Lord of the Ascendant of the revolution of the year were joined with the benefics or with the malefics, or were found in the places in which it was at the hour of the elevation, and judge according to that, and according to the luminary who is the authority.[550]

Having diligently inspected everything individually, and having considered well, you can know the durability and end, and likewise the deposing of anyone promoted, from his power or rule or office.

---

[549] Maybe Bonatti means this is less good because mere stability is not as good as having great strength and wealth, too.

[550] I.e., the sect ruler. Bonatti must mean the sect ruler of the original chart for the elevation, since that is the chart for which he has emphasized the importance of sect.

ON THE ELEVENTH HOUSE

Chapter 1: On trust or hope which someone has about some matter

As hope is one of those things in which all men rejoice and which make them to be delighted, it comes as no surprise if men have hope in having things which they desire; and therefore men sometimes hope to have things which it is possible to have; sometimes things which it is impossible to have (and they see manifestly that it is impossible that they should have them)–nevertheless however they want them.[551] Whence if someone were to pose a question to you about something which he wished to have, see if it is impossible, [in which case] do not get involved with the judgment. If indeed it is among the things that are possible, look at the ascending sign at the hour of the question (which is called the 1st house), and its Lord, and the Moon, and the Lord of the 11th, and see if the Lord of the 1st or the Moon were joined to the Lord of the 11th, or the Lord of the 11th were joined corporally to the Lord of the 1st: it signifies that he is going to attain the thing in which he has faith. If it were by an aspect, see what kind of aspect it is: because if it were a trine or sextile without reception, he will get it easily. If however it were with reception, he will get it most easily. If indeed it were a square with reception, he will get it, but not very easily, even if not with difficulty. And if it were without reception, or were an opposition with reception, he will get it with difficulty. And if it were an opposition without reception he will get it with difficulty, perhaps after losing hope.

If indeed the Lord of the 11th were in the 1st or 10th or the 7th or 4th, and the Moon were joined to him by the noted aspects, or she were joined to some planet who received her, he will get the thing in which he has faith, in accordance with his prayers, unless the Moon commits her disposition to another who is poorly disposed. For if the Moon then committed her own disposition to some planet, and he were in Gemini or Virgo or Sagittarius, or Pisces,[552] it signifies that the querent will get something of the thing which he hopes for, but not as much as his mind would be contented with; however he will get it with little labor. If indeed it were in Aries or Cancer or Libra or Capricorn,[553] he will attain it; but what is attained will be not enough, with labor and the greatest difficulty. If however it were in Taurus or Leo or Aquarius, he will attain what

---

[551] See Bonatti's discussion of hope in Tr. 1, end of Ch. 9.
[552] I.e., the common signs.
[553] I.e., the movable signs.

he intends wholly, and without great labor. If indeed it were in Scorpio, he will attain it but not completely, and with labor–unless she[554] were then received by Mars: because if she were received, he will attain it as in the other cases. And if the one to whom the Moon committed her own disposition were impeded, it signifies that the matter reaches almost as though to its effect, and it will be in the process of becoming [real], and it will be wholly believed to be coming [true], and perhaps that he will attain it–however it will be destroyed after it is attained or after it is thought to be arranged. And if he were not impeded, but were in the conjunction of some planet who received him, it signifies the attainment of the thing, and even more perfectly than the querent believed. The same thing will happen to him if the Lord of the 1st were joined to some planet who received him.

Chapter 2: Whether a man the querent speaks about is a friend or not, or will become a friend or not

There are some men who sometimes pretend to be the friends of others, or want to say that they would like to become their friends; but those wishing to be certain consult an astrologer [as to] whether it is so or not.

Whence, if someone came to you to pose a question about this to you, look at the 1st and its Lord, and the Moon, and the Lord of the 11th (just as was said in the preceding chapter), and see if the Lord of the 1st or the Moon is joined corporally with the Lord of the 11th, or by a trine or sextile aspect; or [if] the Lord of the 11th were joined to the Lord of the 1st: it signifies him to be a friend, and that he who says he would like to become a friend, will become one, and they will be joined[555] together in a true and stable friendship. And if it were with reception, their friendship will last forever, including [between] their successors. And if the Lord of the 5th then aspected one of the aforesaid from an aspect of friendship, the friendship will even last with their children and other descendants. And if it were without reception or from a square with reception, the friendship will last a long time, but will not be extended to the generation to come. And if it were from the opposition (whether with reception or without reception), or from a square without reception, there will be whispering and contrariety and contention [in] the friendship, and each of them will be contrary to the other, nor will they be very friendly to one another, nor will their

---

554 I.e., the Moon.
555 Reading *iungentur* for *iungetur*.

friendship be durable. And the opposition will devastate the friendship more so than a square aspect.

On a matter which a querent does not[556] wish to disclose to you

If however someone were to ask of you about some topic which he did not want to disclose to you, but said to you, "See if I will attain the thing which I hope to attain, or not," you must then consider the Lord of the 1st and the significatrix (who is the Moon). If they were both joined to benefics and [the benefics] to them, and the benefics were in angles (or one were in an angle and the other in a succeedent), or they were both in succeedents, say that he will attain the thing which he hopes for. If indeed one were in an angle and the other in a cadent, provided that they were joined together from the noted aspects, and the matter was something capable of being divided, he will attain part of the thing which he hopes for. If indeed one were in a succeedent, the other in a cadent, he will get less of it than that. And if they were joined from cadents, he will attain [either] not enough or nothing, indeed he will reckon what he did attain as being nothing. And if they did not aspect each other, he will not attain the thing which he hopes for.

And see likewise with what planet the Lord of the 1st or the Moon is joined, or of what house he is Lord, because the thing will be of the nature of those matters which are signified by that house. And if he were the Lord of two houses, it will be of the nature of that house which he aspects more, or which he is going to aspect first or into which he enters first.

---

556 Reading *noluerit* for *voluerit*.

ON THE TWELFTH HOUSE

Chapter 1: Concerning a prize race[557] set in any place: which of the horses or other animals (whether rational or irrational) will come in first[558]

If at some time someone came to you to pose a question to you about a race–which horse or other animal will win it, or is going to reach the finish line first–you must not look in this matter as you look in other matters, but otherwise. Because the 12th is given to an animal running in the race; and the hour[559] is given to the race, and the Lord of the hour is likewise given to the animal.

Whence you must see where the Lord of the hour of the question then is: which if it were in the 1st, the animal of the querent will come in first; and if it were not his, but were another's, and he wished to be informed of it, your judgment will be the same, and he will come before all other animals; and all the more strongly and surely if the Lord of the 1st and the Lord of the hour were the same; and he will precede the other animals by a great deal. If indeed it were in the 10th, it will come in second; and if it were in the 11th it will come in third; and if it were in the 7th it will come in fourth; and if it were in the 5th it will be fifth; and if it were in the 9th it will be sixth; and if it were in the 3rd it will be seventh; and if it were in the 2nd it will be eighth; and if it were in the 8th it will be ninth; and if it were in the 6th it will be tenth; and if it were in the 4th it will be eleventh or equal with the last; and if it were in the 12th it will be last or equal to him. If however there were more than twelve (which rarely happens), judge on it according to the aspect which the running animals were to have to the 4th or the 12th house.

For the deliverance of him who rides the horse or other animal,[560] look likewise to the same Lord of the hour: which if he were in his own domicile or

---

[557] *Bravio.* The way Bonatti uses this word suggests an overlap between "finish line" and "prize," like we speak of a "Cup" both as the race itself and the prize. Therefore I will generally translate it as "race" and "finish line" as context demands.

[558] As Bonatti emphasizes below, this particular set of instructions is primarily for querents who actually own a horse or other animal in the race. Instructions for regular spectators are given in the following chapter.

[559] I believe Bonatti means the chart should be cast for the time of the race. Thanks to Deb Houlding for pointing this out.

[560] I note that in the famous Italian horse race called the Palio (held every year in Siena), the race track is square: consequently, riders and horses are frequently thrown against the wooden barricades of the track by their own momentum when making the turns. This frequently leads to injuries to either jockey or horse. I myself saw this happen in 1989. Since the Palio has been going on for centuries, it is quite possible that Bonatti is referring to races much like it.

exaltation, his body will be saved from impediment, unless the Lord of the 8th were to aspect him: because then it signifies impediment without the breaking of his limbs. If however he were in [his] bound or triplicity or face, free from the malefics, he will likewise be saved. And if he were in his fall, it signifies his fall from the horse, but he will be impeded in a bad way. And if he were in his descension, it signifies his falling, and it is possible that even the horse will fall with him. And if then one of the malefics were to aspect him from the opposition, or were joined to him corporally, or by a square aspect, he will break some limb of his body. And if the malefic who impeded him were impeding him from Aries, his head will be wounded; if from Taurus, his neck or adjacent parts will be wounded; if from Gemini, his upper or lower arms or hands; if from Cancer, he will be wounded about the chest; if from Leo, he will be wounded around the back; if from Virgo, he will be wounded around the navel; if from Libra, he will be wounded around the hips; if from Scorpio, he will be wounded around the shameful areas; if from Sagittarius, he will be wounded around the upper thighs; if from Capricorn, he will be wounded around the knees; if from Aquarius, he will be wounded around the legs; if from Pisces, he will be wounded around the feet. If however the Lord of the 1st were in the 8th with a malefic or otherwise impeded, or in addition the Lord of the 8th were impeded, or the Moon were impeded, it signifies his death from the fall.

Chapter 2: When someone who does not own an animal running among other animals in the race: which is the animal who will win

And if perhaps someone who did not own a horse or animal running among the animals or horses in the race, were worried at some time, and were to say "Which of the horses or other animals running in the race will win it?" You will be able to see by this which animal would win, and his color and age and his goodness, and fame. Whence you ought to look at the Lord of the hour with a very true instrument which would not deceive you; which if you were to find him in the 1st or in the 10th or 11th, or you were to find another planet in one of the aforesaid places, you will be able to tell him that the horse or other animal of the color signified by the planet, will win the race; and do not prefer the 11th to the 10th, nor the 10th to the 1st, but the 1st to the 10th and the 10th to the 11th.

Whence, know that the winner may be known by the color of the animal. Then after you have seen the animal which ought to win, look to see if his significator were in its own domicile: it will be a noble animal, as if it is more dexterous among the other horses, and it will be renowned. And if it were in its own exaltation, it will be a more famous and more renowned animal, and of noble stock, and which for a long time will be accustomed to beating other animals. And if it were in its own triplicity it will be much less than this, and it will not be a very renowned animal nor of noble stock. And if it were in its own bound, it will be less than this again, and will hardly be renowned. And if it were in its own face, it will be an animal of little note, or it will be foreign, from another land, as though unknown in this land. If however it were not in these places, it is an unknown animal and not very brave, like a farm-horse and the like. And if the significator of the animal were in its own fall, it will be defective and full of faults, even if perhaps its defect is not very well-known. If however it were in its own descension, it will be more defective again, and its defects will be known.

Whether or not the animal winning the race is of great age

If you wished to know whether the winning animal is of great age, look at the planet through which the animal is signified; which if it were oriental, it signifies a young animal; and if it were occidental, it will be of great age; and if it were before the Sun or after it by five signs or more, it will be in the middle.

Chapter 3: Of what quality is the animal's master

And if you wished to know the quality of the animal's master, Sahl said[561] that if the Ascendant were the domicile of the Sun, he will be a king; [but] to me it seems that he would be greater than all of those who have animals running [in the race]. And if it were of the domiciles of Saturn, it will be an animal of great age and not noble stock, unless Saturn is then in the angles or in an optimal place from the Ascendant.[562] And if it were of the domiciles of Jupiter, it will

---

[561] *On Quest.*, "A question on the age of the beast who wins."

[562] This is a direct quote from Sahl. This term is somewhat ambiguous. (a) In Hellenistic astrology, places that are well-positioned or in a good place for the planets to "do business" are those which are in a whole-sign aspect to the rising sign (except for the third): so, the eleventh, tenth, ninth, seventh, fifth, and fourth. So an optimal place (*locus optimus*), which literally means a "best place," could indicate this. There are etymological reasons to believe that the Latin reflects this: *optimus*, or "best," is the superlative form of *bonus*; and the neuter form *bonum* means not only "good" in a moral or beneficial sense, but "a good," i.e., possessions, wealth, etc. *Optimus* undoubtedly derives from *ops* or *opes*, which means "wealth, resources." So an "optimal place" may be a way of reflecting the connection between success, goodness, and benefit which is established in Hellenistic astrology. But (b) a "best place"

belong to a famous and noble man, who has household familiarity[563] with nobles and magnates; or perhaps he could be a bishop or a great judge. And if it were of the domiciles of Mars, it will belong to some bellicose soldier, or bearer of arms, or perhaps to some general. And that same philosopher said that if it were of the domiciles of Venus or Mercury, it will belong to some magnate or noble or woman or writer or sage or learned person. And if it were the domicile of the Moon, it will belong to a certain sailor or some merchant, who therefore makes him run in order to ascend in fame so that he can promote himself better [or sell his services better].

Chapter 4: Concerning things about which people sometimes fear, whether they will happen in the thing they fear, or not

Sometimes it happens that someone, on account of threats which someone makes against him, or because of an act he has committed, or for any reason he were to fall into fear, will therefore come to you to ask whether or not he ought to be afraid of the thing he fears, and you wished to look into the thing he asks: look at the 1st and its Lord. Which if it were in the 1st or the 10th or even in the 7th or the 4th, free from the malefics and from their impediments, say that the threats will be false, and the fear which he has is empty, and that none of the things which he fears will put [him] into danger.

If however the Lord of the 1st were in houses cadent from the Ascendant (which are the 2nd, 6th, 8th, 12th), the threats were already made publicly against him, and are divulged, and he fears threats made against him. And if they must happen to him or be perfected, then look to the Lord of the 1st: if it were in one of the aforesaid weak places, and one of the malefics were to aspect him from the opposition or the square aspect, or were joined to him by body, announce to him that unless he watches himself well, perhaps he will fall into what he fears, and [into that] from which the threats against him arise. And if the malefics were to aspect by a trine or sextile aspect, without perfect reception, he will fall into difficulties and great horrors, and will suffer detriment; ultimately however, he will escape. If however they received him, they will impede either hardly or not at all. If for instance he were free of the malefics, and from their impediments, the fear is already increased in him, indeed so that it will not be increased more, but rather it will be diminished and he will escape from the threats and

---

could also reasonably indicate the eleventh place or domicile–certainly the eleventh is one of the best of the good houses. Below we will see two other uses (see Index).
[563] *Domesticitatem.*

his fear. And if he were impeded by the malefics (whether [he was] in a cadent or succeedent or in an angle)–and even all the more worse if he were in an angle, and the malefic who impeded were in an angle–likewise it signifies impediment and the greatest detriment will come to him from his fear.

And see if the malefic who impedes is the Lord of the 2nd from the Ascendant: his substance will be carried off because of it. And if it were the Lord of the 3rd, his brother will harm him (if he had a brother; and if not, one of the persons signified by the 3rd house). And if it were the Lord of the 4th, one of the things signified by the 4th house. And if it were the Lord of the 5th, it will be a child or one of the things signified by the 5th house. And if it were the Lord of the 6th, it will be a slave or something signified by the 6th house. And if it were the Lord of the 7th, it will be his wife or girlfriend, or something signified by the 7th house. And if it were the Lord of the 8th, it signifies his death because of it. And if it were the Lord of the 9th, it will be a religious person or something signified by the 9th house. And if it were the [Lord of] the 10th, it will be some noble, powerful person, *etc.* And if it were the Lord of the 11th, it will be some household member of a magnate, *etc.* And if it were the Lord of the 12th, it will be the pain of prison.

And if it were not so, but the Lord of the 1st were in the 12th, and the Lord of the 12th were to aspect him from the opposition or a square aspect, or the Lord of the 7th were joined to him by any aspect or corporally, it signifies detriment and difficulties, and that an enemy or someone he fears could conquer him and harm him. And if none of them aspected him, he will be liberated and escape from all of the dangers, and his enemy will not be able to conquer him, and [the enemy] will flee from him, even if he began as an enemy.

And if the Moon were joined to some malefic not receiving her, or who was not the Lord of the house in which the Lord of the 1st was, and [the querent] were to flee, detriment and difficulties will happen to him on his flight. And if the malefic did receive the Moon, and were the Lord of the house in which the Lord of the 1st was, he will be liberated from all of the aforesaid. You may understand the same about anything which is feared.

Chapter 5: On the diversity of many topics at once, which a question is sometimes about

Oftentimes certain people come to an astrologer, indiscriminately asking him about many and diverse topics. And they believe that it is just as easy to respond as it is to inquire.

And it can easily be responded to them about everything at once, as about a single [topic], though it is second-best. Whence, when you do not have a narrowly-determined Ascendant for it, you must give a more general thing to the querent, and this is the Moon; and the rest of the planets signify the quaesited matters.

Whence you must consider the number of the quaesited matters. If they are six topics or less, you will be able to judge about them according to the conjunction which the Moon makes with the six planets. For you will be able to know the nature of the first topic by the nature of the planet to whom the Moon is first joined after the question is made; and see the disposition of the planet, and according to how it is disposed, and you will judge the effect of the matter according to it. For if it were well disposed in a strong place, like in the angles or in those succeedent to the angles, and in its own dignities, and free from the impediments which I have listed for you many times, the effect of the matter will be good. If indeed it were the contrary of what I said, the effect will be contrary.

Then see to whom the Moon is again joined after she were separated from [the first planet]; and see what sort of disposition his is, and judge concerning the second topic according to it. Afterwards, look to see to whom the Moon is again joined after the separation from the second one, and judge concerning the third topic according to the disposition of the third planet to whom she is joined. Then look to the fourth to whom she will be joined after the separation from the third, and judge concerning the fourth topic according to its disposition. Then see to whom she will be joined first after her separation from the fourth, and judge concerning the fifth topic according to its disposition. Then see to whom she is joined after her separation from the fifth, and judge concerning the sixth matter according to its disposition. And may you understand the same with regard to an aspect as to a corporal conjunction.

And if the topics or questions were more than six, judge afterwards by the Lords of the triplicities of the domiciles in which the planets are when the Moon is joined to them (whether by body or by aspect). For example, the

Moon was joined to Mars in the first conjunction which she made after the question was made, and Mars was in Virgo: by the method with which you completed the number of the six planets, you must now judge about the seventh topic according to the primary Lord of Virgo's triplicity, who is Venus. [The Moon] made the second conjunction with Saturn (after she was separated from Mars), who was in Cancer; now you must judge about the eighth topic according to the primary Lord of Cancer's triplicity, which is likewise Venus. In the third conjunction (after the separation from Saturn), the Moon was joined to Mercury, who was in Libra; now you must judge concerning the ninth topic according to the primary Lord of Libra's triplicity, who is Saturn. And after the separation from Mercury, the Moon was joined to Jupiter, who was in Sagittarius; now you must judge concerning the tenth topic according to the disposition of the Sun, who is the primary Lord of Sagittarius's triplicity.

After you have completed the primary Lords of the four triplicities, and [if] the topics were more than ten, judge again through the secondary Lords of the triplicities, just as you judged by the primary ones.[564]

If again the topics overflowed, judge again by the tertiary [or participating] Lords of the triplicities, just as you judged by the primary and secondary ones.

And if again the topics overflowed for you, which has never happened to me, judge according to the Lords of angles. And if again it overflowed, judge according to the Lords of the triplicities of the angles.

Similarly, if you were asked about some thing, whether it was genuine[565] or not, look at the Lord of the 1st and the Moon: if they were well-disposed, the thing will be genuine in its nature. And if the thing were gold, see if the Sun were well-disposed: it will be genuine; lacking this, however, it is false. If it were silver, look at the Moon: if she were well-disposed, it will be genuine silver; if

---

[564] It is unclear exactly why Bonatti is starting with the secondary triplicity rulers now. In his second run-through, he has used the rulers of Mars, Saturn, Mercury, and Jupiter. What about the Sun and Venus? Perhaps he skips them because, since they themselves are primary triplicity rulers, they are already being used in a way similar to the planets with whom the Moon joins.
[565] *Verax*.

she were poorly disposed, it will be false. If they were pearls, look at Venus: if she were well-disposed, they will be genuine. If she were poorly disposed, they will be false. You may understand the same about all precious stones, and about all things expensive and fragrant, as are musk, amber, balsam, and the like. If they were *denarii*[566] or other things sculpted in metal, use Mercury in their testimony. If they were the apparel of religious people, work with the testimony of Jupiter.

And[567] if someone asked concerning multiple things (namely two or three) which of them is better or more useful or more genuine [or truthful], whether they are rumors or something else, like concerning two or more things which he will attain, look at the Lord of the 1st and the Moon, and see which of them is stronger: operate with that one. If the stronger of them were in an angle, free from impediments and were received, it signifies that the one which was named first will be more true and better, and will be gotten by the querent. If indeed it (namely the Lord of the 1st or the Moon) were impeded, as was said, it will be the [first-] named thing,[568] but afterwards it will perish; and if he had gotten the quaesited thing, it will be destroyed after getting it. If however the Lord of the 1st were to aspect the 1st or the Moon, and were received in a succeedent house, or [were] free from impediments, it signifies that the second of the quaesited things will be the true one, and he will get it; and if it were impeded, it will be destroyed after getting it. And if it were in a cadent house, and received, he will get the thing named third, or it will be more worthy or true. If indeed it (namely the Lord of the Ascendant or the Moon) were impeded, and were in a cadent house, nothing will come of those things which were named to you.

---

566 A type of coin.

567 This passage is based on Sahl, *On Quest.*, "A question, which of two or three things is more worthy, and which one will be acquired."

568 *Erit nominatio de re illa.* I have replaced Bonatti's words with Sahl's (*Illud quod prius nominatur erit*). Sahl says: "Look at the Lord of the Ascendant to see if it were in angles, free from the malefics, and received: that which is named first is more worthy, and he will acquire it. And if it were impeded in the angles, it *will* be that which is named first–[but] after this it will be destroyed. And if the Lord of the Ascendant were to aspect the Ascendant, and it were in the succeedents of the angles, free from the malefics, received, he will acquire the thing named second, and it is more worthy. If however it were impeded, it will be gained; afterwards, [though], it will be destroyed. And if the Lord of the Ascendant were cadent, free from the malefics, and received, the third one of those named will be more worthy, and he will acquire it. If it were impeded, it will be nothing of those things which I said, and the question will be destroyed. And judge likewise concerning the Moon."

Chapter 6: When someone is invited to a banquet, whether he ought to go or not, and what foods will be there

Sometimes banquets take place in certain places, and certain regions more than in others, which most often the Italians are wont to hold, and especially the Romanioli, and above the rest the soldiers of Ravenna. And many people are invited to these banquets (which they cannot willingly avoid), and even to weddings and other great occasions for eating. Whence sometimes they wish to be informed by the astrologer, as to whether one must go to the banquet or the feast, or not, and [the querent] would put a question to you about it. Or if you yourself were invited to the banquet, and you wished to know whether you had to go there or not.

Look at the sign which was then ascending, and see if the Moon were in it alone, joined to no one: because then it signifies that you could go to the banquet, nor will you be held in much reverence there, nor will you (or the querent) be held in low esteem. And if she were in the 10th it will happen almost the same, except that you (or the other person who asks) will be held in greater reverence. In the 7th its signification will be less than that of the 1st. In the 4th, less than the 7th, which is less than all the other places, and according to which any house is weaker than the others, indeed he who goes to the feast will be held in less esteem.

If indeed the Moon were joined to some [planet], and were in the 1st, see to whom she is joined: because if she were joined with Saturn, it signifies that at the feast there will be unfit and unclean foods, and poorly prepared, and not well displayed or ordered, and pungent, and the tastes which will be there will not taste of the nature they ought to, nor will one going to the feast rejoice over these foods, nor from the flavors, [and] he who has gone will repent[569] of those tastes; whence it is better that he not go to the banquet he is going to.

If however she were joined with Jupiter, you will be able to go to the banquet with confidence, because the feasting there will be good, and there will be foods there of good flavor, and sweets, and there will be delicacies, and there will be foods there made with laughter and the like,

---

[569] Omitting *nec.*

and you will be honored there, indeed so that few will be honored more than you, or perhaps none [more so than you].

If indeed she were joined with Mars, you should not go to the wedding or banquet, because there will not be foods proper for tasting there, and they will taste bitter, and it is feared lest there be fights and discord between those [at the wedding or banquet].

If however she were joined with the Sun, you could go if you wished: for there will be foods of good flavor there, made with white pepper[570] or mustard; or country food; and similarly-flavored things that are good to taste, and received with foresight, and appropriate.

If for instance she were joined with Venus, go with confidence: because it signifies that there will be delicious foods there of good flavor, and there will likewise be gladness, and games, and many delights, and dishes of many sorts will be multiplied there, and diverse drinks, and there will be things which will please you (or him who is going to the banquet), and in which he will delight. Or the majority of the foods will be rich and very oily.

And if she were joined with Mercury, it signifies well that you can go, because there will be many types and diverse [sorts] of foods, and drinks, and the eating of them, and of things pungently flavored to taste. And good words will be said there (namely, words of wisdom), and even the deeds of the ancients will be narrated there, and many new things will be said there, and heard and unheard things, and believable and unbelievable things will be recited, and likewise a uniting of many men.

And Sahl said[571] that if the Moon were joined to Saturn from a watery sign by a trine or sextile aspect, they will eat trout. And if he aspected her from a square or the opposition, it signifies that they will eat cold meats, like sulz[572] and the like. And if the Moon were in Libra, it signifies the eating of beans. And if she were in Gemini or Aquarius, it signifies the eating of meats, birds. And if

---

570 *Eruca.*
571 *On Quest.,* "A question about a banquet, and what the banqueters will eat."
572 *Sulzium.* Sulz is a mixture of meats pickled in gelatin (similar to headcheese), sliced and served cold. Sahl does not mention sulz in particular.

Jupiter were to aspect her, it signifies the consumption of delicacies. And if Mars were to aspect her, it signifies the consumption of hot foods and roasted meat. And if the Sun aspected Mars then, it signifies that part of the meat is burned. Other planets do not impede her.

If however the Moon were outside the Ascendant, and she were in the 10th, the banquet will be like it is when she is in the 1st, [but] more renowned. If she were in the 7th it will be less than this. If she were in the 7th it will be less than this. If however she were in the 4th it will be less than this again. In the other houses it will be less, in proportion as one of them is less strong than the others.

Chapter 7: Whether the banquet is being held using one or more condiments

In order to know whether one manner of foods will be eaten at the banquet, or more, look then to see what sign is found on the line of the east.[573] Which if it were a fixed sign, and its Lord were in a fixed sign, and likewise the Moon, they will have breakfast [or lunch] confined to one kind of food. If however the Lord of the 1st were in a common sign, they will have another food (namely, a second), but one that is inferior to the first. If however in addition the Moon were in a common sign, the second dish will be better than the first, or it will be twice as much.[574] If however the Ascendant were a common sign, and its Lord of the Moon were in a fixed sign, they will have two dishes. If indeed the Lord of the 1st and the Moon were in common signs, they will have three dishes. If in movable signs, they will have something after the three dishes. If for instance the Ascendant were a movable sign, and the Lord of the 1st and the Moon were in a fixed or common sign, they will have three dishes, and something else after those three. And if the Lord of the 1st were in a movable sign, whoever is consuming[575] will have four diverse dishes, and something after those four. And if in addition the Moon were in a movable sign, they will have five kinds of dishes, and something else after them. And if in addition the Part of Fortune and its Lord were in movable signs, they will have many kinds of dishes, perhaps six or more, or[576] of fruits from trees and the like (which are not counted among the dishes at banquets).

---

[573] The degree of the Ascendant.
[574] *Duplicabitur.*
[575] *Habebunt quatuor fercula diversa quilibet comedentium.*
[576] Reading *sive* for *sine*.

Chapter 8: Knowing why the banquet is held

Sometimes uncouth and jealous people (and whose hearts do not suffer well), as though in the manner of a rebuke, when one of the nobility of his own desire (or perhaps for another reason) holds a banquet, are wont to say, "Why is he doing it?" And perhaps you wish to know the reason for yourself, or someone person asks you about it.

Look at the Ascendant at the hour of the inception of the banquet or of the question, or when you are called to the banquet, and see from which of the planets the Moon is separated, and to which of them she is joined: because if she is separated from one of the malefics, and is not joined to another, but is void in course, he is not holding the banquet for any manifest, apparent reason, but he holds it as though led by a certain insipid [reason].

If however she were joined to the benefics by the opposition or a square aspect, he is holding the banquet for such a reason that he cannot avoid it, as by reason of a marriage, or that such a thing is coming to his own home, which he cannot do [or avoid] without blame if he did not feast, and the like. If however the aspect were from a trine or sextile, he held the banquet in his own honor, and so that he could be happy and rejoice with the attendees; or perhaps that someone held a banquet for him, and he wishes to return the favor, and the like.

How long the banquet will last

If you wished to know how long the banquet will last, look at the planet to whom the Moon is then joined; which if it were in an angle and in a fixed sign, the banquet will be ended after one meal. If indeed it were in a common sign, there will be two meals. And if it were in a succeedent house and in a common sign, it will not be finished by two meals. And if it were in a cadent house and in a movable sign, or even a common one, the feast will last two days or more.

If those at the banquet will fight

And if the planet to which the Moon is joined, were the Lord of her domicile,[577] some people will fight together at the banquet, nor however will the banquet be put to an end before they have eaten.

---

577 I.e., of the domicile in which she is at the time.

When the food will be served at the banquet[578]

To know how the food will be brought to the banquet, you should look at the Lord of the hour of the inception of the banquet, or of the question or the beginning of the journey when someone goes there, [to see] whether he himself may be found in the 1st or the 10th: everything will be obtained and prepared, and well, and ordered, by the sound conditions stated above; and the things to be served will be served on a dish before they sit down. And if it were in the 7th or the 4th, they will sit first and the place for eating will be filled up before the dishes are served.

When one must beware of the foods at a banquet

And if you (or another going to a banquet) were to fear that there are foods to avoid there, look to see if the Moon were then in Cancer or Libra or Capricorn, in conjunction or aspect with one of the malefics (unless Saturn or Mars aspected her from Capricorn): because the plants—whether cooked or raw—are not to be eaten; nor should you even eat beans when she is in Libra, nor even in Virgo, if one of the malefics aspected her, or were joined to her corporally.

And Sahl said[579] that if the Moon were in Scorpio with the Tail, you should not eat fatty or rich things. And if she were in Leo or Sagittarius, you should not eat the meat of forest animals. And if she were in Pisces, you should not eat trout nor other salty fish. And may you understand all of these things when the Moon is in the aforesaid signs in the aspects of the malefics by squares or oppositions without reception.

Chapter 9: Which house signifies the banquet, its reason, and the like

And Sahl said[580] that the Ascendant signifies the reason for the banquet. And he said that if the Ascendant of the banquet were one of the domiciles of Venus, that it will be because of a marriage. And if it were of the domiciles of Mercury, it will be because of a child. And if it were of the domiciles of Jupiter, it will be because of a friend.

---

[578] One wonders if this sort of question is asked by one who just wants to go for the food, and not for the socializing.
[579] *Ibid.*
[580] *Ibid.*

And the 2nd from the Ascendant signifies the drinking vessels and the furniture of the home. Whence if the 2nd house were a common sign, their vessel will be colored. And if Mars were then in the 2nd, the vessel will be [made] with bronze [or copper]. And if Venus were in it,[581] there will be silver in it. And if it were Jupiter, it will be silver and gold. And if it were Saturn, the vessel will be wooden or ceramic. And if a benefic were in the 2nd, it will signify the beauty of the home's decorations. And if the benefic had a dignity in the 2nd, the decorations will be their own. If however it were peregrine, it will be borrowed.

Indeed the 3rd signifies the attendees: if a benefic were there, they will be men of good condition. If indeed Saturn were there, they will be low-class. If however Mars were there, they will be whisperers, or they will be bellicose men, or cutters of roads, and the like.

The 4th signifies the place of the banquet. If a benefic were there, it will be a beautiful place, and fit and decent. If however a benefic were there the place will be unsuitable and shameful or stinking. And Sahl said[582] that if the sign were common, the place of the banquet will be on a porch. And if the Sun or Jupiter were there, their banquet will be in a closed room of the house, or in the south.[583]

And the 5th signifies their beverages. If the 5th were a fixed sign, they will drink from one [form of] drink. And if Jupiter or Mercury were in it,[584] their drinks will be sweet and tasty. If indeed Mars were there, the drink will taste bitter. And if Mars were impeded by Saturn, the drink will be sour [like vinegar]. And if the Sun were there, it will be sharp[585] or harsh. And if Venus were there, it will be milky or something else tasting sweet and good to the taste. If however the Moon were there, the drink will be weak.

---

581 *Eo*, indicating a place or sign.
582 *Ibid.*
583 *Meridie.* This could also mean at midday.
584 *Eo.* See footnote above.
585 *Acerbum.* Like unripe fruit.

The 6th signifies the servers at the banquet. If a benefic were there, they will be fit and decent servers. If indeed a malefic were there, they will be inept and dirty, not knowing how to serve.

However the 7th will signify the cooks and bartenders. If a benefic were there, they will be fit; if a malefic were there, they will be unfit.

The 8th signifies the stewards.

And the 9th signifies those serving and carrying the dishes on the plates. If there were benefics in them, they will be fit for it, and will know how to do it well. If however there were malefics there, they will not do well at it.

The 10th signifies the general goodness and merriment of the banquet which the attendees have together. And if a benefic were [there], it will be a decent and praiseworthy banquet, and the attendees will rejoice and be happy together. And if a malefic were there, it will be an indecent banquet, indeed so that the attendees will be hateful to each other.

The 11th signifies if the host of the banquet[586] and the attendees are friends.

The 12th signifies the one hosting the banquet, or the authority of the house;[587] if a benefic were in it,[588] it shows the joy and happiness which he will have from the banquet. If a malefic were in it,[589] he will be saddened within himself, and will be pained at hosting it.

And whenever you were to see a benefic in any of the aforesaid places, and it were made fortunate, it signifies the increase of good. And if it were a malefic [or] made unfortunate in any of the aforesaid places, it signifies the increase of malice.

---

[586] *Convivato.*
[587] *Maiorem illius domus.*
[588] *Eo.* See footnote above.
[589] *Eo.* See footnote above.

BIBLIOGRAPHY

Abu Bakr, *Liber Genethliacus* (Nuremberg: Johannes Petreius, 1540)

Abū Ma'shar al-Balhi, *The Abbreviation of the Introduction to Astrology*, ed. and trans. Charles Burnett, K. Yamamoto, and Michio Yano (Leiden: E.J. Brill, 1994)

Abū Ma'shar al-Balhi, *Liber Introductorii Maioris ad Scientiam Iudiciorum Astrorum*, vols. VI, V, VI, IX, ed. Richard Lemay (Naples: Istituto Universitario Orientale, 1995)

Abū Ma'shar al-Balhi, *The Abbreviation of the Introduction to Astrology*, ed. and trans. Charles Burnett, annotated by Charles Burnett, G. Tobyn, G. Cornelius and V. Wells (ARHAT Publications, 1997)

Abū Ma'shar al-Balhi, *On Historical Astrology: The Book of Religions and Dynasties (On the Great Conjunctions)*, vols. I-II, eds. and trans. Keiji Yamamoto and Charles Burnett (Leiden: Brill, 2000)

Abū Ma'shar al-Balhi, *The Flowers of Abū Ma'shar*, trans. Benjamin Dykes (2nd ed., 2007)

Al-Biruni, Muhammad ibn Ahmad, *The Chronology of Ancient Nations*, trans. and ed. C. Edward Sachau (London: William H. Allen and Co., 1879)

Al-Biruni, Muhammad ibn Ahmad, *The Book of Instruction in the Elements of the Art of Astrology*, trans. R. Ramsay Wright (London: Luzac & Co., 1934)

Al-Fārābī, *De Ortu Scientiarum* (appearing as *"Alfarabi Über den Ursprung der Wissenschaften (De Ortu Scientiarum),"* ed. Clemens Baeumker, *Beiträge zur Geschichte der Philosophie des Mittelalters*, v. 19/3, 1916.

Al-Khayyat, Abu 'Ali, *The Judgments of Nativities*, trans. James H. Holden (Tempe, AZ: American Federation of Astrologers, Inc., 1988)

Al-Kindī, *The Forty Chapters (Iudicia Astrorum): The Two Latin Versions*, ed. Charles Burnett (London: The Warburg Institute, 1993)

Al-Mansur (attributed), *Capitula Almansoris*, ed. Plato of Tivoli (1136) (Basel: Johannes Hervagius, 1533)

Al-Qabīsī, *Isagoge*, trans. John of Spain, with commentary by John of Saxony (Paris: Simon Colinaeus, 1521)

Al-Qabīsī, *The Introduction to Astrology*, eds. Charles Burnett, Keiji Yamamoto, Michio Yano (London and Turin: The Warburg Institute, 2004)

Al-Rijāl, 'Ali, *In Iudiciis Astrorum* (Venice: Erhard Ratdolt, 1485)

Al-Rijāl, 'Ali, *Libri de Iudiciis Astrorum* (Basel: Henrichus Petrus, 1551)

Al-Tabarī, 'Umar, *De Nativitatibus* (Basel: Johannes Hervagius, 1533)

Al-Tabarī, 'Umar [Omar of Tiberias], *Three Books of Nativities*, ed. Robert Schmidt, trans. Robert Hand (Berkeley Springs, WV: The Golden Hind Press, 1997)

Alighieri, Dante, *Inferno*, trans. John Ciardi (New York, NY: Mentor, 1982)

Allen, Richard Hinckley, *Star Names: Their Lore and Meaning* (New York: Dover Publications Inc., 1963)

Aristotle, *The Complete Works of Aristotle* vols. I-II, ed. Jonathan Barnes (Princeton, NJ: Princeton University Press, 1984)

Bloch, Marc, *Feudal Society*, vols. I-II, trans. L.A. Manyon (Chicago: University of Chicago Press, 1961)

Bonatti, Guido, *Decem Tractatus Astronomiae* (Erhard Ratdolt: Venice, 1491)

Bonatti, Guido, *De Astronomia Tractatus X* (Basel, 1550)

Bonatti, Guido, *Liber Astronomiae: Books One, Two, and Three with Index*, trans. Robert Zoller and Robert Hand (Salisbury, Australia: Spica Publications, 1988)

Bonatti, Guido, *Liber Astronomiae Part IV: On Horary, First Part*, ed. Robert Schmidt, trans. Robert Hand (Berkeley Springs, WV: The Golden Hind Press, 1996)

Boncompagni, Baldassarre, *Della Vita e Della Opere di Guido Bonatti, Astrologo et Astronomo del Seculo Decimoterzo* (Rome: 1851)

Brady, Bernadette, *Brady's Book of Fixed Stars* (Boston: Weiser Books, 1998)

Burnett, Charles, ed., *Magic and Divination in the Middle Ages* (Aldershot, Great Britain: Ashgate Publishing Ltd., 1996)

Burnett, Charles and Gerrit Bos, *Scientific Weather Forecasting in the Middle Ages* (London and New York: Kegan Paul International, 2000)

Carmody, Francis, *Arabic Astronomical and Astrological Sciences in Latin Translation: A Critical Bibliography* (Berkeley and Los Angeles: University of California Press, 1956)

Carmody, Francis, *The Astronomical works of Thābit b. Qurra* (Berkeley and Los Angeles: University of California Press, 1960)

Dorotheus of Sidon, *Carmen Astrologicum*, trans. David Pingree (Abingdon, MD: The Astrology Center of America, 2005)

Grant, Edward, *Planets, Stars, and Orbs: The Medieval Cosmos, 1200–1687* (New York, NY: Cambridge University Press, 1994)

Haskins, Charles H., "Michael Scot and Frederick II," *Isis*, v. 4/2 (1921), pp. 250-75.

Haskins, Charles H., "Science at the Court of the Emperor Frederick II," *The American Historical Review*, v. 27/4 (1922), pp. 669-94.

Hermes Trismegistus, *Liber Hermetis*, ed. Robert Hand, trans. Robert Zoller (Salisbury, Australia: Spica Publications, 1998)

Holden, James H., *A History of Horoscopic Astrology* (Tempe, AZ: American Federation of Astrologers, Inc., 1996)

Ibn Labban, Kusyar, *Introduction to Astrology*, ed. and trans. Michio Yano (Tokyo: Institute for the Study of Languages and Cultures of Asia and Africa, 1997)

Ibn Sina (Avicenna), *The Canon of Medicine (al-Qanun fi'l tibb)*, ed. Laleh Bakhtiar (Great Books of the Islamic World, Inc., 1999)

Kennedy, Edward S., "The Sasanian Astronomical Handbook Zīj-I Shāh and the Astrological Doctrine of 'Transit' (Mamarr)," *Journal of the American Oriental Society*, v. 78/4 (1958), pp. 246-62.

Kunitzsch, Paul, "Mittelalterliche astronomisch-astrologische Glossare mit arabischen Fachausdrücken," *Bayerische Akademie der Wissenschaften Philosophisch-Historische Klasse*, 1977, v. 5

Kunitsch, Paul, trans. and ed., "Liber de Stellis Beibeniis," in *Hermetis Trismegisti: Astrologica et Divinatoria* (Turnhout: Brepols Publishers, 2001).

Kunitzsch, Paul and Tim Smart, *A Dictionary of Modern Star Names* (Cambridge, MA: New Track Media, 2006)

Latham, R.E., *Revised Medieval Latin Word-List from British and Irish Sources* (Oxford: Oxford University Press, 2004)

Lemay, Richard, *Abu Ma'shar and Latin Aristotelianism in the Twelfth Century* (Beirut: American University of Beirut, 1962)

Levy, Raphael, "A Note on the Latin Translators of Ibn Ezra," *Isis*, v. 37 nos. 3/4 (1947), pp. 153-55.

Lilly, William, *The Starry Messenger* (London: Company of Stationers and H. Blunden, 1652). Reprinted 2004 by Renaissance Astrology Facsimile Editions.

Lilly, William, *Anima Astrologiae*, trans. Henry Coley (London: B. Harris, 1676)

Lilly, William, *Christian Astrology*, vols. I-II, ed. David R. Roell (Abingdon, MD: Astrology Center of America, 2004)

Long, A.A. and D.N. Sedley, *The Hellenistic Philosophers*, vol. I (Cambridge: Cambridge University Press, 1987)

Māshā'allāh *et al.*, *Liber Novem Iudicum in Iudiciis Astrorum* [Book of the Nine Judges], ed. Peter Liechtenstein (Venice: 1509)

Māshā'allāh, *De Receptione* [*On Reception*] and *De Revolutione Annorum Mundi* and *De Interpraetationibus*, in *Messahalae Antiquissimi ac Laudatissimi Inter Arabes Astrologi, Libri Tres*, ed. Joachim Heller (Nuremberg: Joannes Montanus and Ulrich Neuber, 1549)

Māshā'allāh, *On Reception*, ed. and trans. Robert Hand (ARHAT Publications, 1998)

Maternus, Firmicus Julius, *Matheseos Libri VIII*, eds. W. Kroll and F. Skutsch (Stuttgard: Teubner, 1968)

Michelsen, Neil F., *The Koch Book of Tables* (San Diego: ACS Publications, Inc., 1985)

Mantello, F.A.C. and A.G. Rigg, eds., *Medieval Latin: An Introduction and Bibliographical Guide* (Washington, DC: The Catholic University of America Press, 1996)

New Oxford Annotated Bible, ed. Bruce M. Metzger and Roland E. Murphy (New York: Oxford University Press, 1994)

Pingree, David, "Astronomy and Astrology in India and Iran," *Isis* v. 54/2 (1963), pp. 229-46.

Pingree, David, "Classical and Byzantine Astrology in Sassanian Persia," *Dumbarton Oaks Papers*, v. 43 (1989), pp. 227-239.

Pingree, David, *From Astral Omens to Astrology: From Babylon to Bīkāner* (Rome: Istituto italiano per L'Africa e L'Oriente, 1997)

Pseudo-Ptolemy, *Centiloquium*, ed. Georgius Trapezuntius, in Bonatti (1550)

Ptolemy, Claudius, *Tetrabiblos* vols. 1, 2, 4, trans. Robert Schmidt, ed. Robert Hand (Berkeley Springs, WV: The Golden Hind Press, 1994-98)

Ptolemy, Claudius, *Tetrabiblos*, trans. F.E. Robbins (Cambridge and London: Harvard University Press, 1940)

Ptolemy, Claudius, *Quadripartitum* [Tetrabiblos], trans. Plato of Tivoli (1138) (Basel: Johannes Hervagius, 1533)

Sahl ibn Bishr, *Introductorium* and *Praecipua Iudicia* [The Fifty Judgments] *De Interrogationibus* and *De Electionibus*, in *Tetrabiblos*, ed. Girolamo Salio (Venice: Bonetus Locatellus, 1493)

Sahl ibn Bishr, *De Electionibus* (Venice: Peter of Liechtenstein, 1509)

Selby, Talbot R., "Filippo Villani and his Vita of Guido Bonatti," *Renaissance News*, v. 11/4 (1958), pp. 243-48.

Seneca, *The Stoic Philosophy of Seneca*, ed. and trans. Moses Hadas (New York: The Norton Library, 1968)

Stegemann, Viktor, *Dorotheos von Sidon und das Sogenannte* Introductorium *des Sahl ibn Biŝr* (Prague: Orientalisches Institut in Prag, 1942)

Thomson, S. Harrison, "The Text of Grosseteste's *De Cometis,*" *Isis* v. 19/1 (1933), pp. 19-25.

Thorndike, Lynn, *A History of Magic and Experimental Science* (New York: The Macmillan Company, 1929)

Thorndike, Lynn, *The* Sphere *of Sacrobosco and Its Commentators* (Chicago: The University of Chicago Press, 1949)

Thorndike, Lynn, "A Third Translation by Salio," *Speculum*, v. 32/1 (1957), pp. 116-117.

Thorndike, Lynn, "John of Seville," *Speculum*, v. 34/1 (1959), pp. 20-38.

Utley, Francis Lee (review), "*The Legend of the Wandering Jew* by George K. Anderson," *Modern Philology*, v. 66/2 (1968), pp. 188-193.

Valens, Vettius, *The Anthology*, vols. I-VII, ed. Robert Hand, trans. Robert Schmidt (Berkeley Springs, WV: The Golden Hind Press, 1993-2001)

Van Cleve, Thomas Curtis, *The Emperor Frederick II of Hohenstaufen: Immutator Mundi* (London: Oxford University Press, 1972)

Weinstock, Stefan, "Lunar Mansions and Early Calendars," *The Journal of Hellenic Studies*, v. 69 (1949), pp. 48-69.

Zoller, Robert, *The Arabic Parts in Astrology: A Lost Key to Prediction* (Rochester, VT: Inner Traditions International, 1989)

Zoller, Robert, *Bonatti on War* (2nd ed., 2000)

INDEX

Lightning Source UK Ltd.
Milton Keynes UK
UKOW01f2005070817

306875UK00012B/537/P